Mitzvah Girls

Mitzvah Girls

Bringing up the Next Generation
of Hasidic Jews in Brooklyn

Ayala Fader

PRINCETON UNIVERSITY PRESS • PRINCETON AND OXFORD

Library of Congress Cataloging-in-Publication Data

Fader, Ayala, 1964–
    Mitzvah girls : bringing up the next generation of
Hasidic Jews in Brooklyn / Ayala Fader.
        p.   cm.
Includes bibliographical references and index.
ISBN 978-0-691-13916-6 (hardcover : alk. paper) —
ISBN 978-0-691-13917-3 (pbk. : alk. paper)
1. Jewish girls—New York (State)—New York—Conduct of life.
2. Jewish religious education of girls—New York (State)—New York.
3. Jewish women—New York (State)—New York—Conduct of life.
4. Hasidim—New York (State)—New York—Conduct of life.
5. Women in Judaism. 6. Borough Park (New York, N.Y.)—
Religious life. I. Title.
    BM727.F33 2009
    296.8′3320820974723—dc22   2008053073

British Library Cataloging-in-Publication Data is available

This book has been composed in Palatino

Printed on acid-free paper. ∞

press.princeton.edu

Printed in the United States of America

10   9   8   7   6   5   4   3   2   1

For Adam

Contents

Acknowledgments

IN BORO PARK, BROOKLYN I was privileged to meet and spend time with many Hasidic women and children. I am especially grateful to the women I pseudonymously call Rifky, Mindy, Esty, Gitty, Mrs. Silver, *morah* 'Teacher' Chaya, Malky and Chaya for sharing their astute insights and inviting me so warmly into their homes and classrooms. Thanks also to the Bnos Yisruel school, its administration, and its wonderful teachers. While I do not always see eye to eye with the women I met in Boro Park, they have greatly impressed me. I admire their strength, sincerity, and their commitment to their families and Jews everywhere. I hope that this representation of my experiences with them will be interesting and not offend.

In a way, I have grown up with this book, so it is a great pleasure to publicly thank the institutions and individuals who have generously helped me along the way. As an undergraduate at New York University, conversation with Fred Myers led me to eventually continue there for graduate school. Don Kulick was a wonderful reader, both for my Masters thesis and for later work. My dissertation committee deserves special thanks for their guidance and support over so many years. Steven Gregory and Hasia Diner directed my thinking, reading and writing to new places. I will always be indebted to Faye Ginsburg, whose scholarship I so admire. Faye encouraged me to engage with the politics of my research and always reminds me of its broader significance. Barbara Kirshenblatt-Gimblett's incisive feedback, vast knowledge and unswerving support have been invaluable, as has the model of her own ongoing creative scholarship. I will never be able to fully express my gratitude to Bambi Schieffelin, the chair of my committee: reader, champion, advisor, and friend for so many years. Bambi's commitment to teaching, mentoring and scholarship are an ongoing inspiration.

Participating in a dissertation writing group and later a book writing group created a sense of solidarity. For support of many kinds thanks to Teja Ganti, Barbara Miller, Karen Strassler, Alice Appley, Chris Walley, Lotti Silber and Gerald Lombardi.

I was fortunate to have had two very generous readers for the entire manuscript. Jeffrey Shandler asked key questions, made important suggestions, and offered much needed encouragement. Jonathan Boyarin shared his knowledge and critical eye, pushing me to engage my material rigorously. These readers both made this a better book, and I will always be grateful to them.

Granting agencies made the research and then the writing possible, and I am happy to acknowledge their support. Language training in Hebrew was supported by the Jean and Albert Nerken Scholarship-United Jewish Appeal, UJA Federation. My Yiddish training at the YIVO Summer Program, Columbia University was supported through the generosity of Martin Peretz. The fieldwork was funded by Wenner-Gren Foundation for Anthropological Research, the National Science Foundation, the Lucius Littauer Foundation, the National Foundation for Jewish Culture, and the Memorial Foundation for Jewish Culture. The Spencer Foundation for Research Related to Education supported me during the dissertation write-up period. I was awarded a National Endowment for the Humanities Fellowship when I needed it most. Columbia University Seminar's Schoff award supported the preparation of the index.

Fordham University has also been generous in supporting my research, awarding me first a Faculty Research Grant and then a year-long Faculty Fellowship. I am especially grateful to the Sociology and Anthropology Department, Dean Himmelberg and the university for making it possible for me to extend my leave in order to accept the NEH fellowship. Many thanks to my colleagues at Fordham: Allan Gilbert and Clara Rodriguez helped along the way. Jeanne Flavin gave advice, read drafts, and met me for late night drinks. Rosemary Wakeman and O. Hugo Benavides are mentors and friends.

Other friends, colleagues, and mentors have read my work and provided input at critical points in the writing for which I am grateful. They include: Asif Agha, Jane Hill, Samuel Heilman, Elinor Ochs, Alessandro Duranti, Sarah Bunin Benor, Henry Goldschmidt, Ben Chesluk, Adina Schick, Jillian Cavanaugh, Paul Garrett, Miki Makihara, Peter Schneider, Lanita Huey-Jacobs, Judy Gerson, Courtney Bender, and Myra Bluebond-Langner.

For listening to me so patiently and offering encouragement in many ways over the years, I'd like to give special thanks to friends Stacey Lutz, Pat Moynihan, Laura Johnson, Chris Walley, and Lisa Sussman. I am especially grateful to Irina Carlota (Lotti) Silber, a friend whose support, love and intellectual rigor has inspired me in scholarship, motherhood, and friendship.

Presenting work in progress offered invaluable opportunities to rethink my work. Thanks to the Pew-sponsored Jews, Media and Religion seminar convened by Jeffrey Shandler and Barbara Kirshenblatt-Gimblett at New York University and the Pew-sponsored Secularism seminar convened by Fred Myers and Angela Zito; the Language Socialization conference at the Center for Language in Interaction organized by Alessandro Duranti and Elinor Ochs at UCLA; the Rutgers-sponsored conference, "Beyond Eastern Europe, " organized by Jeffrey Shandler and Yael Zerubavel; and the Columbia University seminar, Religion in the City, convened by Courtney Bender and Lowell Lizevy.

In the final stages of writing, Paul Glasser of the YIVO Institute generously shared his knowledge of Yiddish language, culture, and history by checking my Yiddish orthography and history. Beryl Goldberg took sensitive and beautiful photos. For introducing me to Beryl, among so many other things, thanks also to Susan Katz.

Many thanks to my editor at Princeton University Press, Fred Appel, for his enthusiastic support expressed in such a courtly manner. Thanks also to the staff at Princeton for their help in preparing the book for publication, especially Leslie Grundfest. Dave Luljak expertly prepared the index.

I am very happy to have the opportunity to publicly thank my parents, Larry and Yael Fader, for their ongoing and unconditional love and support. Babysitters par excellence, article clippers, and Hebrew consultants, I know I am lucky they live nearby. Thanks to my sisters, Nava and Jumi, my brother, Oren, and my in-laws, George and Evelyn Idelson, for their love.

My son, Simon, and my daughter, Talia, have been patient and encouraging, always reminding me what matters most. Watching them grow brings surprises and joy every day.

My greatest debt is to my husband, my partner, Adam, who helped me every step of the way. I rely on him for the clarity of his judgment, his sense of humor, and most of all his love. And it is with my love, gratitude, and admiration that I dedicate this book to him.

Several articles were published earlier in different forms, portions of which are reproduced and expanded in this book. These include:

Learning faith: Language socialization in a community of Hasidic Jews. *Language in Society,* Volume 35, Issue 2, April 2006, pp 205–229. Copyright © 2006, Cambridge University Press. Reprinted with permission.

Reclaiming sacred sparks: Linguistic syncretism and gendered language shift among Hasidic Jews. *Journal of Linguistic Anthropology,* Volume 17, Issue 1, June 2007, pp 1–22. Copyright © 2007, Wiley-Blackwell Publishing. Reprinted with permission.

Literacy, bilingualism and gender in a Hasidic community. *Linguistics and Education,* Volume 12, Issue 3, 2001, pp 261–283. Copyright © 2007, Elsevier Ltd. Reprinted with permission.

Reading Jewish signs: Multilingual literacy socialization with Hasidic women and girls in New York. *Text and Talk*, Volume 28, Issue 5, September 2008, pp 621–641. Copyright © 2008, Mouton de Gruyter Publishers. Reprinted with permission.

Reflections on Queen Esther: The politics of Jewish ethnography. *Contemporary Jewry*, Volume 27, July 2007, pp 112–136. Copyright © 2007, Association for the Social Scientific Study of Judaism and Springer Netherlands. Reprinted with permission.

Notes on Yiddish and Transcription Conventions

A Brief History of the Yiddish Language

Yiddish is one of many post-exilic Jewish languages—including, for example, Judeo-French, Judeo-Spanish (or Ladino), Judeo-Greek, and Judeo-Arabic— that traces its origins to a mixture of several sources, what linguist Max Weinreich (1980) has called a "fusion" language. Yiddish developed during contact among Jews and between Gentiles and Jews in different regions of Europe through migration and resettlement over hundreds of years. Most scholars agree that the four major components of Yiddish are Hebrew-Aramaic (*loshn-koydesh* 'holy language'), Romance languages, Germanic, and Slavic languages.

Yiddish emerged around the year 1000, when Jews, who had presumably been expelled from what would later be Italy and France, resettled in the Rhineland, which Jews called *Loter*, the basin of the Moselle and the left bank of the Rhine, between Cologne and Speyer (Goldsmith 1976:28–30; Weinreich 1980:1–2). These immigrants spoke, what in Hebrew was called *La'az* 'the language of foreigners', which included variants of spoken Latin and early versions of French and Italian all infused with Hebrew elements.

Over time, the Jewish Rhineland community absorbed many lexical and syntactic elements of the spoken Germanic dialects in the area. Yiddish (*yid* 'Jew'; *yidish* 'Jewish') became an indigenous Jewish language used exclusively by Jewish communities and written in a separate, Hebrew alphabet (Harshav 1990:5). Once Ashkenazic Jews began to migrate to Eastern Europe in the sixteenth century, the language also acquired many Slavic components (Goldsmith 1976:30).

Yiddish consists of two branches: Western Yiddish, no longer a living dialect (Schaechter 2004:192), was spoken by German Jews until the nineteenth century and by some small communities in Alsace, Switzerland, Holland, and southern Germany until the Holocaust; and Eastern Yiddish, which is subdivided into three major dialects based on regions in Eastern Europe, although the political borders of the region were constantly shifting from the sixteenth through the twentieth century with empires rising and falling and states forming and dissolving. Popular writer Michael Wex notes that the Yiddish dialects are based on a geography that no longer exists: "Yiddish got a map of Eastern Europe 450 years ago and never bothered to replace it with a new one"

(2005:48). The dialects of Eastern Yiddish include Central Yiddish (Poland, Galicia, and Hungary), Northeastern/Lithuanian Yiddish (Lithuania and parts of Ukraine and Russia), and Southeastern Yiddish (most of Ukraine and Romania).

Although Yiddish dialects are mutually intelligible and share a Hebrew orthography, they each have a distinctive vocabulary and variations in pronunciation systems. One of the most salient distinctions continues to be between Lithuanian Yiddish and Central Yiddish. These two dialects are a legacy of an ideological split that occurred in the eighteenth and nineteenth centuries between the emerging Hasidic movement, based primarily in Galicia and Poland, and the Lithuanian-centered *Misnagdim* 'opposed'. Lithuanian Jews rejected the Hasidic movement, favoring traditional orthodoxy and Torah study in the prestigious yeshivas in Lithuania, rather than the ecstatic, democratizing Judaism of the Hasidic movement (Harshav 1990:79).

One of the defining vowel differences between Lithuanian (*litvish*) Yiddish and Central Yiddish is the vowel ״. Litvish Yiddish pronounces this as /ey/ (like the English vowel in "hey"), whereas Central Yiddish pronounces it /ay/ (like the English vowel in "buy"). For example, Central Yiddish speakers talk about a girl who is *shayn* 'pretty', and Litvish Yiddish speakers call her *sheyn*. Both are written in Yiddish orthography as שײן. Wex (2005:57) further suggests that Central Yiddish rounds and elongates its vowels in contrast to Lithuanian Yiddish. For example, Lithuanians talk about the word "city," *shtot*, but Polish say *shtut*, so that /o/ (aw of "paw") becomes /u/ (like the longer oo in "boot").

Within Central Yiddish there are other, more subtle differences that speakers in Brooklyn find relevant. One of the most important is between Hungarian Hasidic speakers of Yiddish and Hasidic Jews of Polish/Galician descent. There are differences in pronunciation. Hungarian Yiddish uses a palatalized /l/ (similar to the /l/ in Spanish), and diphthongs are elongated. Hungarian Yiddish also has a distinctive prosody, the intonation or melody of a language. Hasidic women I met who were not Hungarian, described Hungarian Yiddish as "singsong." Most likely, the Yiddish of Hungarian Hasidic Jews has been influenced by the emerging nation-state of Hungary in the nineteenth century and its national language which many Hasidic women then learned in school or from private tutors. As I discuss in this book, Hungarian Hasidic women are also the most fluent in Yiddish of all Hasidic women in Brooklyn. Perhaps it is this fluency that additionally marks their Yiddish as "different." Indeed, I knew I had reached a certain level of Yiddish fluency the afternoon I spent looking after a friend's son while she had her wig styled. I took her toddler out to the hall to play, speaking all the while to him in Yiddish. When I brought the child back to his mother, she said, "Oh that was you, Ayala, in the hall? You sounded just like a Hungarian lady from Williamsburg!"

REPRESENTING YIDDISH

I transcribe Yiddish from its Hebrew orthography using a modified version of the YIVO system (U. Weinreich 1990). This was done to best represent the dialect of Yiddish spoken by the Hasidic Jews I met. Speakers' phonological repertoires include a range of pronunciation. For example, in some situations a speaker might use the word *frum* 'religious' and in others use the word *frim*. These variations are represented as accurately as possible in the quoted portions of text.

The system is as follows:

a   similar to a in "father"
u   similar to oo in "boot" but may also be like oo in "cook"
e   similar to e in "get"
i   similar to i in "big" or ee in "feet"
o   similar to o in "dog"
ou   similar to ow in "cow"
oy   similar to oy in "boy"
ay   similar to i in "fine"
ey   similar to a in "hay"
kh   like the German ch in "ach"
tsh   like ch in "church"
ts   like ts in "cats"
r   produced by trilling the tip of the tongue on the roof of the mouth, similar to producing the final r of "door"

Two contrasts in pronunciation with English are important to remember. First, some Yiddish syllables have no vowels. At the end of words, a cluster of consonants ending in *l* or *n* constitute a syllable. For example, the Yiddish word for "girl," *maydl*, has two syllables, *may-dl* as does the word for "language," *loshn, lo-shn*. Second, an *e* at the end of a Yiddish word is not silent but is pronounced as a short English /e/. For example, the Yiddish word *kashe* 'difficult question' is pronounced *ka-she* rhyming with "Sasha" (Wex 2005:xii).

In the transliteration of Yiddish quotes I remain true to the transcription conventions. For example, I write *khsidic* rather than "Hasidic." When translating, however, I use the Standard English spelling, for instance, "Hasidic." When using an English word that has become part of Yiddish, I retain the English spelling for clarity although the word is also italicized and underlined (see below). For example, I represent the Hasidic Yiddish word for jump as _jumpn_ to show its relationship to the English.

Some Yiddish words have acquired a normative English spelling among Hasidic Jews, and I use that spelling in my transcriptions and translations. For example, the word for "father" in Yiddish is _tati_ according to my transcription system. _Tati_, however, is transcribed by Hasidic Jews as _totty_ or _tatty_, even in printed materials. To avoid confusion, when there is a more standard English language spelling, I generally use that in my translations.

On several occasions I deviate from my transcription system. First, personal names in Yiddish are represented throughout as they are in English to facilitate reading. For example, "_Aaron, kim du_ (Aaron, come here)", rather than, "_Arn, kim du._" Second, a Yiddish term that appears throughout the text, _khsidish_ 'Hasidic', I write as "Hasidish," again to facilitate reading. Community members actually use "_chassidish_," but rather than introducing alternative spellings, and for readability, I use "Hasidish." Finally, in the title of this book I use a standard spelling of the word _mitzvah_ 'commandment' for ease of recognition. Throughout the text, however, I maintain my transcription system and render the word _mitsve_.

In my transcriptions of printed Yiddish, I retain the Yiddish oral dialect used by most of the Hasidic women and children I met. I do this in order to accurately represent how the Hasidic Jews I worked with read printed Yiddish aloud.

Conventions for Transcribing Recorded Speech

To represent the mixture of linguistic codes in the everyday speech of Boro Park Hasidim, I devised the following system to facilitate reading transcribed portions of speech:

a. Yiddish is in italics. Yiddish and Hebrew words are italicized at first mention and then given in roman type, although if a word has not been used recently in the text, I reintroduce it in italics with a definition.

b. Words that belong to both Yiddish and English (bivalent) are italicized and underlined. Examples include _Mommy_, _jumpn_, and _nebby_.

c. English translations of Yiddish words are in single quotes. For example, Hasidic men have long, curly _payes_ 'side curls'. Longer quotes are in parentheses in plain type.

d. Yiddish translations of English words are in parentheses in italics. For example, "The girl made sure that she sat down modestly (*tsniesdik*)."

e. Longer segments of interaction are translated and placed below the original in roman type.

f. Hebrew is also italicized and placed in parentheses. Hebrew used by Hasidim is almost exclusively Ashkenazic Hebrew and is rendered thus orthographically.

g. Context notes in longer stretches of talk are in brackets in plain type.

h. Interactions that I have edited for brevity and relevance are signaled by ellipses (. . .)

i. For talk that is inaudible, I use blank parentheses, ( ).

j. When speakers interrupt each other I use an equal sign (=) to show where the overlap occurs.

Mitzvah Girls

CHAPTER ONE

Introduction

HASIDIC JEWS, who claim to be the bearers of authentic Jewish religion, arrived in New York City after the Holocaust and, defying all predictions, flourished. Women and girls are essential to this community's growth, for it is they who bear and rear the next generation of believers. Women's and girls' responsibilities include mediating the secular world for Hasidic men and boys who study the sacred Torah. This book is an ethnographic study of how Bobover[1] and other unaffiliated Hasidic women teach their daughters to take on their responsibilities and become observant Jewish women. Studies of religion often focus on sacred texts, prayer, or special rituals. My research with Hasidic women and girls led me instead to listen to everyday talk in homes, classrooms, and the front yards of the Brooklyn neighborhood of Boro Park. Language organizes social life and is a springboard into broader issues such as the ways Hasidic mothers and girls talk about authority and desire, about the body and autonomy, about power and morality. Everyday talk between women and girls offers insight into how those who critique the secular world imagine it and themselves. Girls' willingness to civilize the secular world through Jewish practice has the potential to create an alternative religious modernity, one with the power to perhaps, one day, transform New York into a modern-day Garden of Eden.

Hasidic Jews (Hebrew, Hasid 'pious one'; Hasidim 'pious ones'), who organize themselves into sects, are a distinctive kind of religious group, what I call a "nonliberal" religious community.[2] In contrast to other nonliberal religious communities in North America, for example, evangelical Christians, Hasidic Jews have neither the ability nor the goal of engaging in national politics beyond lobbying for laws and rights that support their own interests. As sociologist Samuel Heilman (2006) has noted, Hasidic Jews have done so well in New York not in spite of, but because of North American urban diversity, with its increasing tolerance for public displays of religion. Rather than gradually assimilating, as have previous generations of Jews, Hasidic Jews have increasingly become religiously stringent. For Hasidic women and girls, this heightened religious stringency requires new forms of femininity, which include their participation in the secular city around them.

Hasidic women complicate stereotypes about women in nonliberal religions by their involvement in the North American public sphere. In order to facilitate Hasidic men's and boys' study of sacred texts, Hasidic women adapt the cultural, political, and economic life of the city to the needs of their community. Their fluency in secular modernity, evidenced in their education, their relatively unmarked clothing, their use of English (rather than Yiddish, the traditional vernacular of Eastern European Jews), and their work outside the home, enables them to create a sheltered enclave for boys and men who study Torah and later also join the workforce.

The participation of women and girls in the life of New York City is tempered by the critique they make of what they call the "*goyishe* 'Gentile' world," the "secular world," and "modern" Jews. These categories, discussed below, are certainly not monolithic; they are differentiated by, for example, race, class, gender. and ethnicity. In interactions between Hasidic women and children, however, these categories often functioned as ideal types that provided a shorthand for articulating Hasidic distinction. In fact, Hasidic descriptions of the secular world, Gentiles, and more modern Jews are often based less on regular interaction and personal experience and more on Hasidic women's ideological beliefs about an authentic Judaism that includes imagined others. When Hasidic women and children observe and talk about others who represent what *not* to be, we gain insight into Hasidic notions of the nature of Jewish difference.

In the chapters that follow I show how the Hasidic women I spent time with teach girls, through everyday talk, to use their autonomy to "fit in" with communal expectations and how they deal with girls' questions and defiance; how Hasidic girls in first grade begin to speak a Hasidic variety of English (English mixed with Yiddish), which marks them as distinctively Hasidic; and how the embodied disciplines of modesty form the basis for Hasidic alternative narratives of romantic love, consumption, and the family.

Hasidic women I worked with disrupt what anthropologist Webb Keane calls "a moral narrative of modernity," which, he suggests, emerged out of Western liberal thought, rooted in the Enlightenment and entwined with an earlier strand of Protestantism (2007:49). In this narrative, progress is associated not only, for example, with urbanization, industrialization, and secularization but also with increasing individual freedom and autonomy (ibid.:6, 46).[3]

The Hasidic women I worked with engage with this narrative of modernity, but they change its meaning.[4] They do not want to be what they call "modern," meaning Jews who are similar to Gentiles (see below), but they do want to be what they call "with it" in their interactions with other kinds of Jews or Gentiles.[5] The version of Hasidic femininity I describe is defined by the ability to be "with it" enough to selectively use and even enjoy the secular and the Gentile world, while never becoming Jews who are modern or secular. Instead, these women envision a religious way of life, which I call an "alternative religious modernity."[6] Real freedom, progress, and self-actualization, Hasidic women tell their daughters, can only come about through the self-discipline that is learned through Jewish religious practice.

Hasidic women's authoritative version of religious modernity dismantles an opposition between the secular and the religious that is central to social scientific definitions of the modern.[7] In their moral narratives, Hasidic mothers promise their daughters that when they learn to make the religious and the secular, the material and the spiritual, the body and the soul complementary, and not oppositional, they will find true personal fulfillment, be rewarded by God in the afterlife, and even, perhaps, do their part to hasten the final redemption.

This book is about the everyday projects of Hasidic women and girls as they strive to redefine what constitutes a moral society. Anthropologist Saba Mahmood has argued that by creating culturally and historically specific forms of sociability, members of nonliberal religious groups attempt to change the moral terms of everyday life. Movements that advocate moral reform, she notes, though often seen as apolitical, are in fact about how "embodied attachments to historically specific forms of truth come to be forged" (2005:34).

Embodied attachments to truth, however, are produced not only by adults in synagogues, churches, or mosques. Equally critical to a movement of moral reform are the everyday exchanges between adults and children and between children themselves in the more intimate spaces of the home, school, and neighborhood, where children may become very different from what adults intend (Kulick and Schieffelin 2004). A grounded analysis of the Hasidic moral project through everyday talk between women and children reveals a modern religious way of life with redemptive possibilities.

RELIGION, WOMEN, AND CHILDREN

A series of related questions with theoretical implications are central to this book. What do the terms "modern," "religious," and "secular" mean to Hasidic women and girls, and how are these categories engaged in everyday life? This includes Hasidic women's and girls' notions of power, difference, and discipline, as well as the everyday practices that shape the meanings these concepts hold. Further, how do embodied practices across the life cycle (e.g., language, comportment, and dress) produce the desire or its opposite in girls to become Hasidic women? My approach to these questions integrates scholarship in the anthropology of religion and of childhood with linguistic anthropology and Jewish ethnography.

Talal Asad (1993) has persuasively shown that the social scientific categories of the secular and the religious are themselves a socio-historical product of European modernity.[8] According to Asad, any discipline that tries to understand religion must also try to understand its "other," the secular. Contemporary nonliberal religious groups are an especially important topic for investigation, because, despite cultural and religious differences, they often share an explicit critique and rejection of the normative categories of the religious and the secular. Studies of nonliberal religious groups cast into relief the historical lineages to which anthropology of religion has long been tethered.

Ethnographies of nonliberal women, in particular, have made important contributions to increasingly complicated understandings of power and agency. A rich body of scholarship examines the religious practices of nonliberal women. Perhaps attempting to explain why so many women began embracing patriarchal religions since the 1970s, much of the scholarship focuses on the unexpectedly progressive outcomes of women's increasing involvement in religion. For example, evangelical Christian women's participation in North American and Latin American churches and prayer circles have created opportunities for these women to acquire newfound authority in their families, combat inequalities of gender, class, and ethnicity, and even reinterpret secular Western feminism to serve women's religious aims.[9]

More recently, scholars have shifted their focus to nonliberal women's religious goals and desires—for piety or submission, for example—in order to develop new approaches to the study of religion and gender more broadly. Nonliberal religious women's critiques of the secular world, especially goals for individual freedom and autonomy, require that scholars acknowledge the secular liberal assumptions that are at the foundation of their disciplines and research questions. Saba Mahmood (2005), for example, uses her study of Egyptian women's involvement in the mosque movement, part of the wider Islamic Revival, to show how liberal beliefs about action, freedom, and the individual have been naturalized in feminist theory.[10] She argues, based on the time she spent with Egyptian women engaged in religious study, that the desire to grow closer to God and create a more ethical world can be as meaningful and legitimate for some women as gender equality or progressive change is for others. In a different cultural and religious context, R. Marie Griffith's (1997) study of the Women

Aglow movement, an evangelical Christian prayer network in North America, similarly argues for more complex understandings of the concept of agency through an analysis of religious submission. Griffith shows that evangelical women's submission to a patriarchal religious hierarchy does not preclude their individual autonomy or fulfillment. These scholars and others attend to nonliberal women's religious activities in order to develop approaches to the study of religion that are unbound by secular liberal assumptions about the person, power, and action.[11]

I build on this scholarship to propose a different approach, one that focuses on everyday life in order to account for the ways that nonliberal women's lives and desires transgress easy distinctions between the religious and the secular. Analyses that exclusively address nonliberal women's religious practices, I contend, reproduce a definition of religion that is artificially discrete from wider social life. This social scientific category of religion, one informed by Protestantism, cannot account for the realities of nonliberal women's lives. Consider Hasidic women who criticize goals of progressive change without rejecting participation and pleasure in the secular realm or hopes for personal fulfillment. The desire for piety and, say, shopping or romantic love can be complementary if women discipline their bodies and minds to conform to Jewish religious practice. Hasidic femininity is predicated on developing the autonomy to discipline the self to religious practices that include a particular engagement with the secular world. Indeed, Hasidic femininity is formed through the very collapse of the religious and the secular.

Ethnographic attention to children and everyday talk reveals the processes by which nonliberal desires and gendered ways of being in the world are negotiated, produced, and sometimes changed.[12] Scholarship in the anthropology of childhood has shown that children and childhood are critical to understanding the politics of cultural production and change. In this literature, children are approached not as immature adults but as agents themselves who participate significantly in social processes, particularly in the production of differences of gender, class, and race.[13] However, with some notable exceptions, little research has been conducted with children in religious movements.[14] Perhaps this is because nonliberal religious childrearing practices trouble secular liberal thought in much the same ways that women's participation in nonliberal religion has challenged feminist theory and politics. Investigating nonliberal religious childhood requires rethinking what are often naturalized assumptions about children and how childhood should unfold, especially around topics such as creativity, discipline, curiosity, and questioning.

A language socialization approach can be a powerful tool for examining gender, cultural production, and change in nonliberal religious communities, because it makes interactions between children and adults the primary site for delving into broader cultural themes and relationships (Ochs and Schieffelin 1984; Schieffelin and Ochs 1986). A language socialization approach contrasts to earlier anthropological work on socialization, which often treated children as the passive recipients of culture and overlooked everyday language, a key medium of socialization.[15] Instead, language socialization centers on the negotiations, by and through language, between adults and children, and among children themselves, to explore how children acquire or reject culturally specific ways of being in the world (Kulick and Schieffelin 2004:352).

An ongoing challenge to language socialization studies, however, has been how to embed the analysis of micro-level interactions within broader political processes. Recent attention to morality and ethics in the anthropology of religion can clarify how micro-level practices constitute broader frames of knowledge and power, thus politicizing language socialization studies. This is especially true in nonliberal religious communities that legitimize their very existence to their children by laying claim to one moral "truth." A focus on children and their interactions with adults offers a grounded methodology for ethnographically studying the intersection between morality and politics, especially as it is negotiated with the next generation.

Another challenge to the language socialization approach has been to go beyond its exclusive focus on language and begin to examine broader relationships between semiotic registers such as language, clothing, hairstyles, and comportment. Researchers in linguistic anthropology are beginning to theorize how beliefs about language interact with beliefs about the body and material culture in specific historical and cultural ways. In a community where the Torah is believed to be the words of God, the relationship between religious signs and their referents is not arbitrary; it is divinely intended, as scholars working with sacred languages have noted (e.g., Elster 2003; Haeri 2003). A central question in this book is how beliefs about divine truth which shape sign relationships in explicitly religious contexts, such as prayer, interact in everyday signifying practices in other contexts. How, for example, does the belief that Hebrew-Aramaic sacred texts are God's words affect how little girls, who will not study Torah, learn to read and think about texts in other Jewish languages such as Yiddish or a non-Jewish language like English? Or how is God's commandment to dress modestly interpreted on a shopping trip to Macy's? Throughout the book

I examine Hasidic "semiotic ideologies," that is, cultural and religious beliefs about the nature of signs in different contexts (Keane 2007).

This study of the Hasidic women and girls I worked with in Brooklyn, then, engages topics with broad implications, including the cultivation of nonliberal femininity; the relationships between language, the body, and materiality; and what the dynamics between the secular and the religious in a nonliberal religious movement today can tell us about multiple inflections of modernity.

HASIDIC JUDAISM HISTORICALLY AND TODAY

In the eighteenth century, European (Ashkenazic) Jews wrestled with modernity and the rapid social changes it brought, including urbanization, industrialization, religious reform, and, in many places, unprecedented opportunities for Jewish participation as European citizens.[16] Some Jews responded by participating, for example, in the secularizing Jewish Enlightenment (*haskalah*), becoming, what they called in Yiddish, *modern* (Weinreich 2008:733); others became involved in the nascent Zionist movement and its Jewish nationalist dream; and still others were part of a traditionalist response that included the Hasidic movement.[17]

The Inception of the Hasidic Movement

Radical for its time, the Hasidic movement offered a transformed and transformative Judaism.[18] Sparked by the teachings of Israel Ben Eliezer, known as the *Baal-Shem-Tov* 'Master of the Good Name' (a reference to his reputation as a worker of miracles), Hasidism spread quickly throughout much of Eastern and Central Europe where pogroms against Jews were common and many, especially in Eastern Europe, lived in poverty. Hasidism is messianic.[19] Hasidic Jews hope that by fulfilling their religious obligations they will bring the *geulah* 'redemption', which includes an end to Jewish exile and a rebuilding of the temple in Jerusalem by God. The Messiah has been delayed, many believe, because of impieties in the diaspora (Mintz 1992:2–3).

All Orthodox Jews, including Hasidim, lead lives circumscribed by the 613 commandments (*mitsves*) found in the Hebrew Bible, as interpreted by Jewish sages, believed to have been divinely inspired, and preserved in the Oral Law, the Talmud. But the Hasidic movement was distinct from other forms of orthodoxy in its emphasis on Jewish mysticism, the creation of a new style of worship, and a unique social organization. Hasidic teachings asserted that any Jew could commune with the divine through a joyous expression of faith, including singing, dancing, and ecstatic prayer. This contrasted with the existing rabbinic tradition, which was based on ascetic study of the Torah, primarily the domain of the elite (Hundert 1991; Rosman 1996).

Hasidic Jews developed allegiances to different rebbes, who were charismatic, spiritual community leaders. A rebbe, his followers believed, provided an actual conduit to God, and many stories have been handed down about the wonders wrought by particular rebbes. Through his familial dynasty a rebbe cultivated adherents who formed a court (*hoyf*) or sect, with court leadership generally passed from father to son or the closest male relative. Hasidic sects were often named after the region where a rebbe's authority was established. For example, Lubavitcher Hasidism originated in the small town of Lubavitch, in what was then Russia (now Belarus). Followers of different rebbes distinguished themselves through dress, ethnicity, ideology, and religious practice. They were often dispersed across the Eastern and Central European landscape, and Hasidic Jews made pilgrimages, often a long distance from their homes, to visit their rebbe if he lived far away. Hasidim historically have been linked to one another through networks of faith that crossed geographic boundaries and borders.[20]

Other traditionalist Jews based in Lithuania opposed Hasidic Judaism from its beginning, arguing that religious authority should come from scholars in *yeshivas* (institutions of higher Jewish learning). These Jews were called *misnagdim* 'opponents' (of Hasidism) or, alternatively, *litvish* 'Lithuanians' referring to their place of origin or, later on, *yeshivish*. Litvish Jews followed the authority of the head of a yeshiva, rejecting the all-encompassing authority of Hasidic rebbes, the focus on mystical texts, and the ecstatic democratizing forms of worship.

Hasidic Judaism in Postwar North America

By the close of World War II, the vast majority of Hasidic Jews in Europe had been killed in the Holocaust. Some fared better than others as a result of geography and political circumstance. Those living close to the Russian border, for example, had a greater chance of escaping across to the relative safety of the Soviet Union. Similarly Hungarian Hasidim survived in greater numbers than Polish Hasidim, because the Nazis did not take over Hungary (an Axis ally) until 1944. In contrast, the Nazis took over Poland in 1939, and consequently the vast majority of Polish Hasidim were killed in concentration camps (Mintz 1992:27). The Hasidic Jews who survived came after the war and settled in the United States, Israel, England, Canada, and Belgium, among other urban centers internationally.[21] The Holocaust provided Hasidim with a mission of reconstruction that made it their responsibility to rebuild and repopulate their communities.

Hasidic courts and dynastic leadership in New York City today are not simply transplanted from Central and Eastern Europe, nor are they completely discrete communities, although they have sometimes been represented as such in the ethnographic literature. Indeed, almost all the ethnographies of Hasidic Jews have focused on one "community" or court.[22] However, Hasidic courts were created, not re-created in North America.[23] Upon arriving in New York, the Hasidic rebbes who survived the war, such as the Hungarian Satmar rebbe and the Galician-Polish Bobover rebbe, attracted not only their own followers but also European and North American Jews who had very different backgrounds and histories. In his ethnography of Satmar Hasidim, for example, Rubin (1997:46) estimates that in 1961 40 percent of the Satmar court had not been Satmar or even Hasidic in prewar Europe. Hasidic courts established themselves anew in New York by building yeshivas for boys, schools for girls (only Satmar and Lubavitch), *mikves* 'ritual baths' and other community institutions that observant Jewish communities require.

Although Hasidic Jews in New York share many beliefs and philosophies, diverse courts, or "circles" as many women call them, can be distinguished by a number of features that most prominently include their attitude toward religious stringency (*khumre*), religious interpretation and practice, language use, clothing, and level of participation in North American life. This is not to diminish that significant differences also exist within each Hasidic circle based on familial history, religious practice, and opinions on Hasidic politics, to mention only a few.

Over time different courts have become associated with distinct Brooklyn neighborhoods, though these neighborhoods also include other Jews and Gentiles. There are more than thirty courts (Mintz 1992), but I provide a brief discussion of three of the largest and most prominent in New York City: Satmar, Lubavitch, and Bobov. My aim is to highlight the range of Hasidic variation. I also address the rarely discussed category of unaffiliated Hasidim.

Hungarian Hasidim form the largest population of Hasidic Jews in New York; the biggest and best-known Hungarian court is Satmar, with other Hungarian courts including, for example, Pupa, Spinka, Vizhnits (from Bukovina), and Munkacz.[24] Satmar dominate Williamsburg, Brooklyn, where they have had tensions with their Latino neighbors (see Mintz 1992; Rubin 1997) and, more recently, with the *artistn* 'artists' who have moved to Williamsburg and sparked its gentrification. Although some Satmar have great wealth, at least half of the Hasidic families in Williamsburg live below the poverty level.

Satmar have also built a satellite community, Kiryas Joel, in upstate New York, where there have been conflicts over funding for schools that went to the national courts (see Boyarin 2002). In the ethnographic literature and according to different Hasidic women I spoke with in Boro Park (some Hungarian themselves), Satmar are considered the most religiously stringent and isolationist, evidenced in part by men and women's fluency in Yiddish, which is a result of limited exposure to secular education and cultural forms. Satmar have the strictest standards of piety and modesty that include distinctively Satmar forms of Hasidic dress for men and women, as in, for example, the flat, round, black-velvet brimmed hat worn by men on top of their yarmulkes. A number of Bobover and Lubavitcher women described Satmar as "radical" and "very Hasidic" (*zayer khsidish*). Satmar women, however, are also reputed to have a penchant for luxury and to be good cooks who make highly spiced food. Anthropologist Israel Rubin (1997:54) suggests that, philosophically, Satmar place a greater emphasis than other Hasidic groups on an unquestioning belief in God, which leads to an avoidance of questioning more generally. Satmar have had an ongoing dispute most particularly with Lubavitcher Hasidim, with whom there has been a rivalry for the hearts and minds of the young men of the community (Mintz 1992).

Lubavitchers, the majority of whom live in the Brooklyn neighborhood of Crown Heights, are known for their messianic fervor and their outreach efforts toward unobservant Jews.[25] Crown Heights is a predominantly Caribbean/African American neighborhood with Lubavitchers a small but vocal minority. There has been racial and religious tension between these groups, most notably the violence of 1991 (see Goldschmidt 2006). The Lubavitcher rebbe, Menachem Mendel Schneerson, who led the community from 1951 until his death in 1994, inspired unusual levels of devotion, with many suggesting that he was the Messiah himself. Upon his death, and with no successor, the Lubavitcher community was thrown into turmoil, as community members debated how to proceed and whether the rebbe would return as the Messiah. This continues as an ongoing struggle between the *meshikhists* and the anti-*meshikhists* (those who believe him to have been the Messiah [*moshiakh*] and those who do not) (Levine 2003:3). Satmar find this belief particularly objectionable.

In his efforts to rebuild after the war, the Lubavitcher rebbe institutionalized an unusual campaign: the active recruitment of unobservant Jews in order to bring them closer to Orthodox Judaism. Because of their successful outreach, Lubavitchers have the largest population of *baley-tshuves* 'returnees to the faith', known informally by the abbreviation "bts. (singular, baal tshuve "bt")". This has influenced wider Lubavitcher life, as many new members have skills and experiences out-side Hasidic Judaism that they often integrate into Lubavitcher life. For example, I was told many times about a woman who became a Lubavitcher bt and gave up her successful singing career. She now gives concerts exclusively for Orthodox women.[26] In the hierarchical world of Hasidic Judaism, bts, with their dubious Jewish upbringings, are often not considered good marriage partners for Jews who are *frim* or 'religious from birth' or "ffb". Yiddish is not often spoken among Lubavitchers, partly because of the many bts who do not know it. Lu-bavitcher clothing and style is often less marked than in other Hasidic circles. Men, for example, wear dark double-breasted suit jackets rather than the long black coats that other Hasidic groups wear, and young girls often wear very long skirts, casual shirts, and shoes, some-thing other Hasidic circles, such as Bobover, find unfeminine.

Bobover Hasidic Jews also lived for a time in Crown Heights, but when crime began to rise in the 1960s the Bobover rebbe, Shlomo Hal-berstam, moved his community to the Brooklyn neighborhood of Boro Park, where they have grown to be the largest court there today.[27] The Bobover women I met often called themselves "moderates" in terms of religious stringency and openness to North American popular culture. Mintz (1992:123) suggests that in contrast to other Hasidic circles, Bo-bover are "peace-loving," avoid controversy, and practice a "homey" (*haymish*) variety of Hasidism. After the war this welcoming Judaism appealed to many, and an unusually large number of these European non-Hasidic Jews sent their sons to the Bobover yeshiva. This created a strong new generation of young men who became loyal followers of the Bobover rebbe. Following the death of the Bobover rebbe in 2000, struggles ensued over issues of leadership, with one splinter group eventually building its own schools and synagogue. As the moderates of the Hasidic world, Bobover speak Yiddish and English. Men and women dress in a Hasidic style, but they are not as immedi-ately distinctive as the Satmar or Lubavitch. As I discuss below, the neighborhood of Boro Park that Bobov dominate has become increas-ingly bourgeois over the years, with expensive real estate and bustling shopping boulevards, a destination point for Orthodox Jews from all over the world.

Despite these important and real distinctions among Hasidic circles, I found that in everyday life the common goal of religious stringency united Hasidic Jews, especially women, often muting religious, politi-cal, or ethnic differences. I had initially planned to work with Bobover women and children, but even in Bobover institutions, like the girls' school I introduce below, many of the teachers and administrators, and even some students, were from other Hasidic groups such as Satmar,

Lubavitch, Ger, and Vizhnits, or were not even Hasidic at all. Although all the teachers and administrators answered to the Bobover school principal (the rebbe's granddaughter) who is overseen by the Bobover rebbe and his advisers, they differed in terms of religiosity and involvement in the non-Jewish world, especially in their educational level. Nevertheless, they worked well together and often socialized among themselves, inviting one another to family weddings and celebrations. The boundaries between courts were more fluid than I had expected among the women I met. In fact, one of my early questions, "Which court do you belong to?" was always met with uncomprehending stares. Women eventually reframed my question as, "Do you mean, where does my husband *davn* 'pray'?" This seems to imply that Hasidic courts and allegiance to a rebbe may have more salience for men than for women.

Further, in the course of my research I met a number of Hasidic families who call themselves "unaffiliated," meaning they do not follow any one rebbe exclusively. They do, however, identify their level of religiosity and family history with Hasidic Judaism. In response to this population, a school for girls and one for boys opened about twenty years ago in Boro Park. The majority of its students come from unaffiliated families who still consider themselves Hasidic. The school expects girls, boys, and their families to adhere to a certain level of religious stringency, but the administration does not promote the position of any one rebbe. Being Hasidic, especially for women and girls, can be a stance toward religious stringency and a style of Jewish observance. This is evidenced by the terms that the majority of Hasidic women I met used to describe themselves: *hasidish* (*khsidish*) 'Hasidic' and *haymish* 'homey' (idiomatically, Jews like us). I heard these terms far more often than I heard women refer to a particular Hasidic court.

The Wider Geography of North American Judaism

Hasidism is only one variant of Judaism in North America today. There is tremendous variation that ranges from the strictly observant to the liberal interpretation of Jewish law, and even to secular Judaism. Despite the differences between Hasidic Jews, they are generally considered, and consider themselves, the most religiously stringent. But large communities of non-Hasidic Orthodox Jews also exist that continue to be known as *litvish* 'Lithuanian' or Yeshivish (also Black Hat) Jews. Litvish Jews also rebuilt their communities in North America after the war, establishing a network of rabbinical yeshivas, all of which are affiliated with the Agudas Yisroel, the Orthodox Jewish Union, and governed by the Council of Torah Sages, primarily yeshiva deans

(Heilman and Cohen 1989).[28] A large community of Litvish can be found in Lakewood, New Jersey, and the Brooklyn neighborhoods of Flatbush, Midwood, and Kensington are known for their large Litvish populations.

More liberal forms of orthodoxy include the Modern Orthodox, who attempt to maintain Jewish religious practice while participating more fully in North American life, such as, for example, going to the movies or getting college degrees. The Hasidic women I met in Boro Park often called these "Young Israel types," a Modern Orthodox network of synagogues. I heard a number of women gently make fun of Modern Orthodoxy and its efforts at compromise between religious observance and secular participation.

Finally, there are certain religious and social distinctions between Jews in North America that Hasidic Jews do not recognize, although the distinctions are significant for the rest of American Jewry. These include the more liberal Reform, Conservative, and Reconstructionist movements of Judaism.[29] For Hasidic Jews these are all negatively called *fray* 'free' Jews, that is, unbound by literal Torah observance. As I discuss later, Hasidic Jews have negative beliefs about freedom when it includes what they perceive to be a lack of religious discipline.

THE RISE OF RELIGIOUS STRINGENCY: GENTILES, SECULAR, *FRIM* 'RELIGIOUS', AND MODERN

In postwar North America and Israel, Hasidic Jews and other ultra-orthodox Jews, broadly called *haredim* (Hebrew, 'those who tremble before God') have gradually chosen stricter religious observance in their communities where Jewish law offers alternatives.[30] In postwar North America, Hayim Soloveitchik (1994:77) suggests, the "diminution of otherness" evoked a new vigilance among second-generation haredim.[31] He notes that in voluntarily separate communities, or "enclave communities," there must be continual reinforcement and heightening of difference. A central arena where haredim claim Jewish difference is in increasingly stringent interpretations of sacred texts that they cast as the true essence of a shared Jewish past, although the texts actually reflect contemporary concerns with accuracy and authenticity for a community whose transmitters of memory were obliterated or uprooted by the Nazis (Soloveitchik 1994:70-71). This invention of tradition was shaped not only by the experience of historical rupture but also by new opportunities for Jewish participation in North American life as citizens (Soloveitchik 1994:74-75; see also Friedman 1987, 1993; and Heilman 2006).

Despite increasing religious stringency, the Hasidic women I worked with do not withdraw from the wider communities where they live. Instead, they "hyperbolize" their distinctiveness, as they simultaneously participate in a range of contemporary spheres that allows them to flourish.[32] The hyperbolization includes a heightening of the ways that religious observance has been carried out, which especially emphasizes Hasidic gender differences and a renewed effort to mark Jewish difference from Gentiles and other Jews in very public ways. A generation or two ago, for example, many Hasidic women in Boro Park obeyed the modesty laws by covering their hair with a wig upon marriage. These days, women in the same families cover their hair with a wig *and* a hat, hyperbolizing the injunction to cover the hair. Similarly little girls today (third and fourth generation) are given exclusively Yiddish and Hebrew-origin names like Raizy, Tobe, or Chaya. These girls' grandmothers, however, often had English names, like Lily or Rose, along with their Yiddish/Hebrew names. Many of these same women whom I met had now given up their English names and used only their Yiddish names.[33]

The hyperbolization of Hasidic difference is especially notable in the stark contrasts drawn between Jews and Gentiles. Perhaps this is especially relevant in interactions with children who are in the process of learning claims to Jewish distinction amid the diversity of Brooklyn. Hasidic mothers and teachers asserted to me and their children that, based on the biblical text and rabbinic commentaries, Jews had been chosen by God from among all the other nations for special responsibilities and special rewards in this life and the next. Anthropologist Henry Goldschmidt (2006:22–24), in his study of blacks and Lubavitchers in Crown Heights, notes that in the founding text of Lubavitch Hasidim (the Tanya), there is the claim that although Gentiles and Jews share a *nefesh beheymes* 'an animal soul', only Jews have a *nefesh elokis* 'a godly soul'. I also heard from Bobover and unaffiliated Hasidic teachers and mothers in Boro Park that the Jewish *neshume* 'soul' is "just different" (from that of Gentiles). Hasidic women I worked with tell their children (using English terms) that Jews are more "refined," "disciplined," and "civilized," that they have more *mentshlekhkayt* 'humanity' than Gentiles. Gentiles, many suggested, do not have the internal strength to discipline their desires. As one Hasidic woman told me, "*Goyim* 'Gentiles' (sing. *goy*, pl. *goyim*) do whatever they want, do what they feel like." This hierarchy of peoples, legitimated by a God-given soul and developed through the discipline of religious practice, engages with and inverts a particular narrative of modernity where a Protestant-inflected secularism represents the peak of civilization.

Moderate Hasidim, Bobover, and others in Boro Park, however, have different histories and religious texts than do Lubavitchers in Crown Heights, where Jewish and Gentile difference is almost always closely shadowed by racial tensions. For Lubavitchers in Crown Heights, Goldschmidt (2006:22) argues, religious claims supersede what Lubavitchers perceive to be superficial black and white racial distinctions or the cultural claims made by many less observant North American Jews.[34] But in the more diverse neighborhoods of Boro Park and nearby Sunset Park, the religious category of Gentile is not always monolithic, nor is it always framed in religious terms. An illustration is the Hasidic woman who told me that while "on an essential level, goyim are goyim," there are also the exceptional "good goyim." Good goyim are moral, reasonable people who attempt to perfect themselves by fulfilling the Noachide Laws (the seven laws that the Torah requires both Jews and Gentiles to observe).[35] Often good goyim are neighbors with whom a Hasidic Jew has had friendly interactions or a business partner who has proven to be fair and honest.

Some Hasidic women and children I worked with use racist discourse to distinguish between black Gentiles and white Gentiles, creating a racialized distinction within the broader religious trope of Jewish-Gentile difference. Other non-white Gentiles in Boro Park, such as South Asians or Chinese, in my experience, are generally ignored or simply relegated to the category of goy.[36] In addition, a wide range of Muslims, distinguished through their dress, are called "Arabs." Black Gentiles, in contrast, are often called *shvartzes* ('blacks', a derogatory term) and may be described as "scary" and unappealing. The ways that a child learns to recognize and distinguish between Gentiles is a topic of much discussion, both between Hasidic women and children and between children themselves.

Whereas the word "Gentiles" has specific meanings, women used the English term "secular," often coupled with "North American," as a vague description, which, they said, depended on the context. At times it may mean a Jew who is not observant, especially referring to Jews who came before World War II and discarded most forms of religious observance in their efforts to assimilate. At other times "secular" may refer to North American popular culture such as books, movies, fashion, magazines, or North American bodies of knowledge, for example, psychology or education. I believe the term "secular," as it is used most often by Hasidic women I worked with, provides a broad label for North American cultural life that is not explicitly Gentile or Jewish. The secular world is often opposed, in the everyday talk of women and girls, to those who are *frim* 'religious Jews' or to Jews more generally. Hasidic understandings and uses of the terms "secular" and *"frim"* are, however, different from the way most North Americans understand the secular and the religious, a theme I explore throughout this book.

Jews who are less frim than Hasidic women and girls or not even observant at all are much more troubling to narratives of God-given Jewish distinction than Gentiles or secular North Americans. Hasidic girls and women expressed a great deal of ambivalence toward what they call more "modern" ways of being Jewish. Modern activities or objects either bring a Jew in contact with Gentiles or blur a boundary between how Jews and Gentiles live. Technology and capitalism, for example, are not inherently modern if they support a Hasidic way of life, something sociologist Solomon Poll (1962) noted many years ago. In contrast, modern activities include watching a movie, going to dinner at a restaurant where men and women sit together, having a pet dog, or even celebrating one's birthday, because they are activities that North Americans engage in. Being modern is not so much about adherence to Jewish law; rather, the issue is how an observant Jew interprets the spirit of the law. A girl, for example, may be dressed modestly, but if her clothes all come from the Gap, she will be perceived by other observant Jews as more modern because she looks more like the Gentiles around her. These categories—Gentile, secular, *frim,* and modern—are all important for understanding how Hasidic girls come to understand themselves and ways of being in the world.

JEWISH DIFFERENCE: EPISTEMOLOGY AND METHODOLOGY

Dressed in a conservative skirt, blouse, and black tights, with my unruly hair tucked under a black cotton beret, I clutched my backpack on my lap as I sat on the Brooklyn-bound B train. At Grand Street in Chinatown the subway went above ground, snaking through closely packed tenements with laundry flapping on lines strung between buildings. Then the subway crossed the Manhattan Bridge, the sun glinting, first off the steel and glass skyline and then the choppy surface of the East River. This train took me to Boro Park, Brooklyn, where I conducted fieldwork intensively from 1995 to 1998. But because this study is an example of anthropology at home, over the years I have continued to cross the Manhattan Bridge and visit Hasidic women friends, and also keep in touch with them by phone. I have kept track of changes and continuities among the women I worked with, as well as the broader neighborhood of Boro Park, so that mine is both a longitudinal and contemporary account.

I chose to work in Boro Park partly because I hoped to avoid problems of representation given past critiques of anthropology, as I, too, am a Jewish woman from New York. Anthropologist Jonathan Boyarin (1988) has similarly noted that by choosing to work with Jews he hoped no one could accuse him of "cultural imperialism." I also confess to harboring romantic notions about shared history and identity. I knew I would not share a common faith with Hasidic women, but my great-grandparents had been Orthodox and came from the same parts of Eastern Europe that many Hasidic Jews do. I hoped that I would be accepted, at least partially, because of who I was. Of course, this proved to be more complicated than I expected.

The encounter between me and Hasidic women and girls should be understood as representative of contemporary struggles over Jewish authenticity in North America, as well as the politics of contemporary ethnography where the "informants" are literate, politically active, and engaged in their own representation. That I am a nonobservant Jewish woman from New York, and a graduate student in anthropology, shaped the research in many ways. While I was studying Hasidic socialization, I was simultaneously socialized into professional anthropology and, by Hasidic women I met, into appropriate Hasidic femininity. Meanwhile, Hasidic women were using my presence to socialize their own daughters about how to interpret Jewish difference.

Like every anthropologist, I explained that the goals of my research were a doctoral degree and, eventually, a book. However, the Hasidic women I worked with framed my presence in a religious discourse of redemption through return. For them, God had led me to my research topic in order to help me return to the faith. My very presence legitimized their critique of the secular world. That I, who had a liberal Jewish upbringing and such extensive exposure to higher education, might still end up among them was evidence of the power and truth of their Judaism.

As a Jew studying other Jews, I take up a conversation started by other Jewish anthropologists working in Jewish communities.[37] Anthropologist Susan Kahn (2000), in her study of assisted reproduction in Israel, has noted that because of her own identity her research was marked by a blurring of the line between subject and object. For those conducting research with Hasidic Jews, as in any nonliberal religious community, the potential conversion or return of the anthropologist remains a key issue (see Harding 2000), to which I return in the coda to this book. Other Jewish women ethnographers who have worked with Hasidic women in Israel and North America have noted the tension between communal efforts at *kiruv* 'Jewish outreach' and goals for ethnographic research.[38] Like me, these anthropologists struggled with

Hasidic women's expectations of Jewish return and their own hopes for gaining access to communities that are often closed to outsiders, including Jewish outsiders.

In my case, the confounding of observer and observed was increased when I got married during the research period, which meant that I then occupied a series of social positions shared by the very women I was studying: Jewish "girl," bride, wife, and, after a time, mother. When I attended a class for Hasidic brides, there was little separation between researcher and participant. The last class was exactly a week before my own wedding, and the merging of positions challenged my sense of professional self as I wondered who, exactly, was attending the classes. Was it the anthropologist? Was it an observant Jewish bride? A nonobservant Jewish bride who was thinking about becoming more observant? I never considered becoming Orthodox, something Hasidic women I met puzzled over, but my experience did force me to wrestle with many of my own assumptions about religious observance, my commitment to Judaism, and my responsibilities as a Jewish ethnographer.

Hasidic women and I were constantly reframing the meaning of Jewish difference that our encounter personified. My presence in the community could be confusing. The modest dress I wore out of respect for community members and also to facilitate my entrance into the community hinted that I was attempting to participate in a more Jewish life, whatever the reason. Initially I denied that status, claiming simply to be working toward my degree. However, my denials were countered by knowing nods indicating that perhaps I was not ready to accept why I had been drawn to my research topic. I eventually decided to follow the lead of the women I was meeting and neither made claims nor denied the influence of being exposed to their community. Issues common to every ethnographic encounter became especially charged. In everyday greetings, for example, Hasidim often respond to the question, "How are you?" with *burikh hashem* 'blessed be his name'. Although most anthropologists will aim to follow local rules of politeness, my attempts were charged with the uncertain status of my Jewish soul. I was initially uncomfortable to respond with *burikh hashem*, because I felt I was misrepresenting myself. When I did respond this way, several women expressed their approval, as they did to my other attempts at ritual behavior. Motivated by their belief that the first step of Jewish observance is religious practice, followed by understanding, my actions were a step in the right direction, no matter what my motives were. Indeed, this is an issue for Hasidic children that I discuss in chapter 3.

Hasidic women and girls' interpretations of my own Jewish difference helped me recognize certain key themes that shaped the research.
For example, those who first met me often initially asked if I was from
"out of town," or if I was a Beys Yaakov girl (a more Litvish girls'
school). The clues they cited for these impressions were my accent,
which is, in fact, a typically Manhattan one, and my shearling coat,
which was, coincidentally, what all the more modern Beys Yaakov girls
were wearing. These interpretations were the first clues I had that embodied signs, such as a different vowel or a style of coat, formed a
system for understanding and producing Jewish difference among
women and girls.

I tried to accommodate to communal practices and not to be provocative. I said the appropriate prayers before eating. I was always conscious, especially in my work with young children, of my position as
an outsider whose contact with the Gentile world was considered potentially polluting. I felt it was my responsibility (as well as in my research interests) to conform as best as I could to the practices I was
attempting to understand. Perhaps it was my efforts to offend no one
that made my time in Boro Park feel constraining and stifling. Despite
close friendships and the generous invitations of many Hasidic families, I often breathed a sigh of relief as the subway crossed the Manhattan Bridge and brought me back to my own Upper West Side home
after spending part of each week in Boro Park.

My initial entry was facilitated by another anthropology student
who had done research on modesty in the community and introduced
me to a Hasidic woman. Little by little, I obtained the phone numbers
of other women—friends, neighbors, and relatives. In the more formal,
institutional realm of a Bobover Hasidic girls' school, Bnos Yisruel, I
walked in off the street and offered to be a "helper" (cutting out arts
and crafts projects for the children) in exchange for the opportunity to
observe in several classrooms. I believe my research topic, Yiddish and
children's education, aided my entrance. It was not threatening in
terms of challenging gender relations, and their educational system is
an area of which many Hasidic families and educators are proud.

After the several months I spent building social networks within the
community and establishing myself in Bnos Yisruel, my research began
to take shape. I regularly attended and audio-taped in two kindergarten classrooms in Bnos Yisruel and in the second year I followed the
same girls into the first grade. *Morah* 'teacher' Chaya, the kindergarten
teacher, and Mrs. Silver, the first-grade teacher, appear frequently in
the coming pages. Both were young, energetic, and earnest Bobover
women who were recently married. Overall, I had less contact with
older teen-aged girls, who are closely protected, and older boys and

adult males. I was able to attend the Bobover boys' preschool for three months where I also helped out. But when I tried to switch from a nursery class to a kindergarten and began to come more often, the principal telephoned and asked me to come see her. I entered her office with a pounding heart. She told me that parents had seen me in the class and complained, asking about the "strange" woman in the class. They wanted me out. She had to accommodate them, she told me apologetically, and so I stopped visiting there. This experience led to an unexpected and important finding: Hasidic girls are less protected from outsiders than are Hasidic boys.

Over time I developed close relationships with three families who allowed me to collect longitudinal data on their children: the Klein family (Bobover Hasidim), the Gross family (Dobrizhiner Hasidim), and the Schwartz family (unaffiliated Hasidim). I also visited extensively with the Katz family (also unaffiliated). I have made minor changes to everyone's lives in order to protect privacy, and pseudonyms are used throughout.

When I visited the families, I audiotaped and transcribed everyday interactions between women and children and between children themselves. This included bath time, homework, dinnertime, and playtime. Rifky Katz and Esty Schwartz, two young mothers, are especially insightful commentators on Hasidic life, and their thoughts and words appear often. Even though I worked so closely with these women and we have remained friends, they told me years later that they only allowed me to visit them at first because they hoped my research would become more than "just a project for school"; they hoped that I would become more observant.

In preparation for the research, I brushed up on the Hebrew I had learned as a child and learned Yiddish in the YIVO program at Columbia University. However, Hasidic Yiddish, as I discuss, is distinct from the standardized Yiddish I had learned, and so I arranged to have a private Yiddish conversation tutorial with the daughter of a friend, something many Hasidic women found amusing and a bit odd. My tutor, Gitty Fried, was a newly married Bobover woman, just nineteen years old and a recent high school graduate. Our lessons quickly became two-way informal interviews. I brought Gitty all my questions that had come up that week during research and practiced Yiddish, and she asked me many questions about more modern Jews and my own experiences growing up. We met in her house when her husband was in *kolel* (the post-yeshiva institution of higher Jewish learning for married men). Gitty, a bright, matter-of-fact, and curious person, was just enough of a newcomer to married life to be an especially thoughtful commentator.

In addition to my work with women and children, I also attended wider communal events. I went to many Hasidic weddings and holiday celebrations, as well as inspirational lectures for women. I visited the Catskill Mountains to see a girls' summer camp and to visit Rifky Katz's bungalow colony. Finally, in order to understand broader Hasidic community building activities, I regularly attended local community board meetings, interviewed non-Jewish neighborhood residents, and followed local and national media coverage of interactions between Hasidim and others that usually reported conflicts over resources, privileges, or representation.

Throughout the book I often use the term "Hasidic" without qualifying which court. In these instances I refer to the range of Hasidic women and girls that I worked with during my research; many of them were Bobover but others included Lubavitch, Satmar, Vizhnits, and the unaffiliated. As noted earlier, I do this because although court distinctions are often important in marriage, school considerations, or distinctions in ritual practice, these distinction are rarely noted in everyday interactions in school, the streets, or at home by women I spoke with. For this reason, I adopt the local term women used to express widespread commonalities: Hasidish or Hasidic and haymish. Both imply a shared level of religious stringency as well as a shared way of life. Nevertheless, at times when court differences among Hasidic women and girls are important, I note them appropriately.

THE EVERYDAY WORLD OF HASIDIC GIRLS AND WOMEN

Among the Hasidic children I met in Boro Park, boys have very different experiences than girls have as they grow up. They go to separate parochial schools, camps, and social events; they pray in different parts of the communal synagogue, with women and girls upstairs or behind a curtain, hidden from men and boys for whom they pose a potential distraction. Girls can shop in any New York store for skirts, blouses, or dresses as long as they are appropriately modest and do not mix linen and wool, a biblical prohibition. Boys, however, wear distinctive black pants and white dress shirts. From age three on, boys have long side-locks (*payes*), wear black velvet yarmulkes, and, eventually, sport beards and hats appropriate to their Hasidic sect. Boys and girls even come to speak different languages once they enter first grade: boys speak Hasidic Yiddish and girls speak Hasidic English, which I describe in detail in chapters 4 and 5. Boys' and girls' separate socialization prepares them for the gender segregation that increasingly characterizes adult Hasidic Jewish life in Boro Park.

Gender segregation is based on the different responsibilities that women and men have to the Jewish community as a whole. As already mentioned, boys and men study sacred texts, and therefore they are prominent in the Jewish public sphere such as the synagogue, the religious leadership structure of the community, and the social life of the yeshiva. Women and girls mediate the Gentile/secular public sphere and are responsible for interactions with, for example, pediatricians, social service agencies, and the electric company. They are also the ones who keep the domestic sphere running, although Hasidic men are officially the heads of their households.

In the intimate space of the family, however, gender segregation can be more muted. Hasidic fathers and mothers are both actively involved in child care, although, as children mature, fathers become more involved in their sons' educations and mothers increasingly supervise their daughters. Young boys and girls—neighbors, cousins, and siblings—often play together in front of their Brooklyn houses or apartments, riding bikes, playing tag, or jumping rope. Even as they grow older and their lives are increasingly separate, at home brothers and sisters live in close quarters. I was reminded of this whenever I used the bathroom in a Hasidic apartment and saw all the stockings hanging to dry in the shower or when I saw Hasidic boys, teenagers, expertly holding and playing with infants.

Educational Institutions

Educational institutions are a critical factor in boys' and girls' different childhoods. As noted, when Hasidic Jews arrived in New York after the Holocaust, private schools were quickly established for boys, teaching literacy in *loshn-koydesh* 'holy language' used for study and prayer and Yiddish, which was and continues to be the medium of instruction. Once the boys are literate in Yiddish and loshn-koydesh, generally by first grade, in class boys read a line of sacred text in loshn-koydesh, translate it into Yiddish, and then discuss the text in Yiddish. They receive limited secular education.[39]

With no Hasidic school available for girls except Satmar and Lubavitch, other Hasidic parents sent their daughters to existing private Hebrew day schools, which were Orthodox, not Hasidic.[40] Yiddish was not part of the curriculum. Girls (today's grandmothers) learned English and gained passive competence in loshn-koydesh as the language of prayer. Additionally, some Hebrew day schools taught Modern Hebrew (*ivrit*), the language of Israel, which differs from loshn-koydesh. But when rabbinic leaders realized, in the 1970s, that girls were speaking less and less Yiddish and were exposed to more modern ideas, the majority of courts built private schools for girls.

Yiddish is the language used in kindergarten, and girls learn the Hebrew/Yiddish alphabet in preparation for literacy instruction in both languages. Once girls enter first grade, classes are in Yiddish in the morning, when "Jewish" subjects including loshn-koydesh and Yiddish literacy is taught, and English is spoken in the afternoon, when "secular" or "English" subjects are taught. Yiddish for the girls is both a medium for instruction as well as a curriculum subject in that girls are taught Yiddish grammar, spelling, and vocabulary. Girls even have different teachers for their morning and afternoon classes. Hasidic women teach the morning Jewish subjects and Litvish (non-Hasidic, Orthodox) women often teach the English subjects because these courses require a certified teacher with stronger backgrounds in secular education. Because of this educational history, Hasidic girls today are often more fluent in Yiddish than their mothers and their grandmothers, although their fluency starts to break down as they enter elementary school (see chapters 4 and 5).

Boys' schools structurally and pedagogically reproduce the yeshivas of Eastern Europe, but Hasidic girls' schools have adapted North American parochial and public school models. In preschool Hasidic classrooms, there are distinct areas for pretend play, blocks and games, and art. Girls sit in small groups at tables or in a circle on chairs. Colorful posters and students' work are displayed around the classroom, although in most the writing is in loshn-koydesh or Yiddish and the work has explicitly religious themes. In one preschool classroom I observed, pictures of three food categories were displayed (fruit, baked goods, and juice), with the appropriate loshn-koydesh blessing for each.

Once girls enter first grade, the classrooms more closely resemble parochial schools. Girls sit at wooden desks arranged in rows facing the teacher. They also now wear plaid uniforms to school, much like Catholic school girls, but instead of kneesocks and short-sleeved blouses for the warmer months, they wear tights all year round and long-sleeved blouses to be appropriately modest (tsnies). They are also required to have their hair pulled back and are not allowed to wear long earrings or nail polish.

Throughout girls' schooling, activities familiar to any North American schoolchild, such as arts and crafts, school plays, recess, and assemblies, are informed by Hasidic beliefs about gendered childhood, the nature of truth, and religious authority. For example, if a child hits another child, she may be given a "time out" as in any other North American school. The seat where she must sit during the "time out," however, is called, in Yiddish, the tshive-benkl 'the chair of penitence', and the child may wear a red mitten to symbolize that she hit another child.

Two Hasidic women pushing strollers and Hasidic boy on a bike. Beryl Goldberg, photographer.

Hasidic girls' schools, except those that are unaffiliated, are supervised by a Hasidic rebbe and, as noted, directly linked to the authority of particular Hasidic courts. Schools also run sleep-away camps in the Catskill Mountains, where girls can spend the summer months; a number of adult women I spoke with reminisced fondly about these camps. Both boys' and girls' schools are from preschool through high school.

Once girls finish high school at age seventeen or eighteen, they either marry through an arranged marriage or go to a teachers' seminary in Brooklyn or in a Hasidic community abroad such as Toronto (common for Bobovers) or Israel. Most women and men do not pursue higher education, although with local colleges like Touro offering gender-segregated classes at night, attitudes toward higher education are changing (see Heilman 2006). Although they are not allowed to study Torah or, in some Hasidic schools such as Satmar, even to read the Bible, lifelong education has become increasingly important for Hasidic women.[41] Women in Boro Park may attend countless Jewish inspirational lectures and courses, read Jewish books and magazines or *Reader's Digest* which has been communally approved, and listen to cassettes on Jewish themes and self-improvement.

Social Lives and Responsibilities

Hasidic girls and women I met are forbidden to participate in many forms of North American leisure activities such as going to movies, watching television, or reading certain books. However, they are neither isolated nor oppressed by their lives. Levine's (2003) study of Lubavitcher Hasidic teens in Crown Heights, and Davidman's (1991) and Kaufman's (1991) studies of returnees to the faith (bts), all capture the pleasures and strong sense of purpose and community that Lubavitcher girls and women can experience.[42] Levine has shown that at a time when their North American counterparts often lose confidence, Lubavitcher teen-aged girls maintain a strong sense of self and purpose. She suggests this may come from spending most of their time in the company of other girls and women, as well as the especially strong belief among Lubavitchers that each girl's everyday actions have the cosmic potential to help bring the Messiah.

Because Lubavitcher women in particular are exposed to so many unobservant Jews, they are familiar with feminism and other ways of life more generally. Morris (1998), for example, in her historical study of a Lubavitcher women's magazine, notes how Hasidic women have consistently engaged with and rejected North American feminism. This familiarity with the very cultural forms they critique was also common among the Hasidic women I met, although to a lesser extent, as was their elaborations around the Messiah. I should not have been surprised, although I was, when Esty Schwartz, the young unaffiliated Hasidic mother I worked with who is prominent in the upcoming pages, winked at me and told me that her daughter, Leye, "looks just like Cindy Crawford with that beauty mark on her cheek." Hasidic mothers I spent time with liked to show me that they were fluent in much of North American popular culture but rejected its values nonetheless.

When girls are still in school, they get together at one another's houses and have group shopping excursions. At school productions and community events, such as slideshows and lectures, girls can see friends and socialize. Many do homework together or work on school projects. For married women, weddings are important social events where they catch up with friends and relatives, and spend the evening dancing, eating, and chatting. The constant cycle of Jewish holidays ensures time for visiting and relaxing with relatives and friends, as does everyday shopping with their children in tow.

When girls get married and have children, their responsibilities expand significantly. Primarily they care for their children, making meals, checking homework, playing, and teaching their children. Women do most of the housework, although many had a Polish or Russian "cleaning lady" (goyte, feminine form of goy) to help out. As mentioned, they are also responsible for mediating any outside services related to the home or the children, such as paying the bills and taking children to the doctor. Hasidic wives must manage and maintain a strictly kosher home, where, for example, dairy products and meat products do not mix and certain foods are prohibited, such as pork or shellfish. Even vegetables must be checked and cleaned lest they harbor tiny flies or worms which would make them nonkosher. A woman and her husband together must observe the complex laws of family purity (tahares-hamishpukhe), which regulate all conjugal intimacy based on a woman's menstrual cycle. Women are also responsible for all preparations for the Jewish holidays that structure the year. During the spring holiday of Passover, for example, the Hasidic women I knew gave their homes the most exhaustive cleaning I have ever seen in their efforts to fulfill the religious requirement that all leavening be removed from the home. Women commonly stayed up all night preparing their homes for the holiday, and during school recess stressed-out teachers discussed how much they still had to do to get their homes ready. Many women with children continue to work outside the home, as teachers, businesswomen, or providing services to other women such as babysitting or selling ready-to-use bags of lettuce that were already checked for bugs. The women I met who

Boro Park side street. Beryl Goldberg, photographer

feature in the pages of this book are busy, active, strong, and, most of all, pious, certain that their way of life is the only one with any real meaning.

BORO PARK

The urban neighborhood of Boro Park, Brooklyn, has imprecise and expanding boundaries. Noach Dear, the previous city councilman, told me that the neighborhood spans 36th to 60th Streets from north to south and 8th to 20th Avenues from east to west. In 1992 a building boom took off when the city changed zoning laws to allow homeowners to build on 65 percent more of their lots (Heilman 1998; Sontag 1998). Boro Park, along with Kensington and sections of Bay Ridge, make up Community District 12, which is home not only to Hasidic Jews but to a diversity of other ethnic groups including Russians, Poles, Pakistanis, Chinese, and Latinos.

Boro Park is one of the largest, most affluent, and most diverse of the Jewish neighborhoods in New York City. The 2000 Census reports that out of 160,000 residents, 82,000 (51%) identified as Jewish and three-quarters of that figure identified as Orthodox (Heilman 2006:73). But with the birthrate in Boro Park double that of most of the city, that figure, according to community members, is much too low. They claim that there are at least 95,000 Orthodox Jews. The Bobover rebbe, Shlomo Halberstam, descendent of the Galician rebbe Chaim Halberstam, was among the first Hasidic leaders to move his congregation to Boro Park, Brooklyn, in the 1960s. Other Hasidic dynasties followed, transforming the neighborhood into a modern day "kingdom" of various courts mapped onto the streets of Brooklyn. With the influx of Hasidic and non-Hasidic Orthodox Jews, many of the long-time Italian, Irish, and non-Orthodox Jews left for the suburbs or moved to other Brooklyn neighborhoods (Mayer 1978). Today Bobover Hasidim form the biggest community, although they generally comprise less than a third of the Hasidic population in Boro Park. Smaller Hasidic groups, commonly identified by a rebbe, include Krasna, Ger, Skver, Munkacz, Pupa, Karlin-Stolin, and Satmar (Epstein 1987; Schick 1979; Sontag 1998).

Hasidic Jews in Boro Park have built many visible and invisible walls in the diverse neighborhood where they live. But to have influence with the city government in shaping their neighborhood, they participate in much of city and state life. Many Hasidic Jews run businesses, vote in blocs for representatives who serve their interests, sit on community boards, and, when necessary, even use the federal court system to resolve disputes (see Boyarin 2002). Unlike the Amish, who attempt to withdraw into their own communities as much as possible, Hasidic Jews selectively make use of many aspects of contemporary society in order to strengthen their communities. For example, many Hasidim use new technologies like cell phones and computers for business, media for communicating with Jews across national boundaries, and minivans to ferry around their large families. Hasidic Jews have built their own organizations that serve state-like functions such as a volunteer ambulance service, neighborhood watches, and charities. They also have organizations that facilitate the use of governmental social services such as the (now defunct) Council for Jewish Organizations, which routinely helped Hasidic Jews file for state benefits without leaving their neighborhood or even speaking English.

At the same time, Hasidic Jews live in what they call *goles* 'exile'. Despite their participation in the city, state, and nation, for Hasidic Jews in Brooklyn, life is one more phase of historical dislocation and rebuilding, one that will continue until the Messiah arrives. Jewish diaspora reaches back thousands of years, with Jews experiencing multiple dispersals from many of the lands where they had established communities, sometimes over a thousand-year period (Boyarin 2002). Hasidic Jews in Boro Park were exiled and dispersed during the Holocaust from what they nostalgically call the *alte haym* 'old home' in Eastern Europe (most generally what is now Poland, Ukraine, Hungary and Romania). These Hasidic Jews yearn for their former destroyed Eastern European home, as well as the ultimate return to biblical Israel, which will come only with the Messiah.[43]

The experience of dispersal creates ties of memory and everyday practices that cross time and space. Most Hasidic Jews have family members in enclave communities across the globe, and these ties to the diaspora are periodically activated through visiting, business, marriage, and study. Marriages are made across national boundaries, between Brooklyn and Argentina, for example. Young men and women from Brooklyn go to study in yeshivas and teachers' seminaries as far away as London, Israel, Australia, or Montreal. Through their own privatized transit system, Jewish networks are kept active. Buses (with separate sections for men and women), for example, regularly leave Boro Park for New York State (Monsey, the Catskill Mountains, and Monroe), New Jersey (Lakewood), and other places with large Jewish populations such as Montreal. These ties reinforce the experience of *goles*, allowing Hasidic Jews to claim allegiance to no nation, while simultaneously using the resources of any nation. As a religious diaspora their ultimate loyalty is to other Jews whom they call *haymishe yidn* as well as to Jews more generally.

Through an appropriation of urban space, Hasidim in Boro Park have built an alternative city that can, at times, cast its shadow over the mainstream New York City landscape. Hasidim attempt to control the morality of the built environment by patrolling its borders. For example, thanks to a wealthy Australian Hasidic donor, many Boro Park bus shelters display posters of Jewish holiday celebrations and products, rather than sexy underwear ads. Individuals monitor immodest store displays, and, on one occasion, photographs of women's faces were spray-painted out of an advertisement considered immodest. Several months later, the storekeeper changed his display. To further shield themselves from unwanted and unnecessary contact with the world outside their community, Hasidim have built political shortcuts through bureaucracies that enable them to get prompt and effective attention. Hasidic political power stems from their control over Hasidic votes, though they have become intricately involved in the political process, too. Officer Miller, a member of the local police force in the 66th Precinct told me that Hasidim call on their elected officials to put pressure on civil servants who are not accommodating.

One of their strategies for interacting with the city and state government of New York is to use the language of minority status, that is, democratic notions of tolerance for difference in order to define and protect their own communities—communities which themselves explicitly reject tolerance of others as a principle. Hasidic Jews also strive to control their image as it is portrayed in secular presses and popular entertainment; a frequent response to an unflattering portrait is to protest using a lexicon based on North American ideals of protest and civil rights regarding ethnic minority communities. When a film crew came to shoot scenes for the film *A Price above Rubies*, which is about a Hasidic woman who leaves her community and takes up with a Latino boyfriend, Hasidim physically stopped the shoot, using a peaceful sit-in to disrupt the filming and making it impossible to continue.[44] I spoke with assemblyman Dov Hikind (an observant Jew himself), who had issued a public statement boycotting the film. He suggested that although Hasidim are the same as any other group, they are not accorded the same rights as other ethnic minorities. "You know being politically correct," he told me, "applies to minorities, to the gay community, it does not apply to the Hasidic community . . . it's very unfortunate." In this conflict, Hasidim actively and through their spokespeople, attempted to dismiss what they thought was an unfair portrayal of their lives.[45]

Hasidic attempts to maintain a protected enclave community while selectively participating in the political, economic, and cultural life of New York City can create conflicts with others who live in Boro Park, including neighbors, customers, and sometimes even friends. Some neighborhood activists and non-Hasidic residents of Boro Park suggested to me that Hasidim do not share an "American" vision of community, in which shared space and common interest override ethnic difference. The president of the local community board, Mrs. Canelli, told me that rather than build "community" in Boro Park, Hasidim want to protect themselves from the communities that already exist:

> I think they always do that [i.e., take over a community], so that they could put an invisible fence around the area and nobody would come in ... they want to do like the ghetto, you know, this is an invisible one. This is what they tried to attain and they did."

Mrs. Canelli criticized Hasidic community building practices that were premised on the exclusion of those who are different. When I told Rifky Katz about complaints I had heard from non-Jewish community members regarding neighborhood politics, she smiled and shrugged, saying, "That's *goles.*" She elaborated that Jews have always lived among yet kept apart from those who are different from them. Life in New York, she told me, is just one more phase of a journey. Many Hasidic women told me, nevertheless, that it is their responsibility to provide a model of a moral community to Gentiles and to other Jews. Hence they do not like to see divisiveness among Jews publicly aired, or defections or deviant behaviors, which exist in any community. Hasidic women I worked with told me that by building up *klal yisruel* 'the Jewish nation' rather than any "American" form of community, they do their part to live according to God's commandments.

BOOK OVERVIEW

In this book I look across the Hasidic female life cycle, from infancy to girls on the threshold of marriage, to understand how Hasidic women teach girls to discipline their desires and their bodies as they redeem Jewish meaning from North American secular and Gentile life.

Chapters 2 and 3 focus on nonliberal Hasidic notions of the self. Through discursive practices such as praising and questioning, Hasidic women try to teach their daughters the desire to "fit in" (a local English term), to fear being like Gentiles, and to shape their curiosity in distinctly nonliberal ways. Hasidic women elaborate beliefs about the person and the nature of children and childhood that are specific to Hasidic Judaism. At the same time they draw on North American popular psychological models of child development and education. A distinctive nonliberal goal for Hasidic socialization is the cultivation of individual autonomy so that girls can fulfill their communitarian responsibilities to their families, other Jews, and God. Girls who fail to fit in, who ask the wrong kinds of questions or are defiant (*khitspedik*), are silenced, shamed, teased, and eventually may have to leave the community.

Chapters 4 and 5 focus on the dynamic ways that Hasidic women and girls use bilingualism (Yiddish and English) to mediate both the secular world and differences between Orthodox Jewish women. For Hasidic Jews, no matter which language is used or how mixed Yiddish and English become, the mode of communication is always Jewish. I describe two emerging gendered varieties of Jewish languages, Hasidic Yiddish and Hasidic English. Hasidic men speak predominantly Hasidic Yiddish, whereas Hasidic women speak Hasidic English, transforming English into a Jewish language. However, girls sometimes express ambivalence about not wanting to sound too "modern" or "too Hasidic." These two chapters show the complicated work that language is doing among Hasidic Jews today: separating Jews from Gentiles, Hasidic men from Hasidic women, and creating hierarchies of piety among observant Jewish women and girls.

Chapters 6 and 7 shift the focus from language itself to talk about the bodies and minds of Hasidic girls in the practices of modesty (*tsnies*). Women and girls' ways of speaking (regardless of which language), clothing, reading, and comportment are shaped by a belief that public embodied signs produce and provide evidence of Jewish women's interior souls. I analyze the ways that Hasidic women socialize girls to imagine their embodied difference from a range of others and to encourage the desire to be like Jewish "princesses." As girls mature and prepare for marriage, they are taught how to talk about new forms of intimacy in modest ways. Hasidic women and girls do not deny the value of secular materiality, knowledge or goals for individual fulfillment. Rather, they claim that they enjoy the "true" pleasures of consumption, beauty, sexuality, and romantic love because they have the strength to elevate them through the religious disciplines of Hasidic modesty.

In the coda I suggest the contributions this specific study of Hasidic women and children makes to wider conversations in anthropology about alternative modernities. I also discuss the challenges an ethnography of nonliberal Hasidic women poses to the possibilities of an ethical practice of anthropology.

The world today has become increasingly polarized by religion, particularly in the aftermath of 9/11. Anthropology, with its potential for offering critical yet humanizing close studies of everyday life, has a political responsibility to complicate the analytical categories of the religious and the secular. Discursive and embodied practice between nonliberal religious women and girls unexpectedly bridges what too often these days seem to be unbreachable chasms between modernity and tradition, the secular and the religious, cosmopolitanism and enclavism. My approach has broad implications for documenting the historical and cultural processes by which communities lay claim to authoritative versions of modernity, legitimized by religion or secularism. Robert Orsi has commented on the importance of studying "the despised religious idioms," not in order to impose a normative grid but to make us challenge our own ways of understanding (2005). My goal is to do just that—to provoke new ways of thinking about nonliberal religion through the everyday words and lives of Hasidic women and children.

CHAPTER TWO

Fitting In

ONE WINTRY EVENING I sat at Mindy Gross's kitchen table while she gave her children supper. Mindy had been a preschool teacher until the birth of her fourth child just a few months back. She was an easygoing woman with brown eyes and a shoulder-length brown wig with bangs. I met her at a "salad party" Esty Schwartz had thrown for some old high school friends, where each woman brought a salad to share. When Esty told Mindy about my research, Mindy invited me over to hear how her children spoke "only Yiddish" at home. Although this did not turn out to be completely accurate, it is how I came to be visiting as she spooned up macaroni and frankfurters for her children. While her children ate, she turned to me and said, "Do you know, Ayala, that this morning I gave Yitsy (age two) a *mitsve-tsetl* 'good deed note' to bring to school? " She explained that she had written a note for Yitsy's teacher telling her that he had gone to synagogue with his father early that morning and prayed *azoy shayn* 'so nicely'. His teacher had read the note in front of the class, told him how proud of him she was, and gave him a prize, a piece of candy. Yitsy beamed from his seat. Then Mindy turned to Yitsy and chanted in a singsong voice, "Do you want to get another *mitsve*? *Vus vet zan dan mitsve*? (What will your good deed be?) What can you do to get a *mitsve*? You can eat your supper!" Yitsy said emphatically, "No!"

Although Hasidic children, like Yitsy, do not always respond just as their mothers and teachers would like, most of the Hasidic women I met, in a historical shift from the practices of their mothers and grandmothers, use praise and rewards to create the desire in their children to take on the personal responsibility for obeying God's commandments. The Hasidic women I worked with regularly read popular North American parenting books and, during their schooling, are exposed to educational materials that draw on North American popular psychology, educational incentive models for behavior, and self-help genres.[1,2] These women use contemporary North American childrearing practices and beliefs, however, to cultivate nonliberal Hasidic conceptions of the self, conceptions that simultaneously draw on Hasidic religious philosophy regarding the soul, good, evil, and gender difference.[3] In practices of *khinekh* 'moral education', Hasidic women engage the modern notion of the self as a project but with a key difference: the modern Hasidic child realizes fulfillment by independently conforming to a religiously communitarian society rather than to one that promotes pride in individualism. When Hasidic children learn to use their individual autonomy to "fit in" (a local English term) and fulfill their responsibilities to other Jews and God, they are ultimately participating in the Jewish moral narrative of redemption, for as Rifky Katz remarked to me, one never knows which Jew's pious actions might just "tip the scale" and bring the Messiah.[4]

My discussion of Hasidic children's moral education (*khinekh*) in this chapter and the next integrates Foucault's (1997) work on morality and ethics with a language socialization approach. My approach extends the contributions of language socialization to psychological and developmental paradigms to include the political dimensions of cultural formation, particularly the socialization of morality. Studies of children's moral socialization have concentrated on micro-level interactions between adults and children, and on how these interactions prepare children to participate in local structures and processes.[5] But this scholarship often does not examine these local relationships within broader historically and culturally specific forms of power and knowledge.[6] The language socialization paradigm also tends to limit attention to language. Foucault's approach requires that the language socialization paradigm include a broader perspective that accounts for the discursive and embodied practices by which children come to participate or reject particular ways of being in the world.

Inspired by Aristotelian ethics, Foucault distinguishes between moral codes that establish certain forms of power and knowledge as opposed to ethics which are practical activities central to a certain way of life.[7] Foucault writes, "Ethics are a modality of power which allow people to transform themselves by their own means or with the help of others to become willing subjects of a particular moral discourse" (1997:262). Foucault lays out four aspects to a study of ethical self-forming practices that breaks down the study of morality into distinctive components, creating opportunities for observing change and comparing moral systems (Robbins 2004b:216). First is the part of the self that needs to be cultivated to become an ethical person (the ethical substance). Second is the nature of moral authority (the mode of subjectivation). Third are the "techniques of the self," or the practices by which people learn to be or become ethical beings. Fourth are those whom people hope to emulate by these self-forming practices (*telos*) (Foucault 1997:263–266).

I draw on Foucault's framework in this chapter to analyze how Hasidic women talk about the Jewish soul, gender, personality and child development. Then I describe everyday exchanges between adults and children, where certain behaviors are praised, and adults explicitly draw a connection between love and behavior that conforms to communal and divine authority. Hasidic women engage with popular North American psychological and educational practices to teach children to use their individual autonomy to fit in to a nonliberal moral narrative of modernity. This is a narrative where the goal is fulfillment, not of an individual's will or desires, but rather of an individual's divine destiny.

Transforming the Material World

Hasidic beliefs about the ethical Jewish person originate in shared texts and oral commentary by religious sages. In Foucault's terms, sacred texts form the basis for moral authority because they are believed to be the words of God to his chosen people. In addition to normative Jewish texts, Hasidic Judaism draws on medieval Jewish texts, which, unlike North American Conservative or Reform Judaism, describe an afterlife (the Garden of Eden), angels, reincarnation, and Satan, and retains a continuing hope that the Messiah will arrive one day. Most Hasidic religious philosophy that I learned did not come from texts but from observing the everyday experiences of Hasidic women and children, witnessing how beliefs are taught to young girls, and even young boys, in the Bobover schools, and from extensive conversations with Hasidic women who are mothers and often teachers. Girls, as I noted in the introduction, do not study Torah, but they do have religious instruction in school, and many continue to attend lectures throughout their lives. My account of certain religious philosophies, then, is a gendered one that most likely differs from what Hasidic men might say. In addition, much of the religious philosophy is aimed at children and the relatively unschooled (me) and is, perhaps, simplified.[8]

Rifky Katz was one of the most helpful in explaining Hasidic beliefs about the person and their implications for everyday practice. This was partly because Rifky is a deep thinker who has the ability to reflect on and articulate complicated aspects of her own social and religious life. A young mother with four girls, Rifky wears a short, dark-brown wig and has sharp brown eyes set in a thin face. She is unusual among Hasidic women (most often not a compliment) but is admired by many who know her. In contrast to many other Hasidic women I met, Rifky reads widely, both Jewish religious texts and more secular nonfiction. She even listens to the radio, telling me she is a big fan of Dr. Laura.

(Dr. Laura is a Jewish returnee to the faith who has a radio talk show where she promotes "traditional" values as the real path to "liberation"). Rifky was also involved for a time in La Leche League, which provides information and support for nursing mothers, and had a number of other unconventional interests including yoga. Rifky's husband accepts her explorations and interests, because, she told me, he knows that she is so strong in her belief. He only asks that she not show her children any secular news magazines she sometimes reads.

I asked Rifky to explain some basic religious concepts to me that other women had mentioned, as we sat together one day in a new little coffee house, one of the few places to get a cappuccino in Boro Park back then. She did not usually go to restaurants because of the potential for mixing with the opposite sex, which is immodest, but because it was the middle of the day and the place was managed by a Hasidic Jew she agreed to meet me in this café, and she brought along her daughter and her niece. As the little girls sprawled on the floor coloring, she began to tell me about the struggle to infuse everyday life and the material world with divine meaning, a goal that marks the Hasidic life cycle.

Through prayer, ritual, and learning, Rifky said, Hasidic Jews strive to elevate the physical world of the body in order to serve God and eventually be rewarded in the world to come *gan-eydn* 'the Garden of Eden' (Paradise). The Hasidim see a constant tension between the body (*gif*) and the soul (*neshume*), the material and the spiritual. Men and women (as I elaborate in chapter 6) engage in this struggle differently because of their innately distinct qualities. Although women have more control over their bodies than men—which I learned in a class for brides—both men and women attempt to elevate the body through ritual, making it sacred. In Rifky's words: "Our purpose is to live with our body, with our animalistic desires and soul and channel all that, and focus all that, through our neshume . . . infusing these [materialistic] things all with holiness and not making a separation [between the material and the spiritual]."

Every Jew is given a soul by God at birth. Souls are believed to be linked across time and space; all Jewish souls, past, present and future, are thought to have been at Mount Sinai for the giving of the Ten Commandments. The struggle to have the body elevated by the soul plays itself out in everyday activities. Physical needs and desires are not denied. Rather, the goal is to use conscious thought and ritual practice to sanctify the satisfaction of physical needs. This requires that individuals exercise considerable self-control and awareness around everyday physical activities. Rifky, for example, described how eating can be made into a sacred act:

I have to eat, so I'll channel it . . . I'll concentrate on how I eat, and what I eat, and why I eat, and what I say before and after I eat [i.e., appropriate blessings]. And if you apply all those things thoughtfully, not just by rote . . . and if you put thought in it and you put your *neshume* 'soul' into it, automatically all these physical actions get uplifted and are on the same road, the same path as your neshume.

Jews must consciously control their minds and bodies, their autonomous will, to make the material and the spiritual complementary. This is what Foucault calls the "ethical substance," the aspect of the self that needs to be developed. Hasidic women suggested to me that Jews' strength and willingness to tame their autonomous will is the benchmark differentiating them from Gentiles. Hasidic women portrayed Jews as the only people who have the strength and maturity to take on God's commandments, providing the Jews with a sense of purpose as well as divine rewards.

Hasidic women's vision of the ethical Jewish person is partially defined in contrast to their perceptions that Gentiles and the secular are weak, immature, and often degenerate. Hasidic women I talked to often criticized what they defined as "American" values of "individualism"—which they label "selfish and childish"—and goals for gender equality, which they claim are "unnatural" and lead to dissatisfaction and divorce. Hasidic women and children frequently commented that Gentiles are unable or unwilling to control their bodies and their desires. Gitty, my Yiddish tutor, told me on a number of occasions that Jews and Gentiles eat differently, "*Yidn* 'Jews' don't just dig into a plate of food. *A yid est vi a mentsh*" (A Jew eats like a human being). She also noted that Jews never "eat in the street like dogs," the way so many New Yorkers do.[9] Both comments suggest that Jews master their physical urges (hunger, in her example), whereas Gentiles have no ritual obligations or sense of higher purpose to elevate animalistic physical desires to a holier level. Jews' willingness to submit to their religious obligations heightens their consciousness of the sacredness of everyday life and allows them to try to attain a higher, more meaningful level of existence.

THE HASIDIC CHILD: *MIDES* (INDIVIDUAL CHARACTERISTICS)

Hasidic mothers told me that each Jew is born with an innate inclination toward three traits: charity or compassion, good deeds, and modesty. Growing up is thought of as a process of bringing out these inherited Jewish traits by teaching children to control their impulses and thus develop into *mentshn* 'decent human beings'. Women suggest that although young children are "100 percent innocent," they are also only concerned with satisfying their physical needs, much like animals. In fact, women constantly scolded girls for acting like wild animals (*vilde khayes*) or for sounding like a "chicken market." It is the responsibility of adults to inculcate ritual behavior and make it feel natural, while also teaching children to talk explicitly about their behavior. As children gradually learn to discipline themselves in this way, the culturally appropriate feelings, such as awe of God (*yiras-shemayim*) and satisfaction with a Jewish life, develop and emerge in children. *Khinekh* 'moral education' works on the body, the mind, and the soul to allow children to reach their inborn potential as Jews. In particular, khinekh teaches children how to work on the will in order to make the material world sacred. Working on the will is what Foucault calls "a technique of the self." Learning to control one's body, thoughts, desires, and language is conceptualized as a process whereby the child goes from a pure, animalistic, need-driven state to one of striving toward higher, more spiritual aspirations.

The personal characteristics of an individual determine the sort of struggle that each Jew has in order to reach the level where his or her will can be controlled. At birth, God gives each Jew a complete set of positive and negative *mides* 'measures' (personality traits or temperament), but each individual gets different ratios of these qualities. One person might be born with a greater measure of pride than modesty or more patience than anger. This determines, and is a local explanation for, personality and individuality. "Working on one's mides," or "working on oneself," is a lifelong process of learning to control the negative mides and bring out the more positive ones, a concept that fits with a therapeutic framework central to the North American self-help movement, as I discuss in the next chapter.

Each individual has her own struggle to become an ethical person. In a conversation with Rifky about mides she offered the example of someone born with the mide of anger, a temperament that causes her to often experience anger and manifests as an actual physical need to express anger. A person like this has to realize her need and learn, as Rifky put it, to "channel that energy in some other way." The mide of anger is not inherently bad or good. It is how the individual controls and expresses any mide that determines its final value. The overarching goal for women is to help children become independent enough to take on the individualized work of constant self-vigilance and self-improvement.

When girls *can* fit in, when they use their autonomy to fulfill communitarian ideals rather than individualistic ones, they are closer to more moral, past generations of women: biblical women, their great-grandmothers from prewar Eastern Europe, and even their own mothers today, although, this genealogy is a contemporary construction (see chapter 5). By aspiring to be like past generations of Jewish women—Foucault's notion of the telos—Hasidic women today counter the moral narrative of progress that underlies secular modernity where the progression of time parallels the progression of knowledge and morality. Indeed, Hasidic women today differ from previous generations of Jewish immigrants who wanted to fit in, not to their memories of the past, but to the new North American ways of life that often meant abandoning the ways of their grandmothers. Hasidic women, in contrast, talk about the higher spiritual levels of their grandmothers, and they claim that they aspire to return to past levels of piety, although this telos is achieved through relatively new, North American technologies of the self.

I heard various, sometimes contradictory, explanations for why individuals get certain mides. To understand more clearly, I asked Esty Schwartz, Rifky's cousin, to explain one day when I was visiting her. Esty, like Rifky, was interested in religious study. She worked part-time in an Orthodox but non-Hasidic girls' school where she taught the Hebrew Bible. As the mother of twin toddlers, a boy and girl, Esty often compared her two children, using them to confirm the innate gender difference that has become increasingly important to Hasidic life. She told me about the idea of a *gilgl* (the reincarnation of a soul into a new body). God, Esty explained, gives the gilgl the mides that he or she most needs to work on and improve. For example, if a soul in a previous life had a problem with stubbornness, in the new life he or she might be given the same mide in order to give the soul the opportunity to overcome this negative trait. Esty also suggested that certain mides run in families. Her mother-in-law, she noted, is a very giving person, as is her husband and her son. Her daughter, Leye, however, is not as generous as her son, Aaron. Leye, Esty said, "will keep a toy forever." These two different explanations for mides did not present a contradiction for her; each explanation was appropriate in certain situations, because, as she noted with a smile when I asked, "It's all part of a higher plan." Multiple, parallel explanations for complicated phenomena provide alternatives for Hasidic women trying to understand the logic of God's plans, secure in the knowledge that there is a plan though they may not yet understand it.

Parents and teachers frequently accounted for, but did not excuse, disruptive behavior in children by claiming that "it isn't really their fault. They can't help it. It's their nature." Children are not held accountable for the mides they have been given; but as they grow older, they are expected to learn how to control mides that are unacceptable. Rifky explained that when children are young, the most basic mides that are common to all Jewish children are addressed. As children mature into their teens, a parent has to work more individually on each child's mides:

> When they're younger, we still have to focus on the basics, the foundations: you're not allowed to yell, and you're not allowed to fight, and you're not allowed to be jealous, and you have to *fargin* (not begrudge another something good), you have to be *mevater* (give in or yield to others), you can't be insistent, you can't be an *akshn* 'stubborn.' All these things are basics. And then as their personality develops and becomes more clarified, then you have to work more individually ... this one needs to be taught more calmness, and this one needs to be more stimulated, etcetera, etcetera, etcetera.

Some of the qualities Rifky mentions, such as self-control and consideration of others, are also important, of course, to most North American parents, but for Hasidic children these qualities have cosmic implications.[10] Hasidic women's interpretation of mides emphasizes the moral obligation each child has to other Jews and, ultimately, to God. Rifky's examples of how children should behave are all related to Jewish children's ability to control their egocentric desires and anticipate how their actions affect other community members and God. Bad mides have the potential not only to shame the child but also reflect badly on all Jews. The concepts of *kidesh-hashem* 'sanctifying God's name' and *khilel-hashem* 'blaspheming God's name' remind children that their behavior has wider ramifications for how Jews are perceived, not only by other Jews, but also by Gentiles. For example, Mrs. Silver, a gentle yet charismatic first-grade teacher at Bnos Yisruel, warned a student who was yelling during a class trip that she was committing khilel-hashem, showing Gentiles that she was no better than they. While a discourse of individual fulfillment is expressed (e.g., getting one's needs met), there are also religious ramifications; for instance, children who use their autonomy to fulfill their religious responsibilities provide an example that strengthens the Jewish project of redeeming the world through their fulfillment of God's commandments.

GENDERED MIDES

Gendered temperaments emerge through culturally and historically specific interactions between adults and children (Pufall and Unsworth 2004:13). Hasidic women interpret children's mides through the lens of essentialized gender categories where Hasidic males and females have innate differences. These naturalized distinctions legitimize and produce the gendered division of labor that supports the flourishing of Hasidic Judaism today. Esty frequently noted that her daughter, Leye, had a much stronger personality than her son, Aaron, who was gentle and affable. I observed this as well. I had heard from many different women that girls were naturally softer and more *aydl* 'refined' than boys, whereas boys were wild and more aggressive than girls. I wondered to Esty why Leye would be the strong one, even though she is a girl. Esty explained that softness could be a boy's quality, too, because some boys are not materialistic. Leye's strong will is part of a more general trait that Esty called "pettiness" about toys or treats. Aaron, Esty implied, was less materialistic than his sister, less petty about things, which she interpreted as evidence that he was more suited than his sister to the life of a religious scholar. Esty's reading of her children's different personalities accommodate and legitimize local gender ideologies about responsibility for Jewish continuity, where males are created by God to study Torah and females are created to negotiate the mundane, material world.

As children continue in school, curriculum decisions are influenced by gendered mides, drawing on essentialized notions of male and female innate differences. This was illustrated in a recent addition to the curriculum, Project *Derekh* 'Project Politeness'. Developed by a non-Hasidic, Orthodox Jew in Canada, the project uses classroom materials for teaching children respectful behavior (*derekh-eyrets*), that are drawn from sacred texts. Examples include respecting one's elders and helping out at home. Bnos Yisruel recently adopted some of the materials, translated them from English into Yiddish, and introduced them into the elementary school. Parents and teachers were very pleased with the results.

However, in the boys' Bobover yeshiva, Project Derekh was not taught. Gitty, who was not yet a mother, suggested that this was appropriate because of the differences between males and females. She explained that girls generally need more guidance, "A *yingl* 'boy' is more born to be self-independent, and to know by themselves, and a girl is more undecided. 'Mommy, what should I do now?' " She told me that girls are watched over more, more protected, "so girls turn out more refined." Many mothers of young boys, however, disagreed that this was appropriate. Mrs. Fedder, whose husband publicly speaks on the importance of Project Derekh, told me that "in this world we live in, we need all the extra help we can get." Mothers acknowledge that boys should be learning about respectful behavior from their yeshiva education, but they suggested that the decline in levels of spirituality among

both Jews and Gentiles that characterizes the contemporary period requires more explicit instruction for boys in respectful behavior. This
stance suggests that Jews in the world today need new forms of childrearing, new "techniques of the self", in order to even strive to reach
the heights of past generations. Nevertheless, while boys' mothers
complained to me and other women, no organized efforts were made
to change yeshiva policy, which would involve challenging male religious authority.

Conceptions of gendered mides shape the use of corporal punishment resorted to when children seriously transgress behavioral rules.
During lunch at Bnos Yisruel one day, a teacher told the others about
a nursery school boy who had kicked his teacher. As a punishment his
(female) teacher had taken off the offending shoe, tied it around his
neck and made him walk home with one shoe on and the other off.
Using public humiliation as punishment is not uncommon in girls'
classrooms or in nursery school classes run by women for boys or girls.
Once boys enter first grade and have male teachers, however, corporal
punishment becomes more common. When I asked if girls were ever
hit in school, the teachers at Bnos Yisruel were shocked. "Of course
not," they said. They added, "You can't hit a girl because girls are too
sensitive." Boys, however, whose nature is more inherently wild and
for whom sitting and studying will be increasingly critical, need
stricter discipline, the teachers told me.

INCLINATIONS FOR EVIL AND GOOD:
LEARNING AUTONOMY AND RESPONSIBILITY

While mides and gender shape an individual's struggle for spiritual
growth, two inherent inclinations, one for good (*yaytser-hatoyv*)
and one for evil (*yaytser-hure*), are also present to tempt or guide the
individual in everyday life. These opposing inclinations are important
conceptual tools for teaching children to engage in the constant self-
monitoring and self-improvement necessary for observant Jews. Children do not receive an inclination for good until they reach the age
of *bar/bas-mitsve* 'son/daughter of commandment', age thirteen and
twelve, respectively, for boys and girls. Rifky suggested that the
yaytser-hatoyv requires a certain level of consciousness or awareness
of personal choice that allows individuals to struggle with themselves
and take responsibility for their own actions. There must first be a firm
belief in God, however, before this struggle is possible. Rifky said,
"You have to believe that your *neshume* 'soul' comes from *hashem* 'God'
and it really wants to be good . . . younger children just aren't ready

for that kind of struggle." Younger children, she said, are too involved in fulfilling their physical and emotional needs. This implies that freedom to choose can only be given to a Jewish child once faith (*emune*) in God has been established. Individual choice is a responsibility, not a right, to which one is entitled only after one's faith in God is firm. Hasidic children's agency is developed through moral training that prepares them to use their individuality for divine purposes.

The evil inclination, unlike the good, is present in every person at birth. Esty explained that the evil inclination comes from *Sutn* 'Satan', the fallen angel who struggles with God and speaks to our animalistic urges and selfish desires, encouraging us to lose self-control.[11] For children, parents explain that the evil inclination is a little imp or a *mentshele* 'a little man' who lives inside them, goading them on to be disobedient. Gitty explained in response to my question about these inclinations:

> A klayn kind maynt take az s'iz du a yaytser-hure (a little kid thinks that there is really an evil inclination). It's a little *mentshele* (a little man) jumping around and er makht mikh <u>punchn.</u> Er makht mikh zugn nayn (and he makes me punch. He makes me say no.).

The evil inclination is anthropomorphized, much like Jiminy Cricket represented Pinocchio's conscience in the fairy tale. There is a critical difference between the two, however. The moral of the Pinocchio story (written in 1883 by the Italian author Carlo Collodi) is that in order to become fully human, one must love another more than oneself and be ready to sacrifice for that person. Hasidic beliefs also emphasize the importance of putting the needs of community members before one's own, but when Hasidic children fight their inclination for evil they are fulfilling God's will for them individually and for all Jews everywhere, and this is what makes them fully human.

Gitty suggested that, as an adult, she knows that "there's no such thing as an evil inclination in the shape of a man." This does not make the evil inclination any less real, however. The evil inclination is a "fact" Gitty told me. There is something, she said, that makes you do good and bad. Then she gave me an example of what the evil inclination meant for her. She may go into the grocery store and see a snack that looks good but does not have a reputable *hekhsher* (a mark stamped on products that a rabbi has approved as kosher). If she eats it anyway because she is not "strong enough" to resist, though the snack may be delicious, she will feel regret (*kharute*) later. Her failure to resist her greedy physical desire is the triumph of the evil inclination.

For adults, the evil inclination is real, just as God is a social fact, but the evil inclination is more abstract. Adults have the capacity to understand that the evil inclination is a part of their own soul given to them by God so they may struggle with themselves for good. Children, however, need to have this aspect of the self described in concrete images, because adults believe that children are unable to understand ethical abstraction. Teachers, camp counselors, and mothers frequently invoked an anthropomorphized evil inclination who was out to get them, warning children that their yaytser-hure was "winning." In one of the Bnos Yisruel kindergarten classrooms I observed, Morah Chaya disciplined disobedient children by saying, "*Dan yaytser-hure arbet shver hant*" (Your evil inclination is working hard today). Similarly a camp counselor warned a child to put away a toy before "your yaytser-hure makes you take it out again." Children, for whom growing up is a gradual process of learning to control the mind and body and take responsibility for their own struggles, see the yaytser-hure as a concrete image of something that could lead them astray, something to fight against.

This belief in good and evil is a powerful force for Hasidic children. Mindy told me that her eight-year-old son, Chaim, had confided in her that he had decided to become a *tsadek* 'holy man' even though he was afraid of all the trials God would give him in the process. Mindy chuckled to me about this, although she was also proud that her son was grappling with these serious issues at such a young age.

Women teaching children to struggle with their inclination for evil can transform secular images or figures to address Hasidic techniques of the self that include self-monitoring and self-improvement. In this way secular life is put in the service of the Jewish struggle to control the autonomous will for oneself, one's family, all Jews, and God. In Foucault's terms, secular and Gentile North American cultural forms can be transformed into resources that help Hasidic children work on their ethical substance. In the following example, kindergarten teacher Morah Chaya appropriated secular urban images and used them to teach her kindergarten class about the Jewish struggle with the inclination for evil and, more subtly, about the difference between Jews and Gentiles.

Morah Chaya is a petite newlywed with a luminous complexion, a short brown wig with a pill-box hat on top and an imposing sense of authority for a twenty-two-year old (perhaps a legacy of being the eldest of thirteen). One day she had the girls cut out red stop signs that they mounted on sticks. Then each girl colored a paper hat that had a police badge predrawn on it. First, the five-year-old girls learned to recognize the English word "stop," and they also discussed what policemen do, such as help children cross the street, make the streets safe for all the "good" people, and put all the "bad" people in jail. Their teacher then told the girls that, although as Jewish girls they could not "really" be policemen, they could police their own behavior and that of their peers. Then she explained what it might mean to be a policeman over their inclination for evil:

> MORAH CHAYA: *Vus maynt a policeman iber de yaytser-hure? A policeman iber de yaytser-hure maynt az indz zol me trakhtn far zikh alayn.*
>
> STUDENT 1: I know why.
>
> MORAH CHAYA: *Azoy vi s'iz du gite mentshn in shlekhte mentshn, azoy oukh iz ba yeyde mentsh du gite zakhn vus zay tin, in shlekhte zakhn vus zay tin. Ikh vil yeyde maydl zol trakhtn tse zikh in ir kop, in ven zi vil khas-veshulem tin a shlekhte zakh, zol zi shnel ufhaybn ir stop sign, in stop.*
>
> STUDENT 2: It's backward [Referring to the sign].
>
> MORAH CHAYA: *Nisht backward. You point to yourself. Nisht far de mentshn zoln stop ven zay gayen af de gas, dos tit oukh a police, but indz gayen zan a police far indz. Stop! Nisht redn lushn-hure. Stop! Nisht redn khitspedik! Stop! Gedenk az di darfst tsihern tse a morah de ershte mul! In oyb di zeyst a andere maydl vus, khas-veshulem, a morah redt in zi hert nisht tsi de ershte mul, vus tit men?*
>
> STUDENT 3: Stop!
>
> MORAH CHAYA: *Stop, in dermant far yene maydl az stop!*

> MORAH CHAYA: What does a policeman over the evil inclination mean? A policeman over the evil inclination means that we should think for ourselves.
>
> STUDENT 1: I know why.
>
> MORAH CHAYA: Just as there are good people and bad people, in each person there are also good things that they do and bad things that they do. . . . I want each girl to think to herself, in her head, and when she, God forbid, wants to do a bad thing, she should quickly raise her stop sign and stop.
>
> STUDENT 2: It's backward [Referring to the sign].
>
> MORAH CHAYA: Not backward. Not that people who are in the street should stop. A police does that also, but we are going to be policemen for ourselves. Stop! Don't talk badly about someone else. Stop! Don't talk defiantly! Stop! Remember that you need to pay attention to a teacher the first time. And if you see another girl and, God forbid, a teacher is talking and she does not listen the first time, what do you do?
>
> STUDENT 3: Stop!
>
> MORAH CHAYA: Stop, and remind that girl to stop!

Morah Chaya used the props of a policeman—the hat and the stop sign—to have an embodied, visual form for the girls to understand their internal personalized struggles against their inclination for evil. Girls interrupted her throughout the presentation, but she ignored these interruptions and only acknowledged girls who gave her the response she was looking for. Morah Chaya's lesson taught girls, implicitly, how to understand the presence of Gentiles in their urban landscape. Good Gentiles, like policemen, can make the streets safer for Jews by helping lost little girls or by locking up bad (Gentile) people. In some sense this is an explanation for the very existence of Gentiles: to facilitate Jews' ability to live safely as Jews. But even the efforts of good Gentiles to make the world a better place remain at a very limited level compared to Jewish efforts. Gentiles do not, Morah Chaya implies, have the depth or strength of will to focus on the inclination for evil that lies within their own souls, whereas Jews work on their souls all the time. Their internal struggle and their efforts at self-improvement ultimately distinguish them from Gentiles.

Girls are not only encouraged to monitor themselves. They are also responsible for reminding one another to fight against the inclination for evil by holding up their signs to one another. Morah Chaya framed the internal struggle as a contest, warning her students not to "let the inclination for evil win." She ended her lesson by asking the excited students if they were going to be "good policemen over the yayster-hure." The girls responded enthusiastically, and their teacher said, "*Ikh vil zeyn!*" (I want to see!). She hung a stop sign on the wall and told the girls that every time she saw a student remind another student to fight against her yaytser-hure by quietly saying "stop" (in order not to shame her), she would put a smiley face on the stop sign. It is considered a good deed to discourage another Jew from giving in to her evil inclination, but this must be done discreetly and not for public recognition. She warned the girls not to run up to her and tell her that they had told another girl to stop. Their teacher would be watching, and she would decide when a girl was fighting the yaytser-hure far real 'for real'. The message from this arts-and-crafts activity was that girls are responsible for one another, as well as themselves, although the teacher remains the judge who decides when the struggle is "for real."

In this kindergarten activity, girls bodily experience their peers' and their teacher's constant surveillance, a more concrete version of the all-seeing *aybeshter* 'one above' to whom girls are ultimately responsible. On another day Morah Chaya told her students, before leaving them unsupervised for a few moments during morning prayers, "You don't pray to a teacher, you pray to God, and he is everywhere!" (*Me davnt nisht far a morah, me davnt far de aybeshter in er iz iberal!*). Morah Chaya, in effect, constructs a religious panopticon, Jeremy Bentham's (1984:18) model of a prison which Foucault adopted as a paradigm of modern disciplinary technology. A prisoner in the panopticon is isolated from all other prisoners though ever visible to a guard. Because the prisoner knows he is always watched, he ultimately disciplines himself, thus perpetuating, according to Foucault, the systemic forms of power and knowledge that characterize modernity. Hasidic girls are presented with a panopticon where adults and peers all model God's omniscience. The goals of this religious panopticon are different from what Foucault describes, however. Hasidic surveillance is intended to prepare girls as they grow up to discipline their bodies and minds to serve God rather than any modern form of authority, like the state. Further, girls' efforts at stopping their evil inclination and that of their peers can have both everyday and cosmic effects, as God rewards each individual in this world and the world to come. At an assembly at Bnos Yisruel, the principal told the girls that having an evil inclination is "our *skhar*" 'our merit' because it gives Jews the opportunity and the challenge to work even harder to fulfill God's commandments. She implied that the fight against the evil inclination is one more way that Jews show God that they are deserving of being his chosen people.

MODELING THE JEWISH COVENANT:
PRAISING AS A TECHNIQUE OF THE SELF

In addition to anthropomorphizing religious philosophy, Hasidic women I worked with use praise to give children a concrete connection to the complicated relationship with God for which they are being prepared. Praising is a technique of the self where women reward children who fit in with love, communal acceptance, and material gifts. Women suggest that in this way children learn that fulfillment of the commandments eventually brings rewards from God. This is the Jewish covenant. Women told me that this covenant is too abstract for children, who cannot be expected to curb their physical needs and desires based only on a future reward. Instead, women provide an immediate reward when children fit in, training them to emotionally reap the rewards of fulfilling the covenant. Effectively, Hasidic women model the Jewish covenant for children by having them experience the emotional and material pleasures that come with disciplining themselves to communal and hence divine expectations.

Hasidic women's emphasis on praising as a technique of the self is relatively recent. Esty commented that what she called the "European" childrearing of her grandparents' generation was much stricter and emotionally more reserved than childrearing today in Boro Park. She told me, for instance, that her grandfather felt it was appropriate to kiss his children (i.e., show his love) only when they were asleep. The anthropologist Jerome Mintz similarly notes a shift in the postwar generation quoting from an interview with a Hasidic father:

> The old European school of religious people . . . their way was to punish when the child was bad and to give very little praise when the child was good . . . When a child is being good it is natural that he be good; he is not doing anything out of the ordinary. But when he is bad, he should be punished. And most European parents were that way . . . I hit my children, but I kiss them too. And when they do something good, I praise them. Because if I don't praise them, somebody else will praise them when they do something wrong, and they'll go looking for that praise (1968:69).

Changing practices of praising and disciplining children today reflect the historical give and take between Gentile and Jewish practices, especially, perhaps, around childrearing and family life. For example, the historian Elisheva Baumgarten (2005) points out that beliefs about gender, praise, and discipline in Jewish texts published in Medieval Jewish Ashkenaz (what is now Germany and France) are similar to Gentile childrearing manuals of the same period. Among both Gentiles and Jews, fathers were responsible for children's spiritual development through discipline rather than expressions of love, for "according to the letter of the law, one need not love children before they begin to fear and love God" (*Sefer Hasidim*, quoted in Baumgarten 2005:163). A Jewish father's love, Baumgarten suggests, was shown through his own study of Torah and the demands he made on his children. One source declares that "a man who feels pain when his children cry but does not approach them because he wishes to keep studying Torah will be greatly rewarded" (Baumgarten 2005:163). A mother's love, in contrast, was considered more "natural, like the love of a female dog toward her pups" (164). In North America today, frequent praise and expressions of love by both mothers and fathers is a modern innovation, the "American" way to raise Hasidic children which, I argue, draws on the broader North American beliefs about childrearing rooted in the disciplines of contemporary psychology and education.

The story of how Esty toilet-trained her twin toddlers illustrates how the Hasidic women I worked with compared and drew on what they called "European" and "American" childrearing practices. After the children had turned two and a half, Esty read a popular North American book on toilet-training techniques that stressed rewarding children through incentives and praise when they used the potty instead of a diaper. Esty also asked her parents for advice, and they told her that the only way to train a child was by threatening a *patsh* 'smack'. She told me that she tried the American way, but her children kept on having accidents on her floor. Finally, in addition to the rewards in place, she told them that if they did not start using the toilet she would give them a patsh. This proved quite effective. Esty told me that she decided that a combination of both European and American Hasidic childrearing was probably best. Esty's adventures in toilet-training her children shows how Hasidic women effectively draw on both Jewish and secular/Gentile North American childrearing (as represented in popular texts), making distinctions between secular and religious forms of knowledge irrelevant.

Applying the postwar North American approach of praising and building self-esteem, Hasidic women today encourage children to develop the desire to shape themselves into ethical Hasidic Jews. Praising, as noted, often draws from mainstream North American school-based behavior charts and incentive models that are used throughout the public school system and in many North American homes as well. In Hasidic homes and schools, however, these charts and rewards are used not only to help children master a skill or achieve control over objectives such as toilet-training or doing homework independently (although these kinds of achievements are also recognized); Hasidic forms of praising also support the efforts of children to fulfill God's commandments, as they create emotional experiences in the child that associate positive feelings of love and rewards with the desire to be particular kinds of people.

When Esty's children were three years old, she wanted to start teaching them about the importance of *mevater zan* 'to be yielding', where people use their autonomous will to put the wishes of others (Jews) before their own—a trait that God rewards. Esty explained to me that because young children cannot be expected to understand abstract concepts such as controlling jealousy or yielding to others, she initiated a "mevater prize," which was given to the child who got hurt or lost out on a coveted item. Affectively the "loser" experienced the pleasure of a reward like candy or a cookie, whereas the child who would not give in experienced the disappointment, anger, or jealousy at having to see the "loser" enjoy a treat. One day while I was visiting, chubby dark-haired little Aaron came into the room crying. Esty picked him up and put him on her lap, quietly saying to herself: "There's something she [her daughter, Leye] did to him." Aaron responded:

AARON: Leye bite.
ESTY: *Leye hot dikh gemakht a <u>bite</u>?* (Leye gave you a bite?)
AARON: [silence].

ESTY: Must have bit him. [Aaron whimpers.] *Mommy geyb* (is giving) Aaron a good thing. [Aaron continued to cry softly, saying again, "Leye bite."]

Leye, with short dark hair, came in just in time to hear the exchange and hung her head. She started to cry when Esty took some jelly candy out of the cupboard, saying, "Jelly, jelly, Aaron's jelly." Esty turned to me and said, "She *khaleshes* 'faints/dies' when this happens . . . I don't even reprimand her anymore. She feels terrible." Leye continued to cry, "Jelly, jelly, I want jelly." Esty commented on Leye's tears and then sent her out of the room to get her swimsuit as they were off to go swimming. Aaron meanwhile had stopped crying and was sitting contentedly on his mother's lap. He held the piece of candy, smiled, and said, "Mevater prize." Esty laughed, "You got it, you." Then she said to me, "You see what happens? She feels bad, he stops crying, and it works all ways." Esty was concerned that the culturally appropriate emotions and rewards were put into action for the children to see and experience. Leye got upset (apparently over the candy, not hitting) and the victim, Aaron, was rewarded. Esty, like a number of other mothers I observed, did not explain to Leye what she had done wrong or ask her to imagine how it might have made her brother feel. Indeed, Hasidic women often make fun of what they perceive is the secular North American practice of explaining everything to a child. Further, Leye's intention or understanding was less important than the fact that she experienced a loss from her own aggressive behavior and cried. This model for understanding is essential to Hasidic elaborations of unquestioning religious faith cultivated through religious practice, which I address in the next chapter.

Esty told me that the children had even "cracked" the system. Once when there was only one cookie left in the box, Leye told her mother to give it to Aaron. She knew, her mother concluded, that she would get a mevater prize which was usually candy. She would rather have candy than a cookie. Esty was not concerned that Leye used the concept of the mevater prize to satisfy her own desires. The important thing was that Leye gave way (whatever the reason) to her brother's desire. Children's active participation in their own socialization is an important theoretical contribution of the anthropology of childhood and the language socialization approach, in particular. Leye's manipulation of the mevater prize is not unusual. With a clear-cut system in place, children can use the system in their own negotiations. For example, when seven-year-old Yehudis Klein spilled her bubbles, she asked her younger brother, Shimmy (five years old), and her sister, Malky (three years old), if they would share their bubbles with her. Her sister refused, but her brother quickly gave her his. "Well," said Yehudis, "Shimmy gets the mitsve 'good deed commandment'." She was announcing that her brother would certainly be rewarded sometime by God (and impress adults like me) for his generous behavior. Her sister, by implication, had lost the chance to "get a *mitsve*" because she was selfish. Malky did not respond to her sister, but she also did not give her the bubbles.

Mitsve Notes, Charts, and Prizes

A distinctive aspect of Hasidic socialization practices is the consistent moral framework presented across contexts. As noted, the Bobover Hasidic school for girls, Bnos Yisruel, is directed and overseen by the Bobover rebbe and his male advisers. Most of the teachers are Hasidic or Litvish women, and in order to attend, parents have to agree to maintain the same level of religious practice at home that the girls have in school, creating continuity across home and school contexts. Raising Hasidic girls to become wives, mothers, and homemakers, and boys to become Torah scholars is embedded in the school curriculum. Parents and teachers work together to monitor, report on, and evaluate children's behavior in terms of moral and scholastic development. Boys and girls are expected not only to learn Jewish and secular literacy in school but must learn to live in the spirit of mitsves. This means they have to learn, for instance, to be respectful to elders, considerate, compassionate, helpful, obedient, and hard-working.

Teachers extend their moral and educational influence into homes, as they send home behavior charts that parents must sign and grade, reporting what time the child went to bed, whether he or she was respectful and helpful, if he or she reviewed the lesson. This not only requires parents to be involved in the lessons of the week, but it is also a resource for parents to assert their authority. I heard Raizy Klein reprimand her son, who ignored her request to wash up for dinner, by simply quoting a line from the behavior chart he had brought home from school. She would, the implication was, give him a low grade next to the column marked "*derekh-eyrets far a totty in a mommy* (respect for a Daddy and a Mommy)." Her son quickly complied and washed up.

Parents, in turn, extend their influence into the classroom by writing their children *mitsve-tsetlekh* 'good deed notes'. The notes recount for the teacher and other students a particular praiseworthy action by the child. The notes were often written on post-its, hastily scrawled in Yiddish or English by a mother or older sister. One note, written in English, read: "Dear Mrs. Silver, Malky cleaned up all of her toys right away. Sincerely, Mrs. Goldman." Even at a very young age, mitsve-tsetlekh are gendered, reporting different praiseworthy events for boys and girls. Although all children are praised for praying alone, helping with siblings, or going to bed on time, girls are more often praised for helping around the house, and boys are more often praised for participating in ritual behavior, all of which supports and encourages the strict gender segregation that is presaged by entering nursery school. Children bring the notes into class, where teachers read them aloud for the entire class as the child, standing in front of the room, is often caressed, patted, or hugged by the teacher who engages in parental kinds of behaviors often discouraged in North American public schools. After reading the note, teachers would almost always express how proud they were ("Morah is so proud!") and declare the child a "real *mitsve-yingl/maydl*" (a boy or girl who obeys the commandments). A teacher or parent would often cry out "mitsve-yingl" or "mitsve-maydl" when a child, unbidden, did something unselfish or helpful. Through mitsve notes, children's thoughtful behavior at home has real consequences for their reception and reputation at school and at home. Children appeared to glow with pride when they had a mitsve-tsetl to be read in class, and parents often used the event to encourage children to "get another mitsve" at home.

Using charts and prizes, teachers and mothers help create the desire for children to fit in to what is expected, as well as to strive toward their own individualized improvement. In the middle of the year, for example, Mrs. Silver brought out a gumdrop dispenser. If, during the reading of the prayer book, a girl knew where to continue reading out loud when she was called on, and read clearly and fluently, Mrs. Silver gave her a gumdrop. There were other small prizes: the girl who most often remembered to bring a penny for the charity-box got an extra gold star by her name, and each time girls did their homework they got a different colored star. If they brought a "healthy" snack, they got a smiley face near their name on a chart, and if they brought in a story about how *ales vus hashem tit iz far indz git* (everything that God does is good for us), they also got a smiley face.

In addition to general classroom competitions and rewards, teachers would make arrangements with certain girls who were having problems. Mrs. Silver, for example, made a chart with Esther and her mother, where every time she went to bed on time and did her homework she got a check. After a certain number of checks, she got a little prize, either stickers or a small toy. Tallying points and giving prizes was not done publicly, however. The teacher always called Esther to her desk and whispered or took her outside in the hallway. This form of praising is different from the public acknowledgment usually given.

In Esther's case, Mrs. Silver was "working on her," helping her to overcome some fault and improve herself, setting an example for how Esther would, Mrs. Silver hoped, "work on herself" as she got older.

GENDERED PRAISING

Praising, prizes, and public recognition are for both boys and girls.
Gender, however, determines what qualities and achievements get
praise at home and at school. For preschool boys, frequent and lavish
praise is given for those who reach certain markers of Hasidic masculinity, which leads to their eventual inclusion into the world of male
Torah study. For instance, boys go through an important ritual transformation during their first year in school. When they turn three, they
get their first haircut (shaved heads with side-curls), a *kapl* (yarmulke),
and *tsitses* (a ritual fringed undergarment), all markers of being a Jewish male. The third birthday is marked by parties in school and a great
deal of loving attention from family and teachers.

For boys, praising and public recognition make communal expectations for males explicit and pleasurable. Every morning the preschool
teacher called forward all the boys who were three and had them bless
their tsitses in front of the class. Appropriating a North American children's song popular in secular preschools across the city, Hasidic boys
sang a song to the tune of *Frère Jacques*:

> *Ikh hob shoyn tsitses. Ikh hob shoyn payes.*
> *Ikh bin shoyn groys. Ikh bin shoyn groys.*
> *Ikh vaz de gantse velt, ikh vaz de gantse velt*
> *az ikh bin a yid!*

> I have tsitses already. I have side curls already.
> I'm big already. I'm big already.
> I show the whole world, I show the whole world
> that I am a Jew!

Girls are also publicly praised and rewarded, although for different
achievements. In girls' preschool classrooms, praise focused on neatness, organization, and listening. Teachers praised girls for lining up
neatly, coloring only in the lines, having nicely organized "briefcases"
(backpacks), and having neat arts-and-crafts projects (no glue leaking
and all the pieces glued on straight). Neatness, organization, and listening become increasingly important as girls get older. Being organized and efficient (*geshikt*) and obedient are considered important
qualities when matchmaking gets into swing (see chapter 7).

The monthly assembly in the school auditorium is a forum where girls (from first grade through high school) hear explicitly the kinds of girls they should be, as well as the very real potential for them to reach their goal if they only can use their autonomy for others and for God. At each assembly and for each class a girl of the month is chosen. Girls' mothers, grandmothers, and extended families are invited to attend. Each teacher chooses a girl who has been "super" or "excellent" that month and gives her name to the principal. At the end of the assembly, after speeches, dances, and singing, the principal announces the names of the girls of the month and the qualities that make them so special. As her name is called, each girl walks to the front of the auditorium and climbs onto the stage. The whole school then applauds them. When they return to their seats, their teachers hug and kiss them and tell them that they are so proud of them. Mothers who are present usually take pictures and give their daughters small toys, balloons, and treats.

During one assembly, before the principal announced the girls of the month, she told the girls that three important characteristics provide insight into a girl's "nature": how much effort she makes (*vi azoy zi flast zikh*), how she prays (*vi azoy zi davnt*), and respectful behavior (*derekh-eyrets*). These qualities are about a girl's relationship to herself, to God, and to other Jews. They are a litmus test for a girl's nature, the criteria for being an ethical Jewish girl. Other categories the principal rewarded regularly over the course of a year included: good in learning, always ready with a smile, effort, prays sincerely, nicely behaved at lunch, always ready to help another, satisfied with everything, speaks with refinement (*limidoys toyvos, ale mul mit a shmaykhl, flas, davnt mit kavune, firt zikh shayn bam esn, ale mul grayt tse helfn an andere, tsifridn mit ales, redt mit aydlkayt*).

These qualities explicitly stress that girls must be respectful and satisfied with what they are given. They must be helpful to others and always have a smile on their face. They have to have good manners and speak in a refined way. They also must do their work, pray as if they mean it, and try hard to do their best. The principal ended assemblies by noting that the girls of the month were an example of beautiful mides. However, she said, each girl, as a Jew, had the capacity within herself to achieve this ethical ideal by working on her own mides.

When I asked first-graders what a girl had to do to be best of the month, some seemed baffled and shrugged. Others told me that "you have to be excellent in everything," and another said that you have to *folgn* 'obey' the teacher and do your work. Although first-graders' sense of standards of excellence might be vague, as they go through the grades continuously hearing who gets elected girl of the month and why, the message that girls repeatedly hear is that those who accept what they are told and follow the rules are rewarded publicly at school and by their families, and also by God. Hasidic women provide strong affective incentives for fitting in that include public recognition ceremonies in front of their classmates, mothers' public tears of pride at award ceremonies, or even just getting a gumdrop for going to bed on time. Children who can and do fit in are amply rewarded, emotionally and materially.

For mothers and women teachers, a great deal also rides on their success in having each daughter or student develop the autonomy to "be the best she can be." The cultural concept to *shep nakhes* 'shovel joy' (reap emotional rewards) reveals the notion that childrearing is an investment with potential rewards, not only for the child, but for a mother or teacher as well. Again, this is modeled on the relationship between God and Jews. When Jews fulfill all of God's commandments, God rewards Jews both materially and spiritually. In a way, shepping nakhes (to borrow from Hasidic English) is about getting back all that parents put into children; it is the visible effect of one's efforts at parenting, the public proof that the parent is doing all the right things.

CREATIVITY AND FITTING IN

Hasidic Jews, like other nonliberal religious communities such as Fundamentalist Christians in North America (e.g., Ammerman 1988; Peshkin 1986), possess a moral certitude supported by divine truth. Individual expressions of creativity and imagination can be a challenge to these communities, although certain culturally approved areas exist where Hasidic children can express their individuality and be creative. These frequently include the arts, especially performing in plays, singing, drawing and painting, and reciting. For older girls and young women the domestic arts can become a realm for personal creativity as well. One of the more elaborate *shalekh-munes* (baskets of wine, fruit, candy, and baked goods that are exchanged with family and friends on the holiday of Purim) that I saw was made by a young bride for her future mother-in-law: an edible candy pastoral scene, complete with the engaged couple's portrait floating on a walnut boat in a chocolate lake.

However, despite the opportunities for creativity, the cause and effect, divinely directed universe where Hasidim dwell discourages children from even thinking about things that "can't be" outside prescribed contexts. In school, teachers were not enthusiastic about artistic expression that was not representational or naturalistic. Trees cannot be blue, in much the same way that girls cannot be boys, right and wrong are always knowable, and God is in charge of the universe.

Preschool arts-and-crafts projects are sites where teachers and administrators debate how they should address issues of truth, imagination, and creativity. At least once a week, the girls in Pre-1A (five-year olds) made an elaborate arts-and-crafts project that was taken home to parents. The projects were usually associated with the biblical portion of the week or a holiday. When, for example, the girls learned the biblical story of Jacob wrestling with an angel who descends from heaven on a ladder, the girls made ladders out of popsicle sticks glued on construction paper leading to the sky, which was represented by fluffy, cotton-ball clouds and silver-foil stars. The girls pasted a precut rock onto the ground where Jacob was supposed to have slept. Teachers loved this project, and most of them did it with their classes.

The assistant principal, Mrs. Silverstein, who is Orthodox, but not Hasidic, and college-educated with a master's degree, was troubled by the difference in the educational philosophy she had absorbed in secular higher-educational institutions and the philosophy of Hasidic women. Mrs. Silverstein's goals, based on her training in early childhood education, were to provide arts-and-crafts activities that allowed girls to use their "imagination" and be "creative," she told me. This meant that generally teachers should not precut arts-and-crafts projects for students who then only had to glue on the pieces. The teachers, who were all Hasidic and would not have attended a master's program in early education, disagreed; they felt pressure from the girls' mothers to produce art projects that were clearly identifiable, and the arts-and-crafts project seemed to be a measure of a teacher's facility in putting together a creative project that produced something worthy of display on a refrigerator door.

There was another point of disagreement. Morah Yehudis, one of the preschool teachers, worried that if she did as Mrs. Silverstein suggested and let the girls draw whatever they wanted, the girls would not learn the "right" way to draw. As an example, she showed me a student's paper on which the girl had drawn a blue tree. She did not like them to draw a blue tree because, as she said, "it can't be." Morah Yehudis's argument was that children need to see and represent the world the way it "really" is. If they draw a blue tree, for example, then they might not learn "which way to do it right."

In contrast to their teachers, some kindergarteners seemed to enjoy playing with and testing the boundaries of Hasidic representation, creativity, and imagination. Five-year-old Hasidic girls coloring together in a small group used me as a sounding board for what could and could not be done:

CHRAINDY [laughing]: A *mentsh* 'person' could be purple or orange?
AYALA: Yeah, *far vus nisht* (why not)?
CHRAINDY [laughing]: This dark, dark, dark purple, *ober* 'but' we can have her mouth is also purple and orange?
AYALA: *Ken zan vus me vil.* (It can be whatever you want.)
SURI: A green one.
AYALA: *Far vus nisht?* (Why not?)
SURI: No, a green *mentsh* 'person' *ken nisht zan* (can't be), a green one.
AYALA: Oh yeah, *ken nisht zan* (it can't be). Only in the imagination.
BLIMI: *Ken nisht zan.* (It can't be.)

Despite Chraindy's playful interaction with me about the fantastic colors she can make her person, I am quickly corrected by two other girls, Suri and Blimi, who tell me that a green person just cannot be. This echoes teachers' instructions to their students to use only realistic colors in their artwork. Nevertheless, this small snippet of play by five-year olds shows that children are actively interpreting adult ideas about truth, representation, and reality, and sometimes playing with them, especially with an outsider such as myself.

A number of Hasidic parents and teachers are aware of the pressure to fit in and the implications this has for children's creativity. Some women suggested that a certain amount of "individuality" gets lost once the child enters Hasidic schools. Rifky told me:

> One of the reasons I didn't send my daughter to school up to now ... Because I want to keep that individuality alive in her as long as I can. Somehow you go to kindergarten, and the teacher says we're going to make an apple and everyone takes a red crayon and colors the apple red. But if someone wants to be creative and color the apple purple, "*An apple iz nisht purple* (an apple is not purple)."

The way Hasidic women classify something as "normal" or "not normal" reveals the cultural and religious importance of fitting in. The psychological term "normal" has been given a local idiomatic Hasidic meaning. "Normal" signifies Hasidic normative behavior or what the majority of other Hasidic Jews find acceptable (see also Levine 2003). "Normal" implies a familiar way of being, a known and recognizable set of behaviors. Teachers, in fact, frequently used the word "interesting" to describe a problem child or a child who did not fit in. Being "interesting" was far from a compliment; an "interesting" child was one whose behavior called attention to itself because it was different and unexpected in a negative way.

North American public schooling, of course, also requires that children conform to certain behavioral and educational norms, but in

nonliberal, religious communities, like the Hasidic Jews, nonconform-
ing behavior has religious and moral, as well as social, consequences
because cultural categories are understood as God's design. As Rifky
told me:

> You know, I think in the secular world individuality is much more
> accepted. . . . Your family doesn't obligate you to anything and your
> community. You could have grown up, moved to Alaska and be-
> come a hermit and you'll just be the funny uncle at the Christmas
> party. But here, there is so much more weighing on the conformity
> that people are not really encouraged to allow their individual
> uniqueness to shine. Anything that is different from the norm and
> the acceptable, we worry. How are people going to look? What are
> people going to think? And [she drops her voice to a whisper] how
> can I marry off my children?

Being normal has specific communitarian and heteronormative implications. The very reproduction and growth of the Jewish nation rests
on fitting in.

Across the life cycle, children will increasingly be responsible for
working on themselves, although even adults fear unchecked personal
autonomy. For this reason, institutionalized controls also monitor the
personal autonomy of adults. Hasidic leaders have constructed extensive hierarchies of authority, so that if individuals or families doubt a
course of action or religious ritual, a number of rabbis are on call to
clarify and take responsibility for the decision. Heads of households
frequently call their rebbe to ask which apartment to rent, for example,
or about career choices, schooling issues, or arranged marriages for
their children.

The local term *farkhnyokt* 'overzealous' clarifies how undisciplined
personal autonomy, even if it tends toward religious stringency, can
be a threatening force. Esty told me about a relative of hers who was
farkhnyokt. He had become so religiously zealous that he had decided
he would not sit at the same table with female relatives although the
family had always had men and women at the same table, albeit on
separate sides. Esty was critical not of his stringency but that he had
made this decision on his own, not as part of an institution or under
the direction of an authority figure. Individuals, she told me, do not
make life-altering decisions alone because of the effects they could
have on other Jews. To make an important decision alone is considered
immature, babyish, in much the same ways that, according to a number of Hasidic women, secular North America is childishly selfish in
its search for individual fulfillment. The mature Jew, in contrast, uses
personal autonomy to best fulfill God's plans.

KHINEKH AND THE NONLIBERAL CHILD

Hasidic moral education (*khinekh*) offers an alternative narrative to modern secular self-making, one with distinctive goals despite a shared vocabulary and a similar focus on the autonomous self and contemporary psychology. This is not surprising, given that scholars of nonliberal religious movements have noted more broadly that though members may claim to be adhering to "tradition," in fact, nonliberal religious groups are part of the very processes of modernity that they critique.[12] At times, women talk about distinctively Hasidic beliefs, such as divine truth, reincarnation, or the evil inclination, beliefs that seem outside any narrative of secular modernity. In other aspects of khinekh, however, that narrative is engaged and turned upside down, as, for example, in women's claims that past generations of Jewish women were more ethical than women are today.

Some of Hasidic women's childrearing practices (techniques of the self) share with many other North Americans an emphasis on praising, rewarding, motivating, and exhibiting public displays of love. When, for example, Hasidic mothers celebrate their kindergartners' graduation ceremony with presents, tears, hugs, and huge shopping bags of *nosh* (candy and other treats), girls have the opportunity to experience the physical and emotional rewards for fitting in to adults' expectations of them.

Hasidic women invoke emotional experiences in their children when children conform in order to embody the divine covenant between God and all Jews in a concrete form. Saba Mahmood (2005:141) notes that the evocation of certain emotions in religious practice is not only about creating motivation for adherence to religious doctrine;[13] rather, experiencing culturally and religiously appropriate emotions enables one to make ethical distinctions between good and bad, to actually discern and come to experience pious ways of being in the world. For children in a nonliberal religious community, such as Hasidic Jews, this does not only happen through explicitly religious practice or education but in the everyday contexts of ethical self-formation, from an arts-and-crafts project taped to the family refrigerator to a smiley sticker given for bringing in a healthy snack.

The appropriation from secular North American childrearing, however, is selective. There are North American techniques of the self which Hasidic women firmly reject. As I noted, many women made fun of their perception that secular North Americans believe that everything should be explained to children. A number of women were repelled when they heard from a teacher about a more modern mother who told her child that she was pregnant and even let the child touch her belly. Around issues of the body, asking certain kinds of questions or challenging authority, Hasidic women reject North American child-rearing practices as evidence of the degeneracy and immaturity of the Gentile world (as I discuss in the next chapter).

The anthropologist Webb Keane (2007:5–6) suggests that one version of secular modernity tells a story of human liberation from the false beliefs that hinder individual autonomy and freedom. Hasidic women similarly emphasize the importance of the autonomous will of the child; however, gradual training in khinekh, cultivated both emotionally and physically, persuades children that some freedoms are false, childish, and selfish. Hasidic women told me repeatedly that freedom to pursue self-fulfillment, imagined most frequently as pursuit of a job or a level of income, or even eating without making a blessing, is empty and meaningless. Instead, "true" self-actualization comes when an individual has the discipline to fit into religious hierarchies and practices, the only path to divine truth. Examining how Hasidic girls and boys are formed through everyday interactions with adults and among themselves suggests an alternative formulation of the modern ethical self, especially around issues of autonomy and individuality.[14] The production of ethical Hasidic individuals is not simply a reaction to secular modern self-making. Rather, it emerges from shared processes, even using some shared techniques, but with different goals legitimized through different forms of authority and ethics.

CHAPTER THREE

Defiance

ON ONE OF HER DAYS OFF FROM TEACHING, Esty invited me to visit. We sat down in her airy, newly renovated kitchen that faced her leafy backyard. Esty was wearing the typical outfit of a Hasidic woman relaxing at home: a turban covering all of her hair instead of her usual, blond "China Doll"-style wig (a short bob with bangs), a long-sleeved flowered housecoat, seamed beige stockings, and clogs. Despite her casual outfit, Esty looked elegant. Perhaps it was her bright blue eyes or her willowy build. Esty had been exposed to more modern Jewish girls, having taught in a more modern school and having done some outreach with Jews in Israel before her marriage. Her familiarity with other kinds of Jews seemed to give her more perspective on her own Hasidic life than many, although in no way, as far as I could tell, had it shaken her conviction that her Judaism was the only authentic one.

That afternoon both of her children were in their highchairs waiting to eat lunch. I had asked her about fitting in, and as she fed the children alternating mouthfuls of hot cereal, she told me a story about curiosity, faith, and authority. In fourth grade, Esty said, she accepted that God had made the world, but she wanted to know who made God. This question troubled her, but she was afraid to ask her teachers or her parents. Finally, she pulled aside a slightly older male cousin and asked him. He was shocked by her question and angrily threatened to tell her parents if she ever mentioned it again. "It was a good question," she told me ruefully, "but here we're not so good on questions."

This chapter is about why Hasidic Jews are "not so good on questions," a characteristic that a number of women told me was one of the necessary drawbacks (*khisroynes*) to a Hasidic way of life. The previous chapter looked at the importance of learning to fit in to nonliberal understandings of the person, where individual autonomy is "channeled," as Rifky described it, to fulfill religious communitarian aims. Here I ask how Hasidic women respond to girls and some young boys who refuse to fit in, ask culturally and religiously inappropriate questions, want things they cannot have, or defiantly challenge authority.

Hasidic *emune* 'faith' or 'belief' is the basis for Hasidic cultural beliefs about questioning and authority. Emune requires that each Jew practice Orthodox Judaism despite any individual feelings to the contrary. Women told me and their daughters that understanding and desire develop out of religious practice, not vice versa. An illustration of how emune is cultivated is in the ways that women, older siblings, and peers respond to inappropriate curiosity, questions, or defiance from Hasidic girls (and in some cases little boys). For Hasidic girls there are theological implications for learning the limits of questioning authority that go beyond negative consequences for the individual or the family or a lack of social graces. Because hierarchies of communal authority, based on age, gender, and religious authority, are given divine legitimacy, defiance and questioning of parents or teachers may be tantamount to questioning God. This is unethical on a cosmological scale. Question-and-answer exchanges between adults and girls are the training ground for learning the self-discipline required when a girl's desire must give way if it conflicts with her responsibilities as a Hasidic girl.

In this chapter I show how Hasidic women, older siblings, and peers all help Hasidic girls (and sometimes little boys) develop a form of curiosity that does not ask for too many reasons or challenge the authority of teachers or mothers, male authorities (including brothers), and ultimately to God.[1] When Hasidic girls question inappropriately, Hasidic women respond by *not* answering. Women also look outside their communities, to their perceptions of how Gentiles question and Gentile attitudes to authority, which are an explicit model for Hasidic girls and boys of how not to be.[2]

The question-and-answer exchanges and reprimands that pass between Hasidic women and girls can be understood, in Foucault's terms of ethical self-formation, as discursive technologies of the self; ways that women and girls, in everyday talk, produce Hasidic Jews who willingly fit into hierarchies of communal authority even when they do not want to or understand why. These technologies of the self emphasize the limits of individual reasoning to understand and recognize God's plans. Scholars who have used Foucault's work on ethical self-formation have focused explicitly on religious practice among adults. Joel Robbins (2004b:219), for example, examines two discursive technologies of the self—confession and moral self reflection—through which the Urapmin of New Guinea strive to reach the Christian goal of self-formation: the renunciation of the will and a "peaceful heart."[3] I emphasize that nonliberal gendered forms of curiosity and belief are produced not only in contexts of religious ritual but also in more everyday exchanges. Ethical self-forming practices include what happens when a girl questions her teacher's authority, asks her mother about a ritual practice, or has to be quiet so that her little brother can do his homework. By gradually learning the self-discipline to develop a form of curiosity that does not challenge communal hierarchies of authority, girls come to participate in an alternative religiously civilizing project.

UNQUESTIONING BELIEF AND HASIDIC SELF-HELP

The covenant between God and the Jews is a bargain of sorts, Rifky explained to me in one of our long, open-ended conversations in her small, crowded yellow kitchen. If Jewish men and women observe the 613 commandments which, they hold, God has decreed, they will be rewarded in this life and the hereafter. Of these 613 commandments, 365 are prohibitions and 248 are duties to be performed or observed. Women are excused from the time-bound commandments because of their domestic responsibilities.

Hasidic women I worked with told me that emune is defined by a willingness to acquiesce to God's will, even if they do not always understand God's reasons. This interpretation of religious faith, which privileges deeds over belief, is traced to the book of Exodus (24:7), where Jews at Mount Sinai accepted the Torah from God, saying, in loshn-koydesh, "kol asher diber adonoy naseh venishma" (all that God has said, we will do and we will listen), meaning that obedient action takes precedence over understanding. According to Hasidic women I spoke with, this makes it their responsibility to adhere to the commandments regardless of what an individual desires or intellectually understands.

Still, this does not mean women do not value reasons or search for understanding, because, as Esty said, "There is always a reason." When, for example, Esty's husband's family experienced some trouble with their business, they hypothesized that a recent change in synagogues was to blame, and so they returned to their old synagogue in an attempt to ameliorate their troubles. Much like North American Christian Bible Believers who use the words of the King James Bible as code for uncovering God's intentions for them (Ammerman 1987:54), Hasidic Jews try to discover God's logic operating in their everyday lives. However, Hasidic women I talked to acknowledged that sometimes they were not yet able or ready to understand God's plan for them. In these cases, however much reasons are valued, they do not trump commandments.

Hasidic women's unquestioning belief requires that they try to receive their lot in life with cheerful acceptance, publicly displaying their trust in God. These efforts are sustained by the availability of countless inspirational lectures, books, and even phone services where, by dialing a 900 number, a Hasidic woman can hear an inspiring talk for a fee. This genre of what I call "Hasidic self-help" focuses on strengthening each person's ability to unquestioningly accept God's plans. Similar support for men draws, I believe, more from religious texts and less from North American self-help genres. Examples of lectures available from a popular women's educational center listed: "Understanding Your Personality," "The Importance of Making Goals," "Giving Strength with Words," "Thanking *Hashem* 'God' Brings Good to the World," and *"Ven De Blik Ofn Leybn Iz Rikhtig* [When The Outlook On Life Is Right] [sic]" —all addressing how one develops a positive attitude in life.

These inspirational materials for Hasidic women can be understood as part of an increasing give and take between a therapeutic framework that has informed the self-help movement and religious discourse in North America since the 1960s. For example, Heather Hendershot (2004), in her study of media and evangelical Christians in North America, has noted the ways that evangelicals have embraced and reformulated psychological discourse for Christian consumers. Although Hasidic self-help borrows heavily from the North American self-help movement, there is a significant difference: whereas the North American self-help movement is a form of therapy that encourages people to acknowledge and talk about their troubles—a secular ritual that leads to happiness and fulfillment—Hasidic self-help, though also focusing on happiness and fulfillment, denies the therapeutic value of talking about one's problems. Indeed, persons who complain too much can be seen as lacking faith in God's authority. Real happiness, Hasidic self-help suggests, can only be achieved by accepting God's plans, and disciplining individual reasoning and desires. Hasidic women are secure in the knowledge that, as many remarked to me, "Hashem only gives us what we can bear."[4]

LEARNING UNQUESTIONING FAITH

Hasidic women's conceptions of emune shape self-forming practices with girls and boys, with the goal of cultivating children who will fulfill God's commandments on their own, despite what they feel or think. This is based on the notion that religious practice not only precedes understanding, but that it may prepare the child for understanding when he or she is mature enough. As Rifky told me, "The concept of *khinekh* 'moral education' is that they [children] are ready to be molded, but do not necessarily understand."

Many interactions between adults and girls emphasize adherence to communal gendered hierarchies of authority and a disregard of children's understanding or desire to comply. For example, when a young teacher, Rukhy, was frustrated that her second-grade class showed little enthusiasm for their morning prayers, she asked her grandfather for advice. He told her that when he was a boy he had terribly resented that his father forced him to get up at dawn, in the cold and dark, to study Torah, hours before he began a long day at school. His father kept after him though, demanding that he continue despite his lack of desire. With time and maturity, her grandfather told Rukhy, he came to appreciate his father's pushing him to continue. He even came to cherish his early morning risings, seeing them not as an onerous task but an opportunity to experience the beauty of the Torah. His message to his granddaughter was not to pay much attention to whether her students wanted to pray; just keep them praying and studying, he told her, and they will develop the appropriate feelings of satisfaction and understanding. Ritual practice produces culturally and religiously appropriate desires, not the reverse (see also Mahmood 2005; Jacobson 2006).

The self-forming activities of khinekh help children develop their unquestioning faith, which includes children learning and accepting the limitations of their own independent reasoning. Samuel Heilman, in his ethnography of ultra-Orthodox, non-Hasidic Jews in Israel, points this out in a quote from the Lubavitcher rebbe:

> One should accustom the child to believing without reason and explanation and then, even when he ages and his rationality is strengthened ... he will not depart from the true path and observance even when it does not make sense to him; or when he cannot understand the sense or reach the depths of truth, if he has been trained in such faith from his youth, he will not depart from the faith, and will not depend only on his understanding. (cited in Heilman 1992:175)

The rebbe's assumption is that the limitations of the human mind can stop a child (normatively male in this text) from understanding God's "sense" or the "depths of truth." [5] The child's developing ability to reason is, in fact, a potential danger, because he may be tempted to rely on his faulty and limited interpretation and observations of the world, rather than having the strength to participate in a form of belief that requires submitting to hierarchies of communal and divine authority.

When a child does rely on his or her own reasoning, there can be grave consequences for Jewish continuity. Rifky told me a story about her grandmother who was "too curious." When Rifky herself was a little girl, her mother often told her stories about her grandmother, who, as a young girl, was known for her quick mind. This grandmother would often go to her father (Rifky's great-grandfather) and ask him all kinds of questions, including the question, "Who made God?" Finally, after answering many of her questions, her father grew upset and told her, and I paraphrase the Yiddish, "If you grow up to be a fool, I won't worry, but if you grow up to be a heretic (*apikoyres*), then I'll be worried." Rifky explained that her great-grandfather was warning his daughter that if she continued to "think too much" she might indeed become a heretic and abandon her faith. "Thinking can be dangerous," Rifky told me, "because it can lead you off the path of Judaism.'" Rifky elaborated that if a child does not learn to think, the child becomes, in Rifky's words, "an idiot," which is certainly nothing to strive toward. However, given the choice between a child becoming an idiot or a heretic, any Hasidic parent would choose the idiot.

This attitude toward a child's developing ability to reason contrasts dramatically to an Enlightenment model of the child as described by, for example, Rousseau or, earlier, in some of John Locke's writings, where, given the right environment, children's "natural" ability to reason enables them to become law-abiding citizens. The development of reason makes the law intelligible to individuals, and so makes them subject to its authority (cited in Keane 2007:116). This humanistic view of the child has shaped the contemporary emphasis on child-centered learning currently popular in, for example, North American Montessori preschools (James, Jenks, and Prout 1998:15–16).[6] The humanistic view directly contradicts the Lubavitcher rebbe's view and the moral of Rifky's story about her grandmother. Hasidic women I worked with had no problem appropriating aspects of child-centered learning, as I discussed in the previous chapter, such as praising and building self-esteem. Nevertheless, Hasidic women use these child-centered techniques of the self in order to prepare children to rely, not on their own reasoning, but on that of communal authorities—parents, teachers, religious leaders, and, ultimately, God (see also Heilman 1992:224–225).

Hasidic girls develop an unquestioning emune through their relationships with authority figures at home and in school. Teachers explicitly discussed how learning to respect teachers helps girls develop the appropriate stance to all authority figures. When, for example, a second-grade girl brushed her hair in the middle of class, a teacher asked if she would brush her hair in front of the rebbe at a relative's *upshern* (a boy's first haircut that symbolizes his inclusion as a Jewish male). She was reminding the little girl that she had to give as much respect to her teacher as she would to a rebbe. The teacher told the girl, "*Me darf geybn kuved*! (You have to give respect!)."

Similarly, during recess one day, another teacher complained that a student lacked "sensitivity" to authority. The mother had complained to the teacher about a grade her daughter was given on an assignment; the teacher was angry, she told the other teachers during morning recess, not because of the disagreement over grading but because the mother was teaching her daughter to "question authority."

Obviously, on many occasions in other, more typical North American homes and schools, children are told that despite their own feelings they must obey authority figures. And many times irritated parents, myself included, are questioned too far by a child and may resort to saying, "Because I said so!" But if nonliberal religious girls do not do as they are told, despite their feelings to the contrary, they are not just badly brought up, spoiled, or willful; Hasidic girls who frequently challenge authority figures are ultimately challenging God. Scholarship on nonliberal Christian schooling in the United States has similarly noted the powerful role of authority figures in inculcating nonliberal faith in children.[7] Susan Rose (1993:463) cites a teacher at a North American Christian academy who said, "Don't apologize for telling the kids what is right. They should be taught not to question you." Peshkin (1986) suggests that Christian Fundamentalist parents, as the "bearers of God's truth," command unusually strict authority compared to secular parents.

Among Hasidic parents, authority is determined by age and gender. Male-headed families answer to male religious leaders, whose authority comes more directly from God. Although Hasidic mothers and fathers are responsible for rearing children together, the father is the head of the family. As noted earlier, because of the institutionalized gendered division of labor, fathers, by virtue of their Torah studies, have greater authority at home than their wives do. Over time, fathers become more involved in their sons' Torah studies, leaving daughters more to their mothers. Both boys and girls in a family must submit to their parents' wishes. But girls must also gradually begin to facilitate their brothers' Torah study.

In order to conform to gendered expectations of authority figures, Hasidic girls must learn which kinds of questions are appropriate and elicit approving explanations, and which questions are just not recognized and will not be answered. The formation of ethical Jewish girls who do not question authority or rely too much on their own curiosity, reasoning, or desires is developed through question-and-answer exchanges between women and girls.

JEWISH VERSUS GENTILE QUESTIONS

In preparation for the Passover holiday, where the Exodus narrative is retold during a ritualized meal (a Seder), Mrs. Silver dramatized a portion of the *hagude* (the text used in the Seder) for her first grade class. She emphasized the importance of learning to ask questions in the correct Jewish way. The section she presented was based on a rabbinic commentary that claims there are four kinds of Jewish children, and each one should receive a specifically tailored answer to the ritualized question the youngest child at the table has just recited in Hebrew: "Why is this night different from all others?" The text itself is sparse. Mrs. Silver, the young, quietly charismatic first-grade teacher whose stories riveted her students, added dramatic elaborations. She modeled for her students how good Jewish children ask good questions and how bad Jewish children ask bad ones, making them *almost* but never quite like Gentiles. The loshn-koydesh text describes the four children as normatively male, but Mrs. Silver's dramatization suggests that learning to question in the right way and for the right reasons is an important part of ethical self-formation for both Hasidic boys and girls.

I paraphrase Mrs. Silver's original recitation from Hasidic Yiddish, the medium of instruction in the mornings: One kind of child, a *khukhem* 'wise child' is a good obedient boy who likes to learn Torah. He asks his father respectfully to explain the Exodus from ancient Egypt so that he might fulfill God's commandments. His father rewards him by teaching him all there is to know about the Seder so that he may participate. Another kind of child, in contrast, is a *rushe* 'wicked child'; he is disobedient, does not like to learn Torah, reads Gentile books, does not obey the commandments, and makes fun of all things Jewish. He asks his father disrespectfully what God commanded Jews to do for Passover, excluding himself. His father yells at him that if he had been in ancient Egypt he would not have been redeemed because he asked in such a *khitspedik in narish* 'willfully defiant and foolish' way. The third and fourth children are, respectively, a "simple child" and a "baby." Mrs. Silver told the Passover narrative in its barest outlines for the former and then, to her students' delight, told the story to the baby in Yiddish baby talk.[8]

Wise Jewish children, Mrs. Silver suggests, ask genuine questions for information, and they ask their questions respectfully of the male adult authority, so that they might participate appropriately in Jewish communal life. Mrs. Silver's description of the rushe embodies Hasidic notions of wickedness; the wicked child is defiant, questions authority (his father's and God's), and commits one of the ultimate sins for a Hasidic boy: reading Gentile books and thus taking time away from his Torah studies. He does not respect his father or the Jewish people, as evidenced by the way he asks his father about the Passover story. His questioning is immature and defiant, and, ultimately, even grounds for exclusion from the Jewish people. In Mrs. Silver's telling of the last two children's questions, she implies that questioning is a project which, as they grow up, both boys and girls will continue to grapple with in age-appropriate ways.

In other contexts, girls were taught that Gentiles ask selfish questions that do not respect authority, providing evidence that they do not deserve to be God's chosen people. In kindergarten and first-grade classrooms, Hasidic teachers tell girls that it is Jews' unquestioning adherence to God and the Torah that makes them, what women call in English, "special and different" from Gentiles. For example, Mrs. Silver told her class that when God first created the Torah, God offered it to many nations of the world.[9] Each nation first asked God what it contained or heard some of the commandments and rejected them as too difficult or simply uninteresting. The Jews, however, as noted, upon being offered the Torah, accepted it without even knowing its contents. They recognized God as the ultimate authority and adhered to his commandments without question. Gentiles' questioning of God's authority and their rejection of the Torah explains the selfishness and weakness of Gentiles in their daily lives. Without the commandments to guide them, Gentiles, unlike Jews, lack the internal strength to engage in the personal struggle against the inclination for evil, something Mrs. Silver articulated one day in class:

> *Indz lozn nisht inzer yaytser-hure aranredn. Indz lozn nor de yaytser-hatoyv . . . di bist a yid, in di host nokh a toyre, in di mist folgn vus shtayt in dan toyre.*

> We don't let our evil inclination whisper to us [in contrast to Gentiles]. We only allow the good inclination in . . . You are a Jew, and you still have a Torah, and you must obey what is in your Torah.

Hasidic girls, playing among themselves, sometimes use the category of Gentiles, with all its stereotyped negativity, in their arguments. One day during recess first-grader Chaya Gitty had an argument with a known "troublemaker," Tsini, whom I describe in greater detail below. Chaya Gitty yelled at Tsini that she was acting like a *goyishe rushe* 'evil Gentile'. As soon as they returned to class, the other girls told Mrs. Silver what Chaya Gitty had said. Mrs. Silver instructed all the girls to sit down and asked what had happened. Chaya Gitty denied any wrongdoing, but Tsini confirmed the incident, saying, *"Zi zugt, zi gezugt ikh firt zikh azoy vi a goyishe rushe [sic]"* (She says, she said, I behave like an evil Gentile). Mrs. Silver turned to Chaya Gitty and said:

> *Vilst dertsayln far de <u>principal</u> az ikh hob a maydl vus redt, vi, ikh vil nisht zugn vus? Chaya Gitty, vart far an enfer fin dikh. Dey class, in dey class, <u>vatch</u> me vi'ze red. Indz hobn shoyn gelernt, az de aybeshter hot indz*

gegeybn a moul tse haltn es haylig, redn haylige zakhn, nisht tse redn shlek-
hte, tumedike zakhn.

Do you want me to tell the principal that I have a girl in my class that talks like, I don't even want to say what? Chaya Gitty, I'm wait-ing for an answer from you. In this class we watch how we speak. We already learned that God gave us a mouth, to keep it holy, to say holy things, not to say bad, dirty/impure things, ok?

Chaya Gitty was chastised by Mrs. Silver, who almost, but not quite, compared her unchecked tongue to that of a Gentile ("a girl who talks like, I don't even want to say what"). Chaya Gitty was upset and qui-etly cried at her desk. However, I observed other children sometimes using the category of Gentiles in their play, often taking the more com-mon role of "bad guy" that many other North American children use, as I discuss further in chapter 6. Mrs. Silver was visibly angry over the incident, but when I told Rifky and Esty about this same exchange they both giggled, and asked: "Did she really say that?" While adults can-not condone calling another Hasidic girl an evil Gentile, they seemed to acknowledge, implicitly, that Chaya Gitty's use of the term cre-atively engaged all the bad qualities the category encompasses, which clearly the first-grade girls had already learned.

Hasidic Girls' Good Questions and Bad Questions

In homes and school I saw many young girls ask "good" questions that displayed attentiveness rather than curiosity or challenge. The questions were often about a text and could, for example, refer to an inconsistency or an unusual marking. Parents and teachers in these cases would warmly applaud the young questioner for her careful at-tention and diligence. When a girl asked a good question, she was held up as a model to her siblings or peers for her engagement with the task at hand and the respectful manner in which she inquired. For ex-ample, one Friday evening at Rifky's Shabbes table, her eleven-year-old daughter, Yitty, asked her father why the biblical portion of the week used the word "God" in one part of the text but later used an-other name for God. Her father thought about her question and said he did not know the answer. Her mother told her it was a very good question and that it made her father think. They all agreed that she should ask her teacher. In this case, Yitty showed that she was reading very carefully and had caught something to puzzle over. Her question did not challenge the meaning of the text itself or imply there was a mistake. Rather, because girls learn that the Bible is literally God's words, Yitty asked why God would use two different terms, expecting that there is a reason. She also asked for clarification from her father, the domestic religious authority, in a respectful way. Adults' positive responses to these kinds of good questions may actually be more satisfying than an answer.

When Hasidic girls ask "why" questions that may, just by their asking, challenge the authority of God or the Torah, Hasidic women do not ignore the question, but neither do they answer it. Instead, women offer a statement about essentialized religious authority. Women's responses to "why" questions about religious practice, for example, are used to reinforce the authority of the Torah as God's words, which is done by not answering the question at all. For example, seven-year-old Yehudis, her mother Raizy, and I were on our way to the playground when Raizy stopped off to have a sweater checked by a local expert for *shatnes* (a forbidden mixing of wool and linen). The following interaction occurred:

> YEHUDIS: *Far vus miz me checkn*? (Why do you have to check?)
> [Raizy explained, in Yiddish, that one cannot mix the two materials.]
> YEHUDIS: *Ober far vus*? (But why?)
> RAIZY: *Azoy shtayt in de toyre.* (That's what's in the Torah.)

And that was the end of that. Yehudis did not question further. In this exchange with her mother, Yehudis wanted to know the reason behind the prohibition on mixing wool and linen by clarifying that her question was not about what the prohibition was, but the reason behind it ("But why?"). Her mother's answer was that the prohibition is noted in the Torah. The shatnes rule is believed to have no religious explanation. Hasidic religious commentary (written by male scholars) actually goes out of its way to provide possible explanations. Perhaps a boy asking this question would receive a different answer that included possible reasons given by Torah scholars. However, because women have less access to religious texts and knowledge than men, they end certain lines of questioning, especially with young girls, by appeals to the authority of the Torah. For girls, at least, after some initial attempts at an explanation, the reminder that God made the prohibition should suffice. Girls do not really need to know all the reasoning behind some religious laws.

A similar stance to the Torah's authority and prohibition on questioning one's lot in life occurred during a school assembly I attended. An older Russian Jewish woman had been invited to address the girls on the school's theme for the year: *simkhe* 'happiness'. The speaker told the girls all about the hardships and prejudice she and her family had endured in order to remain observant Jews under the communist regime. Despite everything, she claimed, speaking a Northeastern Yiddish that made the girls giggle, *"Ma mame hot nit gefregt ken kashes. Emune iz simkhe"* (My mother never asked hard questions. Faith is happiness).

In addition to questions, parents' responses whenever a child asks to change familial religious practice teaches girls and boys about communal hierarchies of authority. Although certain laws must be obeyed by all observant Jews, the interpretations of the laws in practice vary. Religious differentiation within Hasidic groups is an important marker of family solidarity, genealogy, and continuity as I noted in the introduction. In fact, despite the unusual continuity across Hasidic home and school contexts, family practices take precedence over the practices in schools (and the Hasidic court) when the issue is one of style, and not level, of observance.

In one case, parents invoked familial authority based on age to reject their son's requests to look different from the family, a result of his exposure to the religious practices of his peers in school. Morah Cohen, a teacher in Bnos Yisruel, told me how she responded to her seven-year-old son's requests to look more like the boys in his school, the Stolin Yeshiva, a Hasidic group that originated in Lithuania. Stolin is known for being very "American," in that males do not look or sound as distinctively Hasidic as some other groups. Among the differences, many Stoliner Hasidic males have short side curls and tuck them behind their ears, in contrast to the long prominent side locks of many Bobover boys. Morah Cohen comes from what she calls a "European" Bobover Hasidic background in Montreal, which is known for its strict adherence to and hyperbolization of the commandments. So when Morah Cohen's son asked to wear a tie and also to cut his long, curly side locks and tuck them behind his ears so the other boys would not make fun of him, Morah Cohen told me that she simply told her son, "We don't wear ties." Regarding his hair, her husband told their son that his mother liked his side curls long and, his mother reported to me: "That was that."

Through appeals to familial authority ("We don't do that"), women and their husbands stressed that conforming to family practice was not open to negotiation or discussion. In the side-curl discussion, Morah Cohen's son not only learned the importance of conformity but also that his desires must give way before his mother's wishes. There are times, then, where age trumps gender, so that even though Morah Cohen is a woman, her preference overrides her son's. But as he grows up, Morah Cohen's son will gradually become an authority figure. Nevertheless, there is the cultural expectation that a change from familial religious practice should not be taken on until a male is sufficiently mature, meaning married with children of his own (see chapter 6).

When girls question Hasidic gender categories, women remind them, again by not answering, of naturalized gender differences where there are strictly defined spheres of interest and activity. As noted, girls often do not have access to certain realms of male knowledge. Requests for knowledge that crossed gender boundaries sparked either teasing or evocation of immutable and divinely sanctioned gender differences that required reminding but no explanation. For instance, Mrs. Silver was telling a story about a famous sage who, at a very young age, had begun to study the Mishna (*mishnayes*, a set of commentary on the Torah). A little girl named Chana raised her hand, was called on, and asked: *"Vus iz mishnayes?"* (What is the Mishna?). Mrs. Silver began to explain that the Mishna was a set of commentaries and then, seeming to get a bit exasperated, told Chana in Yiddish, "When you become a boy, you'll understand" (*Az vest zan a yingl, vest shoyn farshtayn*). Everyone laughed, including Chana and Mrs. Silver.

The teasing tone, laughter, and dismissal of the question reminded Chana that it really did not matter if she, as a girl, knew what the Mishna was. Indeed, Mrs. Silver effectively cut off any further questioning and continued her lesson. Similarly when Esty's daughter, Leye, wanted a ponytail like her brother, Aaron, who had not yet had his first haircut, Esty told her, "Aaron's a boy." Surprised, I asked why such a non-answer would satisfy Leye. "Well," she said, "I'm giving her a reason. That's what's important."

Young boys and girls, like Leye, learning about religious practice and gender differences are taught that certain questions and requests will only be answered through reference to God-given, essentialized differences, and that needs to be enough. These differences legitimate inviolate categories of textual authority (the Torah), gender and age hierarchies, and family religious practice. When a woman perceived a willful challenge to her authority or that of another adult, however, the reaction was very different. *Khitspe* 'willful defiance' is not tolerated. What is labeled khitspe is based on cultural understandings of how intentionality and self-control develop across the life cycle.

REMINDERS, WARNINGS, TATTLING, AND PUBLIC SHAMING

Women do not expect little girls to act like adults. Girls make mistakes in religious practice, defy authority figures at times, and ask difficult questions. The women I observed tried hard to give girls the benefit of the doubt, often reframing defiance as a "mistake." In their mild reminders and warnings, parents and teachers frequently refer to communal hierarchies of authority to remind girls that their will (as children) must be subordinated to the will of adults. On the first day of first grade, for example, a little girl named Chaya Mindy jumped out of her seat before Mrs. Silver had given permission to line up. Mrs. Silver told her to sit down, but Chaya Mindy defiantly said, "No!" Mrs. Silver quietly asked, "*Me meyg zugn nayn far a morah?*" (Can we say no to a teacher?). Chaya Mindy hung her head silently and went to sit down. I heard a number of teachers and parents ask rebellious kindergartners and first-graders the same question. Girls almost always seemed embarrassed and said, "*Nayn*" 'no', or hung their heads and said nothing. Parents similarly disciplined their daughters by asking if one said no to a *mommy* or a *totty*. Through a generalizing strategy, women placed themselves in the category of "teacher" or "mommy," so that rather than a personalized struggle, girls were reminded that certain categories of adults simply had to be obeyed, although, of course, on many occasions children did not obey.

In their reminders to girls who are disobedient, women also appeal to the emotional influence that girls' actions have on authority figures. Mothers and teachers frequently suggested to girls that following the instructions of authority figures made the adults "proud," but not following instructions made them "sad." This occurred also in interactions between mothers and sons. When, for example, Raizy told her first-grader son, Shimmy, to do his homework, he said, "*Ikh vil nisht*" (I don't want to). When Raizy asked, "*Far vus?*" (Why?), Shimmy only said, "*Val*" (Because). Raizy told him that if his rebbe knew that he did not want to study Torah, "*Er vet zan azoy sad*" (He'll be so sad). Eventually, with help from his mother, Shimmy did review his lessons. An aspect to the shaping of curiosity and faith in children is to encourage a sense of personal responsibility for the feelings of authority figures and learn to put them above one's own. In these situations, women suggest to young girls and boys that following the wishes of authority figures is more important than individual feelings or desires. Mrs. Silver once told a student who was going about an assignment in her own way, "*Matty, me miz folgn a teacher, me miz, afile oyb me vil nisht*" (Matty, you have to obey a teacher, you have to, even if you don't want to).

The requirement to obey adults regardless of the children's feelings and to learn to put the feelings of others before one's own is not uncommon in many other North American schools or families, Hasidic mothers and teachers, however, have an unusual authority because the weight of the Torah is behind them, both at home and in school.

The central message girls are presented with is that by accommodating to adult authority, they are fulfilling God's commandments, not just pleasing adult authority figures.

As girls enter first grade, direct challenges to a parent or teacher's authority is publicly named as khitspe. When a teacher or parent labels a girl's behavior khitspe, she often draws in the child's peers or siblings and requires them to ally themselves with her. These kinds of group disciplining activities are often noisy and chaotic, as girls interrupt each other and the teacher in trying to distance themselves from what is often called in English a "troublemaker" (or, in Yiddish, *mekhitsef*). In the following example first-grader Blimi announced to the class that her sister has challenged Mrs. Silver's account of a religious practice that Blimi had passed on to her sister at home:

BLIMI: *Mrs. Silver, man shvester hot gezugt az Mrs. Silver zugt lign.* [Collective gasp from the class.]

MRS. SILVER: *Zug dan shvester az zi iz a groyse mekhitsef. In velkhe class iz zi?*

BLIMI: Fifth.

MRS. SILVER: *Ver iz ir teacher?*

BLIMI: *Ikh vays nisht.*

MRS. SILVER: *Ok, ikh mayn az zol freygn ver iz ir teacher.* [Students call out and seem to agree that her teacher is Mrs. Goldman.] *Ok, Ikh'l darfn redn tse Mrs. Goldman tse zugn az zi hot a groyse mekhitsef in ir class. Me zugt nisht az a teacher zugt lign. Zi vayst nisht vus zi redt.*

BLIMI: *Ikh mayn az ire English teacher iz Mrs. Berman.*

MRS. SILVER: *Ok, zi vayst nisht vus zi redt, dan shvester. Zi iz a groyse mekhitsef.*

STUDENT 1: *Kan teacher zugt nisht kan lign.*

STUDENT 2: *Of course nisht.*

MRS. SILVER: *So indz zeyn mir az ire shvester vayst nisht vus zi redt.*

BLIMI: Mrs. Silver, my sister said that you tell lies. [Collective gasp from the class.]

MRS. SILVER: Tell your sister that she is a big troublemaker. What class is she in?

BLIMI: Fifth.

MRS. SILVER: Who is her teacher?

BLIMI: I don't know.

MRS. SILVER: Ok, I think that I should ask who her teacher is. [Students call out and seem to agree that her teacher is Mrs. Goldman.] Ok, I'll need to talk to Mrs. Goldman to tell her that she has a big troublemaker in her class. We don't say that a teacher tells lies. She doesn't know what she is saying.

BLIMI: I think her English teacher is Mrs. Berman.

MRS. SILVER: Ok, your sister doesn't know what she is saying. She is a big troublemaker.

STUDENT 1: No teacher tells lies.

STUDENT 2: Of course not.

MRS. SILVER: So we see that your sister doesn't know what she is saying.

Perhaps Blimi tells on her sister in order to determine if her older sister is correct in her assessment that Mrs. Silver lied, making Blimi somewhat complicit in the khitspe herself. Mrs. Silver, however, was quick to reframe the challenge to her authority. She ignored the content of the sister's remark (which was actually based on a simplification Mrs. Silver made of a text) and focused on the defiance she displayed by questioning a teacher. By labeling Blimi's sister's a *groyse mekhitsef* 'a big troublemaker', Mrs. Silver showed that there are public consequences for girls who challenge a teacher's authority. The other first-graders were encouraged to rally around Mrs. Silver. Blimi's sister would get the punishment she deserved. Mrs. Silver, however, did try to defuse the gravity of Blimi's sister's comments by repeating over and over, that Blimi's sister simply did not understand her own words or their import. Khitspe can be a serious charge. Mrs. Silver attempted to reframe the breach and bring it down to the level of "mistake."

In this incident, Mrs. Silver distinguishes between tattling and monitoring others in order to help them be better Jews. Part of girls' moral education is learning the appropriate manner and contexts for what is locally termed in English "being someone else's policeman." As noted in the previous chapter, tattling on someone in order to humiliate them is considered a sin. Telling on them in order to help them be a better Jew, however, is fulfillment of a commandment. In this interaction, girls participate in the culturally and religiously appropriate way to monitor their peers. The result of this exchange is to clarify for all the girls that when a girl is defiant, when she is a *groyse mekhitsef*, not only will authority figures like a teacher chastise her, but her own peers will condemn the behavior as well.

Occasions arise, of course, when girls ally themselves against an authority figure or when a *khitspedik* 'willfully defiant' child does not stop what she is doing. From my position in the back of the classroom I witnessed a number of episodes where two students would secretly join forces against Mrs. Silver, just as students often do in other North American classrooms. This happened when, for example, Mrs. Silver told Chana Malky that she would be punished the next day for something she had done; when the girls did an art project, Chana Malky would not join in. As Chana Malky sniffled to herself at her desk, Hindy, in the desk behind her, whispered consolingly. She told Chana Malky not to worry because by the next day Mrs. Silver would have forgotten the punishment and she would participate in the art project after all.

These kinds of student alignments, however, happened much more frequently in English classes, where the teachers generally have less authority than Yiddish teachers. They also tend to happen, from my observations, in the less authoritarian space of the home with mothers more than fathers. Raizy, for example, had a hard time during one of my visits getting her seven-year-old daughter, Yehudis, to stop singing at the top of her lungs and making it impossible for her younger brother, Shimmy, to do his homework with his mother. Despite her mother calling Yehudis's defiance khitspe, Yehudis would not stop, nor would she leave the room as her mother demanded. Finally, Raizy resorted to saying, *"Ikh darf zugn Totty?"* (Do I need to tell Daddy?), which sent Yehudis running into the other room.

The different dynamics between mother and son as opposed to mother and daughter in this disciplining exchange reveals the everyday occasions where girls are trained in and experience their position in gender hierarchies. A boy's homework, even in the case of a first-grader like Shimmy, prepares him for his eventual Torah study. As such, his mother and sister must put Shimmy's learning first by creating conditions under which he can concentrate. By ignoring her mother and continuing to make lots of noise, Yehudis was putting her own desires ahead of her gendered responsibilities to her family. Her mother is quick to discipline her and label this breach of her obligation khitspe, but only when Raizy appeals to the authority of the father, an adult male, does Yehudis finally acquiesce and leave the room. As Yehudis gets older, she will be required to take on many of the same facilitating roles to her brother that her mother has displayed in this interaction. Meanwhile, at age seven she has seen that if she interferes with her brother's Torah study, she will be disciplined.

Indeed, as girls get older, they increasingly take on the role of authority figures when their parents are not around. For example, on a Sabbath morning when Rifky was sleeping, Yitty, her oldest daughter, caught her younger sister, Malky, eating sweet cereal without asking. *"Ganeyve* 'stealing', Malky," said Yitty. Malky guiltily put away the cereal, although I observed other occasions when she ignored her older sister's warnings and did what she wanted.

TSINI THE TROUBLEMAKER

When a girl challenges authority figures repeatedly or in more serious ways, teachers and mothers can become frustrated and resort to more dramatic forms of public shaming to underscore the severity of the transgression. By describing a girl's defiant behavior as similar to the behavior of Gentiles, adults make clear that such behavior will not be tolerated. This form of discipline is illustrated by the case of Tsini, a little girl in the first grade, who, according to students and teachers alike, was a real troublemaker. For most Hasidic girls, the desire to be a troublemaker is most safely enacted in make-believe play. Little girls playing school often claimed the role of troublemaker. There is a certain thrill, apparently, to play at being "bad." When kindergartners played school, one girl was usually the teacher, another was a student, and the third was often the troublemaker who inevitably was soundly reprimanded. Girls often acted out their parts with gusto, and I never heard any commentary about girls choosing to play this role.

Tsini, however, was a troublemaker in real life. She was tall for her age and stocky, with short brown hair. Her clothing was sloppy, her uniform wrinkled, her blouse often not tucked in, and her shoes scuffed. She was also the baby in her family, the last of ten children. Her mother was a third-grade teacher in the same school. When I asked Mrs. Silver about Tsini, she told me that Tsini was "wild and spoiled," perhaps because she was the family baby, but also because she had a *leybedik* 'lively' nature which she "couldn't help." Indeed, she was an impulsive, moody girl, one minute throwing her arms around Mrs. Silver and proclaiming her everlasting love, and the next, losing her temper and openly defying her teacher. Tsini was one of the few students to ever sit in the *tshive-benkl* 'chair of penitence', and also to wear the red mitten showing that she had hit another girl. Other students, aware of Tsini's behavior, often did not want to be her partner on line or play with her, and so Tsini was frequently alone.

One afternoon in class, the other girls had, as instructed, taken out pencils and were waiting for Mrs. Silver to give them paper to do an assignment. Tsini was dreamily doodling on her desk, oblivious to Mrs. Silver's instructions. Mrs. Silver very dramatically called attention to Tsini's activities. As they had in the interaction above with Blimi, the other students chimed in and supported Mrs. Silver, who allowed for an unusual level of calling out, perhaps implicitly encouraging other students to condemn Tsini's behavior:

MRS. SILVER: *Far vus zeyt dan <u>desk</u> ous vi a . . . Mist koydem <u>cleanen</u> dan desk far bakimst a <u>paper</u>. Gay tse de <u>bathroom</u>, nemen a nase <u>paper towel</u>, ken ( ) a <u>paper</u> ( ) . . . Zeyt ous vi a tish in a <u>public school</u>. Goyishe kinder ( ). . . . Host a mul geveyn <u>by</u> a <u>train station</u>? Host gezeyn goyim, zay, vi zay viln shrabn zay, af <u>trains</u>, af hazer, af <u>stores</u>, af <u>gates</u>?*

STUDENT 1: *Azoy zay <u>mess</u>=*

STUDENT 2: *=Zay shrabn=*

MRS. SILVER: *=Zay gayn arup mit <u>spray</u>, zay nemen <u>spray</u> in zay <u>scribbln</u> alts af de <u>desk</u>. Zay <u>care</u> nisht oyb s'iz a <u>gescribbled</u> <u>desk</u>=*

STUDENT 3: *=<u>Right</u>, s'iz azoy vi=*

MRS. SILVER: *=Zay gayn arouf . . . a houz, zay zeyn s'iz a shayne vant, zay nemen a spray in zay shrabn zayer numen. A maydl vus shrabt of ir <u>desk</u>, iz es <u>almost</u> de zelbe <u>kind</u> fin dey.*

STUDENT 4: *A pur mul zeyt me=*

MRS. SILVER: *=Kenst nemen a <u>paper towel</u> in oyb es vet nisht arupkimen, vesti brengn zayf fin dan houz <u>nexte</u> morgn. Darf brengn a klayne <u>bag</u> zayf oder ikh'l rifn dan mame, zol kimen mit a shmate in zi vil ( ).*

MRS. SILVER: Why does your desk look like a . . . First, you have to clean your desk before you get paper. Go to the bathroom, take a wet paper towel, you can ( ) a paper ( ). It looks like a desk in a public school. Gentile children ( ). . . . Have you ever been by a train station? Have you seen Gentiles, how they write on trains, on houses, on stores, on gates?

STUDENT 1: That's how they mess=

STUDENT 2: =They write=

MRS. SILVER: =They go around with spray. They take the spray and they scribble on the desks. They don't care if it's a scribbled-up desk.

STUDENT 3: Right, it's like=

MRS. SILVER: =They go around . . . a house, they see a nice wall. They spray and write their names. A girl who writes on her desk, it's almost like the same kind of thing.

STUDENT 4: A few times, you see=

MRS. SILVER: =You can take a paper towel and if it doesn't come up, then you can bring soap from your house the next morning. You'll need to bring a small bag of soap, or I'll call your mother and tell her that she should bring a rag and she will ( ).

Tsini tried to clean the desk with a paper towel, but it did not remove the doodling. Mrs. Silver then called Tsini over and, in a whisper, read a letter she had written to Tsini's parents. Meanwhile, the other students stared at Tsini, who showed little emotion.

Mrs. Silver's disciplining of Tsini was, in fact, the most severe I saw during my time in her class. By drawing public attention to Tsini's doodling, Mrs. Silver emphasized the gravity of Tsini's offense, comparing Tsini's behavior almost, but not quite, to that of a Gentile child who goes to public school, writes graffiti, and "doesn't care." Observant Jewish children always have to care about what they do and say because God is always watching. As Von Hirsch (1995) similarly noted in her work with haredi caregivers in England, the phrase "I don't care" is a particularly loaded one and elicits strong reactions from parents and teachers alike.

Defacing a desk was seen by Mrs. Silver as a form of defiance and disrespect to authority: the authority of the school, its teachers, and, ultimately, the whole community, because as told to me by Gitty, my Yiddish tutor and an alumnus of the school, "It's the (Bobover) *ruv's* 'rebbe's' school." A number of times I heard mothers and teachers contrast Hasidic schools and children to Gentile children who go to public schools in the neighborhood (see chapter 6). Mrs. Silver's evoking a host of practices that define Gentile children emphasize how the moral boundary separating Jews from Gentiles can be threatened when Hasidic girls are khispehdik. Further, Mrs. Silver suggested that Tsini's mother would have to come into school and scrub the desk in front of everyone. Tsini's behavior not only has the potential for shaming her but also for shaming her parents and her family name. This serves as a warning to girls about their responsibility to respect their parents and "make them proud." Tsini's behavior and disciplining reminded the rest of the girls of the danger of not controlling oneself and not fitting in to the expectations of authority figures.

After witnessing some of Tsini's conflicts in class, I tried to broach the subject with Tsini's mother, Morah Margolis, whom I knew from time spent during recess. During one recess I told her that I had noticed Tsini had been having a hard time. She sighed and told me that it was tough for Tsini to sit still and focus in class. Then she told me how difficult it was to be different "by us" (meaning among Hasidic Jews). Tsini's mother was a bit of an outsider herself, having been brought up in a Litvish household and marrying into a Hasidic family. She seemed to feel the pressure of fitting in more than some other women. Perhaps this was because, as a woman in her mid-forties, she also had grown up in a less religiously stringent environment where she went to the movies and the library. She told me, as had Rifky, "By us, you don't rock the boat. You have to fit in." Just as Esty had said, "We're not so good on questions here," some of the women I met acknowledged that one of the sacrifices of being a Hasidic woman includes "not rocking the boat" either by asking for too many explanations, being too curious, wanting information that only boys need to know, or by being defiant.

Too Old to Ask

Hasidic adults expect that by early adolescence children should know that certain questions and requests cannot even be asked. Gitty described her impatience when her eleven-year-old brother asked her if their mother was going to have a baby; she responded, "Ask a better question." "The others [her other siblings]," she told me, "knew already not to ask, but my brother . . ." Her brother was old enough to have known, she implied, that it was not modest or appropriate, especially for a boy, to talk about having babies. In fact, Gitty was able to reel off a battery of responses that immediately ended a questioning sequence. She reported that in her family when a child inappropriately asked "Why?" in English an adult purposely reframed the question as the letter "y" and responded with the letter "z." If a child asked in Yiddish, "*Far vus?*" 'Why?', the answers might be "*Azoy vi ikh hob gezugt*" (Because I said so), "*Azoy iz*" (That's how it is), or "*Nisht dan business*" (Not your business). Perhaps it is significant that the more playful silencing of questions is in English, and the more serious shutdown of a child's questioning is in Yiddish, which, as I discuss later on, is considered by all Hasidim to be a more moral, more Jewish language, a language especially suited to ethical self-formation.

Parents' and teachers' refusal to answer certain kinds of questions or tolerate defiance does not mean that questioning or defiance simply stops as children become increasingly responsible for fulfilling the commandments. Part of growing up is learning the contexts in which questioning or challenging is more acceptable. Girls in school figure out early on that defiance will be less offensive to adults when it takes place during afternoon English classes. Substitute teachers and teachers of secular subjects, mothers reported to me, confront significantly more defiance than the Yiddish teachers who teach religious subjects. Once, during recess at Bnos Yisruel, some of the teachers laughed remembering how girls had so upset a Russian Jewish substitute teacher by writing "Happy Christmas" on the board in Russian that she cried. Boys also are notorious for tormenting their English instructors, although they would never think of such behavior in their religious studies. Adults give less weight to secular subjects generally taught by outsiders to the community or by less religiously stringent Jews, and children and teens take the opportunity to be defiant in contexts with less potential for threatening communal authority.

Similarly, curiosity can be satisfied when the questioner is safely ensconced in Hasidic life (i.e., married) or when the context of the questioning is of less consequence to the Hasidic community. For example, married women can ask and find answers to more questions than unmarried teens or children. When I expressed surprise to an observant but not Hasidic friend that Gitty was asking me many questions about dating, my friend quickly asked if Gitty was married. When I said she was, my friend seemed relieved. She explained that asking questions out of curiosity was fine, especially once someone is married and part of a tight set of social relationships and responsibilities. If she were single and asking, my friend said, then she would be worried that Gitty was looking for something outside the community.

Indeed, the question about who made God that Esty had so wanted to ask as a child was answered when she was a married woman with children. She told me she went to an inspirational lecture for women and heard a rabbi offer an explanation for that very question. His explanation was that as humans we cannot expect to understand all of God's workings. Although to me this did not seem like an answer at all, she told me the answer satisfied her. Perhaps the main issue was that her question had been acknowledged as legitimate, by a rabbi no less. She had been assured that there was a reason; she was just not yet able to understand it. I met another Hasidic young woman who told me that to answer some of her questions she had gone to a summer class for Jewish returnees to the faith. There, in a context with women who had grown up as secular Jews, she felt comfortable asking some of her more challenging questions that would have been unacceptable at home. Satisfied, she was able to return and participate in her own Hasidic community.

Those who continue to ask inappropriate questions or who cannot or will not fit in sometimes leave their communities and their families. A story reported in the *Village Voice* (July 1997) described four Hasidic boys who left their Brooklyn communities. At the time, all the Hasidic women in the bungalow colony I was visiting in the Catskill Mountains had either heard of the article or had read it. This was not unusual. Whenever an article or a book appeared about Hasidic Jews, no matter the publication, the material circulated in the community, as Hasidic Jews are concerned with and carefully monitor how they are portrayed in the media. The boys profiled in the *Voice* article left for different reasons. For example, one had been gay and another was not a strong scholar and could not find a place for himself. In each story, except for the boy who came out and seemed to be much more comfortable in an openly gay community, the boys spiraled out of control once they left their families. They often got involved in drugs or had other substance abuse problems the article reported. During my stay in the bungalow colony, Rifky and I joined a circle of women who were chatting, sewing, and relaxing on the lawn in chairs under a big tree surrounded by summer bungalows. The women started to talk about the article. Most knew the families of the boys, and they agreed that the boys had problems as a result of their parents' troubled marriages. They lamented that Hasidic dirty laundry had been aired in public to Gentiles and Jews.

In contrast to the *Voice* story about the boys, I spoke with two young women from different Brooklyn neighborhoods, both of whom had broken with their communities. Both gravitated to higher education when they began to question their faith, and this ultimately led to difficult, though satisfying, decisions. Miriam, who grew up in Boro Park in a Hungarian Hasidic family, had a crisis of faith at a relatively young age. She told me that one Sabbath, when she was nine, she sat under a table and methodically ripped up pieces of paper (a forbidden activity during the Sabbath). She ripped and held her breath, waiting to see if God would strike her down. When nothing happened, her whole world changed. She left her community as a young woman and went to a university, pursuing a degree. The background here is that her parents were divorced, and her mother, too, had moved away from her Hasidic faith. Her mother's religious journey was a support to Miriam's own questions.

Chani, another Hasidic girl from a different neighborhood and Hasidic circle, left just at the point of matchmaking (in the last year of high school when girls are between seventeen and nineteen years of age). Chani's parents, in contrast to Miriam's, were returnees to the faith. This meant that in their social world they were never quite as elite as those who are "ffb" or *frum* 'religious' from birth. Chani was a top student and valedictorian of her school. She told me that as she grew up she increasingly felt there was hypocrisy in the community, and she simply stopped believing. She, too, left her family to live with a nonobservant relative and went on to higher education. For both these young women, aside from attending a teachers' seminary, higher education was not an option.[10]

Those who do fit in are always theorizing about why some leave the community. Most blame the children's parents or the lure of materialism (see chapter 6). When there is not a clear person to blame, Esty, Rifky, and other women I met reminded one another that humans cannot always understand God's plan, but there *is* a plan. To echo an address given by the principal of Bnos Yisruel at a school assembly, *"Me tur nisht freygn oder complainen"* (We're not allowed to ask or complain).

CURIOSITY AND AUTHORITY

Hasidic women teach girls which questions they may not ask, what desires they may not have, whom they may not challenge. This happens in everyday exchanges when children's questions or behavior challenge categories of belonging that are considered God-given. Women's responses to transgressions include appeals to a higher authority, silence, shaming, and comparison to the most unethical subjects, Gentiles—all effectively ways to end an interaction. A powerful means by which authority is shored up is through the participation of peers in public disciplining. In class, for example, other students were quick to chime in and support their teacher, even if it meant, as Blimi did, telling on her own sister while, perhaps, simultaneously challenging her teacher's authority herself.

The consistency across socialization contexts means that children are presented with reverberations of a similar moral message from all the Jewish adults, older siblings, and even the peers in their lives. This consistency makes it exceedingly difficult to continue to ask certain kinds of questions, as evidenced by the painful conflicts of Hasidic "rebels" or those who leave (Levine 2003; Winston 2005). In question-and-answer exchanges between adults and children, curiosity is cultivated in ways that do not leave much space for challenges to hierarchies of authority, although children and young adults do find chinks in the system. The cultivation of nonliberal curiosity and relationships to authority are rooted in a particular form of faith that is enacted in sociological hierarchies of age and gender. Though all children must learn to give way before adults, girls must simultaneously put the needs of their brothers and fathers before their own, something they experience in everyday interactions with their siblings, parents, and teachers.

In this and the previous chapter, Foucault's notion of ethical self-formation shows the political implications of moral discourse between adults and children; in other words, how the cultivation of a nonliberal femininity, where girls learn to use their autonomy to discipline themselves, is part of a construction of a Hasidic alternative to their perceptions of Gentile and secular North America. A Jewish girl has to learn what Gitty called *tsirikhaltn* 'to rein herself in'. When I asked Rifky about this, she said she felt that a better way to think about self-discipline might be that a girl has to learn to "channel" her desires, questions, and needs so that they match with what is expected of her. Hasidic women cultivate this by trying to limit the situations where inappropriate curiosity or defiance can occur. They also cultivate a fear in children—which Kulick and Schieffelin (2004) note is the inverse of desire—of being like Gentiles, something I elaborate further in chapter 6. In these interactions of ethical self-formation, Hasidic women engage with modernity's formations of the self but subtly shift the terms: they focus on discipline instead of freedom, faith instead of reason, and action instead of desire.

CHAPTER FOUR

Making English Jewish

AT LEAST ONCE A MONTH I stayed for a Shabbes in Boro Park. In the quiet of Saturday morning, I walked to the Bobover synagogue. The stores were all locked and the streets were empty. Hasidic men, wearing their Shabbes-*bekeshes* (long, black satin jackets tied with a sash), wrapped in striped, blue and white fringed prayer shawls and wearing high beaver hats (*shtramlakh*), hurried by, holding little boys by the hand. I climbed the stairs to the women's section, which was sprinkled with a few middle-aged women and newly married brides. Women with young families generally stayed home. In a Hasidic synagogue everyone prays individually at his or her own pace, so before or after prayer women chatted with one another. I tried to go through the prayers but more often gave up and spent the few hours observing and talking.

One Shabbes morning in synagogue, Gitty's mother-in-law, Mrs. Fried, told me about an inspirational lecture (*shier*) for women that afternoon. The topic was the dangers of books with a non-Jewish outlook (*hashkufe*). After a heavy "Shabbes lunch" at a friend's house and a "Shabbes nap," I walked to the lecture hall on Eighteenth Avenue. Folding chairs were set up in rows, and the room was packed with women. A Hasidic rabbi spoke passionately, warning his listeners about the power of intention and its relationship to language. A Gentile or a heretic, he told us, can scribe a Torah in perfect loshn-koydesh, but his non-Jewish outlook will enter and pollute the very letters, the holy letters, as he forms them. The book must be burned to protect Jews who might read that Torah and be led astray by the outlook of the scribe that has infected the language.

In the same way that a Gentile outlook must be purged from sacred texts written in the sacred language, so a Jewish outlook, rooted in the goal of ultimately bringing about redemption, can transform and uplift the Hasidic vernaculars in Brooklyn, the everyday written and spoken languages, Yiddish and English. Loshn-koydesh, the language of the Bible, prayers, and early rabbinic literature, is believed to be supernatural and non-arbitrary, the actual words of God to his people (Glinert and Shilhav 1991:70–71). However, the Hasidic vernaculars, Yiddish and English, are in a more liminal or in-between space. Both vernaculars are non-standard linguistic varieties that borrow from and mix with each other, blurring the boundaries between the languages. These mixed languages are syncretic, in that they thrive partly because the community wishes to exploit the similarities and differences between them. The very ambiguity of syncretic languages makes them ripe for mediating difference both within and across the community. Just as Hasidic women exploit secular North American psychology for the purpose of producing nonliberal Hasidic persons, so Hasidic speakers, sometimes consciously and sometimes below the level of consciousness, engage with English in order to change its meaning, literally and ideologically. Hasidic Jews, particularly women and girls, use English, but they transform it by integrating features of Yiddish and loshn-koydesh accent, grammar, words, and intonation.

When Hasidic Jews talk about their two vernaculars they most often call them Yiddish and English. But when Hasidic men and women contrast their variety of Yiddish with its particular Central Yiddish dialect and incorporation of English to other forms of Yiddish, they often use the term *"hasidishe,"* or "Hasidic Yiddish," which I have adopted as well. Women I worked with, as well as some men, however, did not agree that their English was nonstandard, although a number laughingly called their English "Yinglish." A few Orthodox, but not Hasidic, women I met told me that Hasidic English was not "proper" or "good" English because it had so much influence from Yiddish. Hasidic women's reluctance to qualify their use of English as nonstandard may be a result of the greater importance they give to "secular" studies for girls, as well as gendered ambivalence to more secular standards of prestige, which I discuss in the next chapter. I suggest, however, that there is a distinctive Hasidic linguistic variety of English; the term I use to describe the influence of Yiddish and loshn-koydesh on English is "Hasidic English."

Hasidic Jews in Eastern Europe and North America have always drawn on and combined different cultural and religious forms, including Gentile folk tales, music and national languages.[1] However, Hasidic linguistic syncretism today is different in that it is part of broader Hasidic efforts to heighten religious stringency in everyday life (see chapter 1). For Hasidic Jews, the blurring of boundaries between Yiddish and English creates distinctively Hasidic ways of talking. The syncretic adaptation of English is a way to produce essentialized differences between Jews and Gentiles. At the same time Hasidic syncretic languages produce essentialized differences between Hasidic men and women: after a period of bilingual fluency, Hasidic girls in first grade begin to use predominantly Hasidic English among themselves, whereas boys speak predominantly Hasidic Yiddish throughout their lives.

Recently, evidence of language purism in girls' schools has emerged. School administrators have begun to ask girls to try to use more Yiddish, especially an unmixed form of Yiddish. Despite these attempts, the majority of Hasidic adults and children continue to use syncretic forms of Yiddish and English, largely because Hasidic children are addressed in syncretic Hasidic Yiddish and Hasidic English. In everyday interactions, Hasidic boys and girls learn that no matter what language they use as their vernacular, their mode of communication is always Jewish.

Especially helpful for understanding the philosophical beliefs underlying Hasidic linguistic syncretism and its meaning in contemporary New York City is the work of ethnomusicologist Ellen Koskoff (2001), who describes the musical practices of Lubavitcher Hasidic Jews. She shows that the Hasidic adaptation of secular, North American music for Hasidic purposes, even for prayer, is based on the belief that a Jew, may liberate the divine sparks embedded in a coarse secular husk through his holy intention. Koskoff describes, for example, the ways that a Lubavitcher composer adapted a Pepsi commercial that the Lubavitcher rebbe used for prayer and meditation. In this way, secular North American consumerism is transformed into a religious tool for the rebbe, the religious leader who is closest of all to God. Although Lubavitchers, perhaps, are especially open to cultural syncretism, given their emphasis on outreach to more secular Jews, I show that similar processes are at work when Hasidic Jews I observed in Boro Park transform English into a Jewish vernacular (in the context of speaking Hasidic Yiddish or Hasidic English): they redeem, sometimes consciously and sometimes unconsciously, the secular vessel of vernacular language through their holy purposes.

For Hasidic Jews, the secular world and its standardized national language are coarse and vulgar. The modern world and its language can be civilized, however, through syncretism with the Jewish languages of Yiddish and loshn-koydesh. The transformation of English into a Jewish language is one more way that Hasidic Jews help to bring about an alternative religious modernity, where linguistic and material vernacular signs provide visible evidence of membership in God's chosen community.

JEWISH MULTILINGUALISM: THE CHANGING MEANING OF YIDDISH

Yiddish has always been situated in a series of multilingual constellations, as Jeffrey Shandler (2005) notes, and it is the ongoing juxtapositioning and integration of languages that informs its changing significance.[2] Historically, among observant Eastern European Jews, Yiddish was one of three communal languages with different social functions.[3] Traditional Eastern European Jewish men and boys experienced, what Max Weinreich (1980) has called "internal bilingualism," where loshn-koydesh and Yiddish supported each other in religious study. Yiddish was also central to "external multilingualism" as the Jewish vernacular (both written and spoken) of everyday life for men and women in contrast to the use of the co-territorial languages (e.g., Polish, Russian, and German) that Jews used to communicate with the surrounding Gentile society (Shandler 2005:12–63; Seidman 1996). The sociolinguist Joshua Fishman (1981) has called the relationship among loshn-koydesh, Yiddish, and a co-territorial, or national, language "triglossia," where each of the three communal languages served a distinct social purpose.

Naomi Seidman has noted, however, that Jewish triglossia has always been gendered. Limited by a passive competence in loshn-koydesh learned in prayer, women were most fluent in Yiddish or the co-territorial languages. Whereas loshn-koydesh was masculinized, Yiddish was often considered a feminized language, suitable for women and uneducated men who were not literate in loshn-koydesh (Seidman 1996). We know less about how the co-territorial language was gendered, although girls from well-off families often had the most access to it through private tutoring or attendance at a secular gymnasium, where boys attended exclusively religious schools.[4] Along with the functional differentiation of triglossia and the critical role of gender, then, Jewish multilingualism has always been marked by dynamic interplay between multiple languages and syncretism.

A turning point in the history of Jewish triglossia began in late-nineteenth-century Europe, when millions of Jews (exclusive of Hasidic Jews) began to debate how they, as a "modern" people, should live, including which language they should speak— Hebrew, Yiddish, German, Russian, Polish, English, or even Esperanto. Out of this historical moment when, as Shandler (2005) notes, language was one of the most widely and passionately debated topics, the Yiddishist movement emerged. Yiddishism was based on the ideology that Yiddish as a language with its own growing literature was essential to the formation of a modern Jewish nation. Up through the interwar years in Europe, secular Yiddish culture flourished. Yiddishists began efforts at standardizing the language, using the literary languages of German and Russian as models and adopting many of the features of the prestigious Lithuanian dialect of Yiddish.[5] Standardization included attempts to standardize Yiddish spelling, grammar, and lexicon. YIVO (the Yiddish Scientific Institute), founded in Vilna in 1925, functioned like a Yiddish language academy, although its authority was contested, especially by both secular and religious Polish Jews (Shandler 2005).

After the Holocaust, Yiddish-speaking refugees to North America found themselves in new multilingual situations, confronting a population of already established American Jews who had abandoned Yiddish for English. In postwar New York, both Hasidic Yiddish speakers and Yiddishists established themselves afresh with their institutions, such as schools, newspaper presses, and publishing houses. There is, however, little formal contact between Hasidic educators or journalists and Yiddishists, who continue to see Yiddish as a vehicle of secular Ashkenazic culture. For Hasidic Jews, their variety of Yiddish distinguishes them both from North American Gentiles and from secular Yiddishists. Nevertheless, as with many other secular (Jewish and Gentile) cultural forms that Hasidic Jews reject, they simultaneously engage those cultural forms in order to change their meaning. For example, the Hasidic principal at Bnos Yisruel, who would have nothing to do with YIVO Yiddish or its speakers, has Uriel Weinreich's Yiddish dictionary (1990), published by YIVO, on her desk and refers to it when she wants to check the authoritative meaning of a word. Secular standardized Yiddish put into the service of Hasidic education allows Hasidic Jews to use any available resources to engage in their world-changing, nonliberal project.

A Linguistic Anthropological Approach to Hasidic Multilingualism

Much of the research on bilingual contexts, beginning with Blom and Gumperz's (1972) classic work on the social meaning of code switching (moving back and forth between languages) in Norway, has focused on oppositions between discrete languages within communities (Woolard 1998). More recent work, however, has suggested that it is sometimes the very ambiguity of two or more languages coexisting in a community over time that makes multilingualism meaningful.[6] This approach shifts the focus from attempting to understand how multilingual speakers distinguish between languages to the "simultaneities" or the blurring of linguistic boundaries that makes definition between languages more ambiguous. Simultaneities are the ways that speakers use the accents, words, grammar, or even speech genres of two or more languages at the same time (Makihara 2004). At some levels—for example, often in accent or words—simultaneities may be conscious. At other levels—often, for example, at the level of grammar or syntax—simultaneities are below the level of individual consciousness.

The linguistic anthropologist Kathryn Woolard (1998) defines three overlapping forms of simultaneity that are helpful for clarifying the subtle ways that Yiddish and English interpenetrate each other in everyday Hasidic talk.

1. Bivalency describes a word or sound that belongs simultaneously to at least two linguistic systems. For example, "mommy" belongs to both Yiddish and English. Similarly the words "is/iz", pronounced the same in English and Yiddish and with the same meaning, is bivalent.
2. Interference is when two linguistic systems are simultaneously applied to the same linguistic system, such as using a Yiddish accent while speaking English. Some Hasidic Jews apply a Yiddish accent, for example, when they talk about the Brooklyn neighborhood of Williamsburg, which, with a Yiddish accent, becomes [Viljamsburg] or Vilyamsboorg.
3. Simultaneous code switching and borrowing[7] is the juxtaposition of passages of speech (code switching) or single words (borrowing) from two different grammatical systems within the same speech exchange (Gumperz 1982:59).[8] Code switching is illustrated by the following examples: I wish *az ets vet kimen* (I wish that you would come); and *ikh hob eym gezeyn fin across the street* (I saw him from across the street). Examples of borrowings include: *Ikh'l hobn dey picture* (I want to have that picture); and *megst jumpn du* (You may jump here).

The ways that speakers exploit similarities or differences between multiple languages in a community is based on cultural and religious beliefs about language and its speakers, what are called "language ideologies."[9] In some communities, simultaneities are used to sustain a tension between two opposed identities, such as the case with Catalan and Castilian in Spain (Woolard 1998). In others, simultaneities can create fluid, urban cosmopolitanism, for example, with Town Bemba in Zambia (Spitulnik 2000) or among the Turkish guest worker youth in Germany (Auer 1998). For Puerto Ricans in New York City, simultaneities between Spanish and English are acceptable only in the "inner" sphere or with friends and family (Urciuoli 1996). In the "outer" sphere, however, based on the dominant Standard English language ideology, speakers may be severely penalized for any syncretic language (Urciuoli 1996:97). Evidence of this is seen in the Ebonics (or African American English) debate that erupted in 1996, where an attempt by a school board to use an Ebonics reader for children as a bridge to Standard English led to outrage on all sides of the issue, mediated as it was by implicit beliefs about race and class.

Hasidic simultaneities have different cultural and religious meaning, because Hasidic Jews, in contrast to many other linguistic minorities in North America, have little desire to participate in North American life beyond fulfilling the needs of their communities, which they have been able to do very well thanks to their political acumen in accessing federal, state, and city resources. In texts and spoken language, simultaneities change English enough to assert the essentialized differences Hasidic Jews perceive between Jews and Gentiles. Because men and women are dominant in Hasidic Yiddish or Hasidic English, respectively, essentialized but complementary gender differences are simultaneously performed and supported in everyday talk. By emphasizing the ways that Hasidic men and women talk about their languages and use them in everyday contexts, the very analytical categories that linguistic anthropologists use can be challenged. These categories are too often rooted in a belief in discrete languages with discrete linguistic boundaries, and in a conception that the bilingual consciously asserts the distinct multiple identities defined by one language or the other. It is the ambiguities, I argue, the bivalencies, the interference, the borrowings and code-switches that allow Hasidic Jews to use English to transform all their ways of speaking as Jewish.

Hasidic Yiddish

The sociolinguist Joshua Fishman (1981:53) noted the dearth of ethnographic research on everyday Yiddish among Hasidic Jews, the only communities today in which Yiddish is actually a vernacular. This is probably a legacy of Yiddishist aversions to Jewish Orthodoxy. Since then, a small body of scholarship has emerged on Hasidic Yiddish documenting that Hasidic men speak more Yiddish than women, that there is an openness among Hasidic Jews to language mixing and borrowing both in the U.S. with English and in Israel with Israeli Hebrew, and that a great deal of variation occurs among Hasidic speakers of Yiddish (Bogoch 1999; Glinert and Isaacs 1999; Isaacs 1998, 1999; Jochnowitz 1981; Katz 2004; and Mitchell 2006). Jochnowitz (1981) and Isaacs (1999) have noted that, although Hasidic children reproduce the dialect of their parents, an informal standard Hasidic variety of Yiddish seems to be emerging. I describe this variety which is defined by bivalences and other simultaneities with English. In contrast to many other bi- and multilingual contexts, parents never corrected or complained about simultaneities in girls' efforts to speak Yiddish. As Rifky said to me, "I'm so happy when my girls speak Yiddish that I would never quip[10] about an English word here or there."

One of the few sites where Yiddish is not open to influence from English is, based on my observations, verb placement. Yiddish verbs occupy the second unit of a sentence. If, for example, a sentence begins with an adverbial of time, the verb must immediately follow. The placement of the subject and object are more flexible. The four-, five-, and six-year-old girls whom I observed in Bnos Yisruel and the children I observed at home all maintained the placement of the verb in the second position when speaking Hasidic Yiddish. An exception was women who were less fluent Yiddish speakers than their daughters because of different educational experiences (see the introduction and chapter 5). These women often used English word order in Yiddish. For example, Raizy Klein, a mother of four from "out of town" who acknowledged her limited Yiddish fluency, said to her three-year-old daughter during a board game: "*Ok Malky, yetst di gayst*" (Ok Malky, now you go). "*Di*" is the second-person pronoun and "*gayst*" is the conjugated verb "to go." The correct Yiddish word order would be "*Ok Malky, yetst gaysti*" (literally, Ok Malky, now go you). In all other linguistic domains, however, Hasidic Yiddish adapted and changed English, making it a productive addition to Yiddish rather than any form of corruption or impurity.

Sounding Yiddish: Interference and Bivalency

Applying a Yiddish accent (phonology) to English words, often consciously, can be transformative. Hasidic community authority figures, such as rebbes, school administrators, and editors, encourage speakers, particularly women, to use a Yiddish accent if in the context of speaking Yiddish they need to resort to an English word or phrase. These authority figures suggest that when speakers are trying to use Yiddish, they can actually religiously uplift the English words they need by making them sound Yiddish. As one writer argued, English used in Yiddish must sound and look different enough, it must be *faryidisht* 'Yiddishized' from the language of Gentiles. There is no need to speak "pure" Yiddish. Indeed, the editor of a Yiddish family magazine (whose work I discuss further below) suggested that a purist approach to Yiddish, meaning not using the English words that have become a legitimate part of American Hasidic Yiddish, made speakers sound "funny." The writer transliterated the English word "funny" in the Hebrew script of Yiddish, פֿאַני.[11] "Funny" has actually become a Hasidic English term which, like "interesting," implies someone who is not "normal" or does not fit in.

One day during a lunch Rifky prepared for Esty and me, they explained how English words in the context of speaking Yiddish could be changed to reflect Yiddish phonology. There was, they told me, a Hasidic school upstate with very strict standards that printed a special handout for teacher comportment. In addition to unusually stringent modesty requirements (e.g., no loud prints or brightly colored blouses), teachers were told to use Yiddish whenever possible. If an English word was unavoidable, the handbook suggested, teachers should try to make English words (or any word) "sound" Yiddish. Rifky described the examples included in the handbook, orally reproducing the written text for my benefit: "Don't say 'Goldberg' (with Standard English pronunciation). Say 'Mrs. [Gɔldbɛrg] (Goldbehrg).' Don't say 'carriage.' Say '[keridʒ] (keridge).' " Rifky told me that at first she had laughed at the school's attempt at what she called "Yiddishizing" English. However, as she thought about it, she told me, she decided the school was right. Hasidim need to do everything they can to support Yiddish.

In Hasidic Yiddish there are certain Yiddish vowels and consonants that are applied to English regularly in order to Yiddishize. These include a flapped [ɾ] (the final /r/ in the English door) instead of the English initial /r/; the pronunciation of initial /w/ with [v] rather than [w] so that the English "wire" becomes "vire"; and the substitution of the vowel [ɛ] (the /e/ of bed) rather than [æ] (the /a/ of hat) so that the English "tan" becomes "ten" or [tɛn].

In their everyday talk Hasidic men, in particular, often make conscious attempts to adapt English phonologically to Yiddish. For example, after talking with me about gendered differences in accent, Raizy told me that she asked her brother-in-law over Shabbes lunch why men had a Yiddish accent in English even after many generations in the United States. He told her that Jews were doing the same thing to English that Jews had done to German when they created Yiddish. He offered an example, suggesting that by saying "vire," instead of "wire" he was making English Jewish, just as Jews had made German Jewish, that is, Yiddish.[12]

Similarly the editor of the Yiddish-language family magazine *Males* 'Virtues' (1998) argued, in an editorial, that as long as spoken language "sounded" different from the "Gentile" language, it was sufficiently Jewish. The editorial, which was directed at policing Jewish women's language, in particular, was spurred when a reader wrote to complain that some of the words used in the "vocabulary building" section accompanying articles were not authentic Yiddish words; as the reader put it, the words *"hot nisht kan yidishe tate-mame"* (Did not have Yiddish parents/roots). The editor wrote back and explained that authors use words that might not be considered "authentic" Yiddish, because Yiddish *"shtamt fin goyishe shprakhn"* (comes from Gentile languages).

Where Jews have been in diaspora, he pointed out, they have fashioned their own language, borrowing freely from languages around them. The language of *amerikaner khsidim* 'American Hasidim' is nothing new; in fact, it is a continuation of a long tradition of adopting and adapting the Gentile language for their own community. The main issue, the editor wrote, is that Jewish languages "sound" different from the Gentile language.

> *Mir darfn nisht fargesn az der tsil fin der yidisher sphrakh iz zikh optsuzindern fin de goyim. Oyb di englishe, english-klingende verter vern mer vi di yidishe, vet nisht nemen tsi lang biz di yidishe shprakh vet gantslikh fargesn vern. Oyb es khapn zikh ober aran etlikhe englishe, ober yidish-klingende, verter, darf es akh nisht tsifil "bodern"; dos mame-loshn blabt nokh alts zayer andersh vi di goyishe shprakh.* (*Males*, no. 3 [1998]: 3–4)

We must not forget that the goal of the Yiddish language is to separate us from Gentiles. If English, English-sounding words, become more [common] than the Yiddish ones, then it will not take too long until Yiddish is completely forgotten. If some English words come into Yiddish, but Yiddish-sounding words, it does not need to "bother" anybody. The mother tongue is still very different from the Gentile one.

The editor emphasized that the purpose of a distinctive Jewish language in diaspora is to keep Jews apart from Gentiles.[13] He suggested that the adoption of English into spoken Yiddish was appropriate if the words "sounded" Yiddish. But if English words with English phonology continued to enter Yiddish, then Jews would begin to forget Yiddish and, ultimately, stop speaking it. As long as English words are modified by Yiddish phonology, the essential difference between Jews and Gentiles would not be threatened. Note that the editor places the Yiddishized English word *bodern* 'bother' in quotes. Not only is the word *bodern* an example of the very process of Yiddishizing that he is discussing,[14] but the term also has a long history as a North American Jewish English borrowing from the turn of the century. Perhaps the author is ironically nodding to a time when Jews from that period used syncretic Yiddish and English (also called Yinglish) with the aim of assimilating and eventually losing their Yiddish. Despite some of the same linguistic processes, the Hasidic project today, especially for women and girls, has the distinctive goal of remaining apart from North American society while still participating in aspects of North American cultural life, in this case using English.

A feature of written Hasidic Yiddish is the ability to signal Yiddish or English phonology systems through the different scripts of each language.[15] For example, in the same Yiddish article the editor of *Males* pointedly included a few English words in English script in the context of written Yiddish. He took issue, in particular, with *khsidishe frouen* 'Hasidic women', who use English phonology when they talk about the Hasidic Brooklyn neighborhoods of Boro Park and Williamsburg. To suggest a preferable Yiddish-accented pronunciation of the neighborhoods, the editor juxtaposed Boro Park and Williamsburg in English script with the transliterated װיליאמסבורג ([viljamsburg]) or Vilyamsboorg and באָרא-פּאַרק ([Bɔra-Park]) or Bora-Park in Hebrew script. The transliterated versions require the Yiddish letter װ, which is typically pronounced /v/ to represent the [w] in Williamsburg, a letter that does not exist in Yiddish, and the Hebrew character ר to represent the use of flapped [ɾ] rather than the English [r] in Boro Park and Williamsburg. Contrasting English and Hebrew scripts creates a visibly syncretic text that clarifies the editor's plug for applying Yiddish pronunciation to English words.

An alternative to this common practice of integrating English words and script into a Yiddish text is to transliterate English words into the Hebrew script of Yiddish with the attendant Yiddish phonological modification for Yiddish pronunciation. This is common in newspapers, advertisements and children's books. In one of the Yiddish classes I took at YIVO, our teacher gave us a copy of a page of advertisements from a Hasidic newspaper so that we could practice reading the Hebrew script. We all laughed at one advertisement for a men's clothing store, which, as we sounded out the Hebrew letters, proved to be almost entirely in English words. In books for Hasidic children, these kinds of simultaneities are also common. For example, a workbook for young children (*Mazel Tov*, n.d.) about the preparations for a party made by an aunt and her niece for a newly married couple (a ritual obligation), proclaimed on the front cover (in English) that the book was in "Chassidishe Yiddish with English Translation." The story was in Yiddish but certain words like "food processor" and "mixer" were transliterated into Hebrew script. When the readers read the text, they would be likely to adjust these words to Yiddish patterns of pronunciation.[16]

Defying Categorization: Bivalencies and Interference

When languages are similar, bivalencies (words belonging to both languages) become more likely, as with the shared Germanic component

of English and Yiddish.[17] The English words "and" or "the," for example, sound similar in speech to the Yiddish equivalent *un* and *der*.[18]
Using Yiddish phonology with English vocabulary also creates bivalencies, words combining Yiddish and English in ways that defy categorization as either Yiddish or English. Rifky told me that until she
was fifteen years old she did not know that *votsh* 'watch' or *tsher* 'chair'
were not Yiddish words. She told me this in the context of saying that
she had grown up speaking more Yiddish than most girls, which made
her proud. A number of mothers told me, with pride, that their sons
made similar errors, unable to keep Yiddish and English distinct. These
kinds of bivalencies indicate that children are sheltered enough to assume that whatever they are speaking is Yiddish, contrary to what
many adults know is actually a give and take between Yiddish and
English. Indeed, many of these bivalent forms eventually get claimed
as Yiddish, having been in circulation for more than at least a generation by Hasidic Jews.

In some cases, the meaning of a Yiddish word may change in order
to approximate its more familiar English meaning (see also Weinreich
1955). The Yiddish word for glasses (spectacles), for instance, is *briln*,
and a different word, *gleyzer* (sing., *gluz*), signifies cups or drinking
glasses. In current Hasidic Yiddish, speakers now use *gleyzer* in place
of *briln*. This shift brings the English and Yiddish closer together in
sound and meaning, as *gleyzer* sounds more like "glasses" than *briln*
does. This change was reported to me by Esty and her nephew, Shmilly
(age ten), who remarked that he had just learned in school that
the "real" Yiddish word was *briln*. Both Esty and her nephew laughed
over the use of *gleyzer* but clearly had no intention of adopting the
"real" word.

These kinds of simultaneities make Hasidic Yiddish a regional
marker of being a North American Hasidic Jew. Yiddish has been a
lingua franca for hundreds of years for Jews dispersed across the globe.
Different syncretic varieties of Hasidic Yiddish used today sometimes
make it difficult to communicate across national boundaries. My Yiddish tutor, Gitty, who is a teacher in a Pupa (Hungarian) Hasidic girls'
school, told me about the difficulty she had trying to talk to the Israeli
Hasidic mother of one of her students. The girl's mother did not speak
very much English, only Yiddish and Israeli Hebrew. Gitty and she
decided to have their meeting in Yiddish, since it was their shared language. However, Gitty said, the two women could not really understand each other. Each woman's Yiddish had so much influence from
the co-territorial language (Gitty's English and the mother's Israeli Hebrew) as to block comprehension. The two reverted to Hasidic English
with a bit more success.

Integrating English into Yiddish:
Simultaneous Code Switching and Borrowing

There has been a long-standing debate among sociolinguists about how to qualify the mixing of languages, when to describe code switching, and when a language has become, by definition, a mixed language with borrowings.[19] My analysis of Hasidic Yiddish shows, however, that, in the case of syncretic languages, the simultaneities, the ambiguous mixing itself, is most relevant, making the analytic distinction between borrowing and code switching difficult and often not relevant. Attempting to qualify and explain each switch or borrowing as meaningful assumes that a speaker's moves between codes are always meaningful. Such a position also involves a great deal of speculation by the analyst. Instead, I show the ways that certain forms of switching and borrowing, often below the level of consciousness, have become definitive of how to speak Yiddish as a Hasidic Jew (see also Stroud 1991). These are switches and borrowings that I heard repeated in myriad contexts by a range of speakers, and, as I discuss, they are socialized from infancy on. In contrast to the strategic uses of bivalency and interference (see also Woolard and Genovese 2007), Hasidic women I worked with told me they were often unaware that they had switched languages at all.

In Hasidic Yiddish, English verbs, nouns, discourse markers (e.g., but, so), and locative phrases (e.g., on the floor) are all integrated into Yiddish. Sometimes these words or chunks of talk have Yiddish phonology and other times they retain their English phonology. I was unable to discern any accent pattern. Borrowings include English nouns and verbs that are inflected like any other Yiddish verb and integrated into spoken or written Yiddish. This includes words borrowed from English in order to fill a gap in Yiddish, such as food processor or freezer. English words or verbs are also frequently used in the context of Yiddish talk despite the existence of a common Yiddish equivalent that is often familiar to speakers. My observations are that boys, girls, and women regularly integrate English verbs into Yiddish that are especially prevalent in the realm of children and school. Again, I have heard speakers use both English and Yiddish accents with these borrowings. Examples include:

1. *Me ken jumpn.* (You can jump.)
2. *Zol ikh fixn de hur?* (Should I fix your hair?)
3. *Vilst dey paper tse coloren un?* (Do you want this piece of paper to color on?)
4. *Di blockst mikh!* (You're blocking me!)

Certain English parts of speech and word categories are regularly integrated into Hasidic Yiddish.[20] The following examples all have Yiddish equivalents:

1. Discourse markers (e.g., already, so, now). Examples include:
   a. *Me ken es zugn, but ikh vays afile nisht . . .* (You can say it, but I don't even know . . .).
   b. *Far vus men all of a sudden redn zayer shprakh?* (Why do we all of a sudden speak their language?).
   c. *So far vus redn azoy?* (So why are you talking like that?)
2. Locatives (e.g., in back of, on top of). Examples include:
   a. *Val de ching-chang iz all the way (by) de floor.* (Because the ching-chang (the jump rope) is all the way by the floor.) Note that "by" is a bivalency, in that it is an English word meaning "near" but is also a Yiddish word meaning "at" [e.g., *Ikh'l esn by ma mame* (I'll eat at my mother's house)].
3. Domains related to children: children's clothing and food, states of emotion, and displays of appreciation (e.g., thank you, please), are usually in English, although, for example, with clothing the Yiddish is also used with no pattern that I could discern. Examples include:
   a. *Sheyndie's mame hot gekoyft kneesocks.* (Sheyndie's mommy bought kneesocks.)
   b. *Ikh hob gemakht macaroni far supper.* (I made macaroni for supper.)
   c. *Ikh bin azoy proud fin Rukhy!* (I am so proud of Rukhy!).
   d. *Dey picture iz gorgeous!* (This picture is gorgeous!). Note, too, that *iz* can be bivalent: English "is" and Yiddish "iz". It is unclear whether the sentence is in Yiddish with English borrowings as I have written it, or if the speaker switches into English after *dey* 'that'. The sentence was spoken by a preschool teacher who usually speaks Hasidic English with her students, commenting on an arts-and-crafts project.

Yiddish bivalency, especially in phonology, can even neutralize a switch in code. Gitty told me that when she is talking to her husband in Yiddish, if she "Yiddishizes" the critical consonant /r/ and the vowels /o/ and /i/, then her sentence remains in Yiddish, despite the fact that she has changed from Yiddish to English in the same sentence. She might say, for example, *"Ikh hob eym gezeyn fin across de street"* (I saw him from across the street). "Is *'across de street'* Yiddish?" I asked. "Sure," she said. By flapping her /r/'s and shortening the vowel of [strit] (street) to [strIt] (strit) and replacing the /th/ of English "the" with a /d/ of Yiddish *de* 'the', the English becomes Yiddish. Note also, again, that the bivalency of *de* 'the' is indistinguishable from the spoken English word "the." The Yiddish translation of "across the street" has no relationship to English and would be read as *fin iber de gas*.

HASIDIC ENGLISH

Hasidic English must be placed in the broader category of Jewish English, which includes ways that Jews living in the United States at different historical moments have created syncretic English for a range of purposes. For example, the Jewish English of the immigrants to North America from the 1880s to the 1920s was similar to Hasidic Yiddish in that it syncretically mixed Yiddish, loshn-koydesh, and English (Gold 1985; Steinmetz 1987). As the children of these immigrants went to North American schools, they eventually stopped speaking Yiddish altogether and their English became more standard, although Yiddish inflections and intonations have affected the sounds of New York, especially Brooklyn, varieties of English (Shandler 2005).

Today, a continuum of Jewish English maps onto a spectrum of Jewish Orthodoxy among North American Jews. Hasidic English is one variety of what sociolinguist Sarah Benor (2004b) calls "Orthodox Jewish English." Another closely related variety is Yeshivish, the language of non-Hasidic Orthodox Jews influenced by male Torah study. Yeshivish has been described by Chaim Weiser (1995), in the popular publication *Frumspeak: The First Dictionary of Yeshivish*, and also by others (e.g., Benor n.d.; Myhill 2004; and Heilman 1998a). Drawing on the intonation, words, and grammar from Yiddish, loshn-koydesh, and modern Hebrew (spoken as a vernacular in Israel), Weiser suggests that Yeshivish was born in today's Litvish 'Lithuanian' yeshivas, where men and boys often read sacred texts in loshn-koydesh and discuss them in English (Yeshivish). This contrasts to the Yiddish discussions that Hasidic boys and men have during religious study. Yeshivish and Hasidic English share many of the syncretic features as I discuss below. There is a significant difference, however, as Hasidic English is being created primarily out of the experiences of Hasidic women and girls in everyday contexts. Most likely, Hasidic men and boys are creating their own variety of Hasidic English as well.

Yiddish Sounds in English: Interference and Bivalency

Hasidic English has a rising-falling intonation which Samuel Heilman (1981) traces to the influence of Torah study among Orthodox Jews in New York. He notes that the chanting from the Talmud called *gemore-*

nign 'Talmud melody' was designed to facilitate reading sacred texts in loshn-koydesh that had no punctuation or vocalization. This prestigious feature of speech, not found in other European languages, was adopted into the everyday speech of Ashkenazic Jewry, Yiddish, and later, when they immigrated to North America, English. Heilman draws on the work of Uriel Weinreich (1956) to point out the prevalence of rhetorical questions embedded within Jewish intonation more generally which he links to Jewish males' discussions of Torah or Talmudic study. He notes, "The rhetorical and rather incredulous question has become closely linked with Yiddish in particular and Jewish inflection in general" (Heilman 1981:247).

These subtle linguistic features are sufficiently marked to allow Hasidic speakers (and the author) to recognize one another in diaspora, even on the telephone. One day I called a local bus company to get information for a trip I was planning from New York City to Washington, D.C., and as the woman who answered the phone began to give me schedules and fares, I recognized her English as Hasidic. The word that tipped me off was "sure," which she pronounced as two syllables with a rising-falling intonation. (She sounded just like my Yiddish tutor, Gitty.) When I asked her, she said that, indeed, she was Hasidic and that their company operated out of Williamsburg.

In addition to intonation, Hasidic English is distinguished by particular aspects of Yiddish phonology, in some cases related to "Brooklynese," which was itself influenced by the Yiddish of earlier waves of Eastern European immigrants (Jochnowitz 1981:737). Yiddish phonology in English, for example, is evident in how Hasidic English speakers pronounce the Yiddish names they give their children. When children's names are said aloud in Hasidic English, Yiddish phonology is maintained. The pronunciation is not assimilated into English phonology. For example, a woman I met, Yitta, had many interactions with Gentiles because, unlike her peers, she had gone to college. She told me that Gentiles she met there always mispronounced her name or its more common diminutive, Yitty, using American English phonology for aspirated double consonants, which rendered her name [Jidy] (Yidie). Other examples include the use of the suffix "-ink" rather than "-ing," so that first graders during the hot weather often complained to their teacher or me, "I'm boilink!" (Rather than "I'm boiling!").

Yiddish in English: Simultaneous Code Switching,
  Borrowing, and Interference

Hasidic English is perhaps most distinct from Standard English in its integration of Yiddish/loshn-koydesh words and phrases, as well as

Yiddish calques, the direct translation of Yiddish into English that produces nonstandard English. I first noticed the prevalence of Yiddish calques in the Hasidic English of women during a Bnos Yisruel teachers' Hanukkah party held one evening after supper (not "dinner"). Gathered around a table laden with desserts, we were playing a game where someone would write the beginning of a sentence on a strip of paper, fold it over, and pass it to another person, who would then complete the sentence and read it aloud to everyone's amusement. One of the completed sentences read: "If I would be an anthropologist, I would look like Ayala." A bit flustered at first, I could not figure out why this sentence sounded grammatically strange to me. Then I realized that it was a partial calque of the Yiddish construction of the irrealis conditional (if I were . . . I would be . . .). In Yiddish, the irrealis conditional has a different syntax (*Oyb ikh volt geveyn . . . volt ikh . . .* 'If I would be . . . would I . . .'). The sentence in Yiddish would be *oyb ikh volt geveyn an antropolog, volt ikh oysgezeyn vi Ayala* (literally, If I would be an anthropologist, would I look like Ayala). However, in the Hanukah game enough of the sentence structure was directly translated into Hasidic English to sound distinctive to an English speaker like myself.

Other common calques are direct translations from idiomatic Yiddish expressions. For example, when the school administration was attempting to have teachers and students speak "only Yiddish" (i.e., not Hasidic Yiddish), a third-grade teacher, Chraindy, told me that she "would break her teeth" speaking Yiddish without any English words. This is a calque from the Yiddish *brekhn di tsayner* 'break the teeth', which implies that it would be linguistically difficult to achieve, the Yiddish equivalent perhaps of the English "tying one's tongue in knots." Yiddish calques in Hasidic English redefine the speech community from Standard English speakers to Jewish speakers of English.

Similarly the integration of Yiddish periphrastic verbs, which often but not always combine Yiddish and loshn-koydesh words, require speakers to have at least a passive competency in loshn-koydesh. Periphrastics are verbs consisting of one undeclined element, usually in loshn-koydesh, and an auxiliary (helping verb), usually in Yiddish, which is conjugated. An example in Yiddish would be *mevater zan* (to be yielding, that is, to give way before the wishes of others). A speaker in Yiddish says, "*Ikh bin eym mevater*" (I gave in to him). In Hasidic English the auxiliary of the verb (to have, to be, etc.) is generally in English, while the invariable element remains in its Hebrew/Yiddish base form (first-person masculine participle). For example, Rifky told me that "children have to learn to be *mevater*." The auxiliary verb *zan* 'to be' is translated into English and combined with the invariable element *mevater* 'yielding' which remains in Hebrew/Yiddish.

Conversational code switching and borrowing from Yiddish or loshn-koydesh also creates the distinctive variety of Hasidic English. In everyday talk, religious concepts, holidays, and aspects of ritual or Hasidic life are not translated into English. When Rifky was giving cooking instructions to her oldest daughter, she told her: "Well, you can make extra. I'll anyway need *flaysh* 'meat' for *sikis* (the Jewish harvest holiday)". In addition to the obvious Yiddish/loshn-koydesh words, note the placement of the English word "anyway" which, in Hasidic English, can be placed most anywhere in the sentence, a feature of the more flexible word order (outside of verbs) in Yiddish. In Standard English the word "anyway" would most likely be at the beginning or end of the sentence, that is, "I'll need meat for *sikis* anyway."

Hasidic women and their children often used Yiddish or nonstandard English words for parts of the body considered immodest to talk about explicitly. What most North American white, middle-class families call "pee" and "poop," Hasidic families call in Yiddish *de klayne in de groyse* 'the little and the big' in the context of speaking Hasidic English or Hasidic Yiddish. Sometimes, rather than use the Standard English word that referred explicitly to the body, Hasidic women used a different English word with a similar meaning. For example, I was invited to share a holiday celebration with a teacher in Bnos Yisruel, Mrs. Hirsch and her family. We gathered around the table for the traditional meal of chicken, kugel (sweet noodle pudding), and vegetables. Mrs. Hirsch turned to me and asked if I wanted a "top" or a "bottom" of the roast chicken. After a few beats of silence, I figured out that she meant the breast or the leg. I was asked the same question by countless Hasidic hostesses, and I also heard one teacher, Devoyre, tell the other teachers that her husband ate a "whole bottom" at a single meal. Perhaps rather than refer to body parts, Hasidic women and girls euphemistically use "top and "bottom" just as Hasidic girls consistently call their ponytails "ponies" without using the word "tail."

In other contexts, Hasidic women and girls use English terms (specifically Brooklyn English terms) that once, but no longer are, used by most Jewish New Yorkers. On the playground, for example, Hasidic children go on the sliding pond/pod, a word that my father, a Brooklyn native, uses as well. Most North American children today call this a slide. Hasidic children eat supper, not dinner, eat frankfurters not hot dogs, noodles or macaroni, not pasta, and they stay in bungalows in the mountains of the country rather than in country houses upstate. Perhaps the use of these words reflects their increasing ability to socialize primarily among themselves, in their own schools. Despite sharing English with other North Americans, then, Hasidic Jews use words and expressions in older New York Jewish English along with Yiddish/loshn-koydesh to make their English Jewish and, specifically, Hasidic.

SOCIALIZING SYNCRETISM: LEARNING TO SPEAK HASIDIC YIDDISH AND HASIDIC ENGLISH

Hasidic Yiddish Baby talk

Before the age of three, Hasidic women and older siblings address babies in Hasidic Yiddish baby talk, which naturalizes syncretic language. A local developmental category for Hasidic children is "baby." This age-defined category overrides all but the most basic gender divisions; children become formally, culturally gendered at age three, when boys have their first haircut, the *upshern*.[21] Although the male circumcision ceremony, *bris*, genders infants at birth, before age three, the semiotics of gender is much more fluid than it will be later in life. For example, before age three girls can wear pants, and boys often have long hair fussed over with by their sisters and put in barrettes and "ponies."

Hasidic Yiddish baby talk socializes children into the specifics of Hasidic syncretism, exposing language-acquiring children to bivalency, interference, and patterns of code switching and borrowings. By addressing very young children, boys and girls, in syncretic Hasidic Yiddish, children learn how to mix Yiddish and English just enough to keep it Yiddish. Perhaps because this is a time of more muted gender differences, children are simultaneously socialized to conceptualize Yiddish as the most appropriate language for bringing up the next generation of male or female Hasidic Jews. As I discuss in the next chapter, Yiddish baby talk socializes the next generation of mothers, in particular, to acquire fluency in Hasidic Yiddish baby talk. Hasidic girls will, as they grow up, increasingly speak Hasidic English, not Hasidic Yiddish. However, their own socialization into Hasidic Yiddish baby talk and their use of it with younger siblings makes them fluent in a register considered best for Hasidic babies for whom they will be the primary caregivers.

Baby talk is a speech register, a variety of speech associated with a particular use within a community. Legalese, for example, is a register lawyers may use. Baby talk, the language directed at very young children, is not universal (Ochs 1988; Schieffelin 1990). However, it is common in many diverse cultural contexts and shares the following features, among others, according to sociolinguist Charles Ferguson (1982):

a. High pitched intonation.
b. Diminutives. In English baby talk, examples include: potty, tummy, shoesies, milky.
c. Specialized words and reduplication. In English baby talk, examples include: boo-boo, poo-poo, go bye-bye.
d. Simplified grammar. In English baby talk, examples include the absence of pronouns and contracting sentences, e.g., Mommy get that? (translation: Should I get that for you?) No more, all finished!

Pitch and intonation are critical markers of a Hasidic baby-talk register. Mothers, fathers, and siblings addressing young children pitch their voices high, vowels are frequently elongated, and there is a repetitive rising-falling intonation. For example, a mother might tell her child that her bowl is empty by showing the child the bowl and saying, "*Geendikt* 'finished'," with the same intonation and elongated vowels that the English baby-talk register uses with a phrase like "all done." Another common phrase with similar high-pitch and rising-falling intonation is: *Blimi makht a brukhe?* (Blimi makes a blessing?) which is how mothers and other caregivers prompt young children to make blessings before eating and drinking.

A good example of the syncretic nature of Hasidic baby talk is the use of diminutives. Hasidic baby talk uses both English (y) and Yiddish (*ele*) diminutive suffixes with Yiddish nouns. Examples of Yiddish diminutives include *kepele* (little head), *trobele* (little grape), and *hentele* (little hand). The English diminutive suffix (-y) attached to a Yiddish noun is also common.[22] Examples include *budy* 'bathy', *zipy* 'soupy', *pitsy* 'small', *sheyfy* 'little lamb', *shlufy* 'sleepy', *kepy* 'little head', and *mouly* 'little mouth'.[23] I rarely heard Yiddish diminutives suffixed onto an English baby-talk word. These words take the English diminutive form. Examples include dolly, botty 'bottle', blanky, cribby, cutey, meany, and mommy (which is also bivalent).

Endearments in Hasidic baby talk often use diminutives that are almost exclusively in Yiddish, and express cultural beliefs about gender roles. These include *tatele* ('little daddy'), *mamele* 'little mommy', *vabele* 'little wife', and *tsadikl* (only for boys, 'little saint'). Other common endearments include *sheyfele or sheyfy* 'little lamb', *ziskayt* 'sweetness', and *neshumele* 'little soul'. In contrast, kin names are in Yiddish, English, or a bivalent form, for example, baby, *shvester* 'sister', *brider* 'brother', *feter* 'uncle', *tante* 'aunt', *kuzin* 'cousin', *bobe* 'grandmother', and *zayde* 'grandfather'. Many of these forms also can be used with English diminutives, so that *tate* 'father' becomes *tatty/totty*.

In addition to diminutives across a range of words, Ferguson suggests that baby talk includes "basic qualities," adjectives that describe the physical states of objects or persons. In Hasidic baby talk, many of these are in English: fun, scary, gorgeous, yummy-delicious, happy, sad, excited, and proud. Some qualities that are central to how children are described are in Yiddish; these include *shayn* 'good, nice' and the negative *nisht shayn* 'not nice', *voyl* 'good or cooperative', *shlekht* 'bad', *shmitsik* 'dirty', *khitspedik* 'willfully defiant', *leybedik* 'lively', and *da-da* 'bad'.[24]

Yiddish baby talk follows Ferguson's (1992:106) description of grammatical modifications regarding simplification. When talking about the self, first- and second-person pronouns are avoided and substituted by proper nouns. Articles and prepositions also are frequently omitted, and verbs are often omitted or not inflected. Examples include *Vi Leye? Du Leye!* (Where Leye? Here Leye! Rather than, Where's Leye? Here's Leye), *Mommy makht clean de fisele* 'Mommy makes clean the footsy', *Breng Mommy Pamper* 'Bring Mommy Pamper'. *Aaron, makh nice Leye* 'Make nice to Leye, i.e., stroke Leye', *Mommy darf es haltn* 'Mommy needs to hold it'. Note that English words (Mommy, Pamper) and Yiddish calques into English (*makh rayn* is calqued as 'make clean' rather than 'wash') are integrated into the predominantly Yiddish talk. In some cases, English and Yiddish words are used seemingly interchangeably. For example, Esty said both *makh rayn* and *makh clean* even during the same interaction.

Hasidic children from an early age verbally play with the fluid boundaries between English and Yiddish. In Mrs. Silver's class I observed six-year-old Chaya Gitty drawing and talking to herself and to me. As she drew a picture of a house, she said, "*A houz*" 'house'. There was a pause, and then she said, drawing on a popular North American expression, "No way, José" (with the accent appropriately on the second syllable). She was playing on the shared and distinctive sounds of *houz* and José. We both laughed. I was also told a joke by a number of different children that played on the shared sounds of Yiddish and English. A child would tell me to begin saying the Yiddish/Hebrew alphabet. I would begin, *aleph, bayz, giml, daled, hay*—and then the child would interrupt and say, "High-chair!" This was a bilingual pun on the Yiddish/Hebrew letter ה (*hay*) and the English word "high," which are pronounced the same in Hasidic Yiddish. This joke brought shrieks of laughter from the children. Punning, which requires knowledge of syncretic language, is similarly reported among French- and English-speaking speaking Canadian children (Heller 1999).

Syncretism in School

When girls enter elementary school and formally begin to learn literacy in loshn-koydesh, Yiddish, and English, they simultaneously learn strategies for incorporating English into Yiddish and Yiddish into English, both spoken and written. While I was doing research, the Bnos Yisruel administration was trying to enforce a new policy that placed more emphasis on the use of Yiddish without syncretism from English. Girls, even teachers, sometimes resisted the new policy, because speakers fluent in Hasidic Yiddish found that they were unable to express themselves in Yiddish to their satisfaction without syncretically incorporating English. Further, among the teachers (and adult women more generally) Hasidic Yiddish and Hasidic English have acquired their own value as a *haymish* 'homey' way of talking. For example, during recess, while a teacher was preparing a lesson, she wondered out loud why she had written the word "steps" in the context of preparing a Yiddish paragraph instead of *trep* which she knew to be the Yiddish equivalent. I asked if using "trep" would sound as if she were trying to be "special." Using Yiddish can be a personal effort a female makes to be at a higher spiritual level that is idiomatically called "special" in Hasidic English. She and the other teachers thought not. "No," she explained, "I've just always talked like that. I wouldn't be comfortable saying "trep." My mother says "steps."

Despite a more purist rhetoric about Yiddish coming from the school administration, girls, in fact, were given the tools and authority to use syncretic forms of language in class and from the language of their own mothers, as I discuss further in the next chapter. In the following episode in Mrs. Silver's class, first-grade girls were taught how to deal with a gap in their Yiddish vocabulary: transliterate the English word into Yiddish orthography and place it in quotation marks. This practice of incorporating and transforming borrowed language is part of a broader set of practices about the transmission of cultural memory and change.

In the lesson, Mrs. Silver was teaching the girls about Yiddish color vocabulary. After the girls learned the basic colors, most of which they knew, they began to ask about colors especially popular that year in clothing, headbands, and boxes of crayons:

MRS. SILVER: *Ikh mayn az mir hobn shoyn ale <u>colors</u>.*
STUDENT 1: <u>*Uh uh, peach.*</u>
MRS. SILVER: <u>*Peach,*</u> *in <u>nectarine</u>, in <u>plum</u>, in <u>meatballs in spaghetti</u>, ale deym vus zan hant of dey <u>crayons</u> zenen nisht kan. <u>Peach,</u> b'emes zol . . . men ya, me ken zugn, but ikh vays afile nisht . . . ikh hob kayn mol*

gehert eymetse zugt es of yidish. . . oyb me vil zugn az me est a <u>peach</u>,
iz du a yidish vort far deym, ober se zugn de color <u>peach</u>, ikh hob nokh
kan mol gehert eymetse zugn in yidish.
STUDENT 2: *Zug, zug, Mrs. Feiffer* [the vice principal].
MRS. SILVER: *Ikh mayn az Mrs. Feiffer vayst afile nisht. Ok, . . . ikh'l*
freygn. Val kinder vil ikh'l freygn.

MRS. SILVER: I think that we already have all the colors.
STUDENT 1: *Uh uh, peach.*
MRS. SILVER: Peach, and nectarine, and plum, and meatballs and spa-
    ghetti, there aren't any colors for all the crayons that we have
    today. Peach should really be . . . you, you can say, but I don't even
    know . . . I've never heard someone say it in Yiddish . . . If you
    want to say that you are eating a peach, there is a Yiddish word
    for that, but to say the color peach, I've never heard anyone say it
    in Yiddish.
STUDENT 2: Tell, tell, Mrs. Feiffer (the vice principal).
MRS. SILVER: I think that even Mrs. Feiffer doesn't know. Ok . . . I'll
    ask because children want me to, I'll ask.

During that recess Mrs. Silver did ask the vice principal and the
principal. The vice principal even looked up "peach" in Weinreich's
Yiddish-English dictionary. All the teachers were stumped, and finally
Mrs. Feiffer told Mrs. Silver to tell the class that *"Mrs. Feiffer vayst nisht.*
Zi vayst nisht" (Mrs. Feiffer doesn't know. She doesn't know). She suggested that the best thing to do, because all agreed that peach was a
very popular color that season, would be to write out "peach" in Yiddish letters and place it in quotation marks.

This color question sparked discussion among the teachers about
their perception that Yiddish had certain lexical gaps. Teachers noted
that they did not know the Yiddish for colors like turquoise or royal
blue. Maybe there is no word for "mixed colors," someone suggested.
Another pointed out that there is a word for "pink," a mixed color.
Mrs. Silver wondered what people in Europe had used. A teacher suggested that these colors were "new" colors. But royal blue, Mrs. Silver
noted, must have been around for hundreds of years.

The conversation ended unresolved. Teachers and administrators
seemed to think it impossible that Yiddish had a word for such a contemporary "fashionable" color as peach. This, as I discuss in the next
chapter, reveals Hasidic beliefs about Yiddish and their Eastern European past rather than any inherent linguistic shortcoming, since English, of course, uses "peach" for both the fruit and the color. The
teachers and the principal actively express their desire to use Yiddish
in order to be like prior generations that are perceived to be at a higher

spiritual level than Jews are today. In fact, however, there is a gap in both cultural and linguistic memory. After the devastation of the Holocaust and at least three generations in North America, not many people are left who really know how Hasidic women spoke in Europe or what their everyday lives were like.[25]

One response to the cultural/religious priority placed on maintaining the practices and languages of past generations, especially in the face of radical change and contact with new cultures, is to enforce linguistic purism, especially by prohibiting the adoption of new or foreign words.[26] But unlike many other linguistic and cultural minorities in diaspora, Hasidic Jews, despite their increasing religious stringency, have not turned to purism. Indeed, gaps in memory or language are satisfactorily remedied by replacing the forgotten language with the new, changing its orthography and bracketing the innovation with quotation marks. This approach creates an unchanging body of Yiddish linguistic and cultural knowledge and yet is open enough to incorporate change from English in order to express today's ideas. Mrs. Silver's first-graders are presented with this model, authorized by the principal of their school and their teacher, and they come to use it too.

Syncretic Games and Books for Hasidic Women and Children

When Hasidic English is written it is much closer to Standard English than when it is spoken. Certain written genres, however, draw particularly on Hasidic English, including fiction for observant Jewish girls, games for younger boys and girls, and inspirational lectures for women. Not only are these genres syncretic linguistically in their use of Hasidic English, they are also syncretic genres that adapt North American cultural forms for the Hasidic purpose of moral edification. Hasidic English in these syncretic genres is marked by its inattention to Standard English rules of punctuation, its code switching into Yiddish/loshn-koydesh words in Hebrew orthography, and its frequent use of Yiddish/loshn-koydesh words transliterated into English script.

For example, on a recent trip to Boro Park to see Esty and her children, I bought a bilingual game of Yiddish Old Maid at a bookstore in Boro Park. The game is put out by *Kinder Shpiel* 'Child's Play', Inc., in Monroe, New York, a suburban (Satmar) Hasidic community. Old Maid, of course, is a classic North American card game for children where the goal is to make as many pairs of cards as possible and, in the process, discard all one's cards. The loser is the person left holding the last single card for which there is no mate, the old maid, generally drawn as a spinsterish old woman. Yiddish Old Maid reinterprets the game for Hasidic and Orthodox Jewish children.

Yiddish Old Maid, Beryl Goldberg, photographer. Reprinted with permission from Kinder Shpiel USA

Instead of an old maid, the single card to be avoided is called *Yeitzer Hora* [sic] 'evil inclination': a deformed male hunchback, covered in pimples, with a huge nose and ears, animal-like sharp teeth and nails, punked-out green hair, wearing a visor backward, a shirt with a skull and crossbones on the sleeve and fashionable Ugg boots, a sword stashed in his belt, holding two spears with eyes, and a computer in a plastic bag. The evil inclination card plays on insider knowledge about the dangers of the secular world (e.g., fashion, computers, and weapons) that have the potential to poison and deform the Jewish body and spirit. Another example of the limited concern with standardization is found on the back of the instructions, which tells children, "The game ends when there is only one player left with the card the 'yetzer hora' and that player loses." Note that "yetzer hora" is spelled quite differently from the actual "Yeitzer Hora" card and is not italicized or capitalized.

The cards in Yiddish Old Maid include drawings of stereo-
typical communal and historical figures, such as "*Shlomke Der Shadkhn*,
Shlomke The [*sic*] Shadchan" 'Matchmaker', who is an older man, ex-
asperatedly trying to answer all his ringing phones. Each card has the
Yiddish phrase on the top of the card in Hebrew orthography and its
English transliteration or translation on the bottom. The nonstandard
capitalization of "The" in the previous example is typical of written
Hasidic English. This is not an influence from the Yiddish/Hebrew orthography which does not have capital letters. The transformation of
North American games and toys to conform with Hasidic values, the
use of English and Yiddish, the lack of consistency in transliteration,
and the disregard for the norms of English orthography are all typical
of games for Hasidic children.

Orthodox Jewish publishers (both Hasidic and Litvish) have similarly transformed North American and Israeli genres of children's literature and changed its meaning, particularly over the past fifteen
years.[27] Often called *yidishe* 'Jewish' books, they are written for girls in
predominantly Hasidic English or Yeshivish. The new genre, published and distributed in North America and Israel, strives to both en-
tertain—the Jewish perception of North American fiction for children—and transmit a specifically Orthodox Jewish moral message. As
the English-language Judaica Press put up on its website: "Our books
(for children) find that delicate balance between teaching important
lessons and still being fun and enjoyable."[28]

Publishers alter the genre of North American and Israeli children's
literature through images, language, and content, effectively transforming the books into morally didactic Jewish texts. For example, in
a book aimed at boys and girls ages five through eight, *The Shabbos
Queen and Other Shabbos Stories* (Fuchs 2002), all males wear large yarmulkes and ritual prayer fringes, and have long side curls and uncut
beards. The mother figure has her hair covered completely with a kerchief (*tikhl*) and wears a modest skirt with her blouse buttoned to the
top. Personal names are also marked as Yiddish, such as Mashie, Mal-
kie, and Dovid. Yiddish/loshn-koydesh words, phrases, and concepts
are integrated into the texts often with no special translations. Many
other books, similarly, include untranslated references to *hashem* 'God'
and Jewish ritual life, which readers are expected to understand.

A tip-off as to religious orientation (Hasidic or other forms of Orthodoxy) or publication site (Israel or New York) is often in the English
spellings of Yiddish or loshn-koydesh words. For example, in an Israeli
publication, a little boy, Efrayim, has to leave a coin on the street because he is not allowed to carry money on the Sabbath. The author
describes how he finds solace while singing in the synagogue,

Examples of Jewish toys and games. Beryl Goldberg, photographer. Reprinted with permission from Scharf's Judaica, Boro Park.

"Efrayim realized that he had bought something better than candy or markers with his coin. He had bought a wonderful mitzvah, the mitzvah of keeping Shabbos and making it holy! " (Fuchs 2002:22). The word *mitzvah* 'commandment' is not translated or marked here, but in a more Hasidic book, the word is transcribed as *mitsve*, which more closely approximates the Hasidic pronunciation of the word. Many Orthodox Jews in Israel and North America do not speak very much Yiddish, and their loshn-koydesh is closer to modern Hebrew spoken in Israel than to the Ashkenazic/Yiddish pronunciation (see chapter 5).

Some of the series for girls are explicitly modeled on secular books for girls, but the content is changed. When I asked an editor at Targum/Feldheim Press about the motivation for the Jewish B. Y. Times series by Leah Klein (1993), she told me, "We had to give them something to read besides the Babysitter's Club series," created by Ann Martin (1988) and aimed at North American girls. In the Babysitter's Club series a group of friends use initiative to earn money, thus gaining a sense of independence. In contrast, the B. Y. Times series depicts a group of Orthodox (not Hasidic) Jewish girls who put out a school newspaper for free while helping others and themselves. In the course of the books, girls often learn to be satisfied with what they have, or they successfully navigate a life-cycle change that they have been anxious about, such as a brother's wedding. These books also integrate Yiddish/loshn-koydesh words and concepts with little marking into an otherwise Standard English text. A number of the older daughters of Hasidic women I worked with read these series and enjoyed them.[29]

Language and Modernity

Political histories, not inherent expressive capabilities, cause people to perceive some languages as more modern than others. Standard English is often considered more modern than Haitian Creole or Persian, for example, because it is linked to the West, industrialization, technological advances, particular political systems and ideologies, and so on (Haeri 2003:13–15). Some scholars have suggested that in cultural contexts with sacred and vernacular languages, the shift to the vernacular allows for certain forms of political transformations associated with modernity. For example, Benedict Anderson, as Haeri (2003:16) notes, suggests that it was the shift from the Latin of the Christian church to European vernaculars, along with literacy, that was an important force in creating the possibility for the imagining of a new kind of national community. Sacred languages are often not considered arbitrary

Created and written by
LEAH KLEIN

REG. PRICE
EICHLER'S
795

The B.Y. Times

15

A lot of good news...or is there?

Secrets!

B. Y. Times, cover. Beryl Goldberg, photographer. Reprinted with permission from Targum/Feldheim Publishers.

because they are given by God (D. Boyarin 1993; Elster 2003). Haeri (2003) suggests that vernacular language, in contrast to sacred language, is believed to be arbitrary rather than divine—the profane property of citizens rather than a moral community of believers—and includes separability of form and meaning that encourages translation (2003: 146–151; See also Pollack 1998).

Hasidic Jews, however, and their syncretic language practices create different tensions and dynamics among vernacularization, sacred language, and modernity. Hasidic Jews do not want to be modern—that is, more like Gentiles—and yet they adapt and redeem cultural forms from contemporary North America, including language, making a so-called modern language, English, sound and look Hasidic. They participate in many of the institutions and processes most often associated with modernity. They are voting citizens and they embrace technology and medical science, participate in the capitalist economy, and are literate in a sacred language and fluent in two vernaculars, including the vernacular of the nation-state. However, by subtly changing the national vernacular they challenge the very idea that the positive features associated with modernity need to be secular.

Syncretic language practices such as those of Hasidic Jews are part of the broader effort, as Woolard (1998:16) suggests, to "dismantle but not neutralize binary distinctions." Perhaps, for Hasidic Jews, binary distinctions between Yiddish and English and the secular and religious have never been that important. Max Weinreich (1980:199) suggested this when he wrote:

> It is misleading to use the term religion to describe traditional Jewishness (in prewar Europe). When we say religion the implication is that there is a sphere in life beyond the boundary of religion. But in Jewishness there is no such delimitation ... All derive from divine relations. There are gradations of sanctity but all nooks of life are sacred.

English becomes a nonmodern language that mediates between the religious and the secular when Hasidic Jews make it Jewish through simultaneities with Yiddish and loshn-koydesh. Through syncretic transformations, English becomes a less arbitrary sign system, one touched with "sanctity," in contrast to Standard English, but not completely religious or secular. In this way, syncretic Hasidic English and Yiddish "dismantle binary distinctions" in order to essentialize the differences between Hasidim and Gentiles, and between Hasidic men and Hasidic women. The linguistic syncretism that creates Hasidic Yiddish and Hasidic English blurs the boundaries between languages and literary genres in order to accomplish a civilizing religious project. By learning to use language syncretically, Hasidic children, especially girls, learn that their participation in the institutions and language of the nation-state is to be used exclusively to follow God's commandments and build up the Jewish people.

CHAPTER FIVE

With It, Not Modern

ONE AFTERNOON, frustrated that her students had switched to Hasidic English during recess after speaking Hasidic Yiddish with her the whole morning, Mrs. Silver scolded them. She compared the biblical Jews in Egypt to her students, as she tried to convince them that English (even Hasidic English) is a Gentile language. The girls listened quietly to Mrs. Silver, and then burst into giggles when she mimicked them:

> *Zay* [the Jews in Egypt] *hobn nisht geredt de goyishe shprakh . . . far vus miz me indz redn de goyishe shprakh? . . . De yidn in mitsrayim hobn gevist az a goyishe shprakh redt me nisht. Ober nebekh, indz, s'iz azoy* <u>terrible</u> *. . . a sakh mentshn hobn beser lib tse redn english vi tse redn yidish . . . Burikh hashem indz kenen yidish, in burikh hashem indz zenen yidishe kinder,* <u>so</u> *far vus darf men zikh sheymen tse redn yidish? A pur kinder sheymen zikh,* "<u>Mommy</u> *red nisht tse mikh yidish. Red nor tse mikh* <u>english</u>."

They [the Jews in Egypt] didn't speak the Gentile language . . . why do we have to speak the Gentile language? The Jews in Egypt knew that we don't speak the Gentile language. But poor us, it's so terrible . . . a lot of people like to speak English more than to speak Yiddish . . . Thank God we know Yiddish, and thank God we are Jewish children, so why should we be embarrassed to speak Yiddish? A few children are embarrassed, "Mommy, don't talk to me in Yiddish. Only talk English to me."

The heightening of religious stringency prevalent among Hasidic Jews today has encouraged the Bnos Yisruel school administration to increasingly express the belief that in school, at least, girls should be using Yiddish among themselves because it is a Jewish language, a language of continuity with past generations of Jews who also always spoke a Jewish language (in addition to praying in loshn-koydesh). The fact is that Mrs. Silver's invocation of the Jews in Egypt who knew not to speak the Gentile language, a subject she raised a number of times over the course of the year, was confusing to some students. On one of those occasions a girl had asked if the Jews in Egypt spoke Yiddish; Mrs. Silver seemed stymied for a bit, but eventually she told them that, of course, the Jews back then spoke *mitsrish* 'Egyptian', a decidedly non-Jewish language.

This incident and others like it highlights an important tension: Yiddish is held up to girls as a vehicle of Jewish continuity when, in fact, important shifts have occurred regarding Yiddish itself and who speaks it. In the previous chapter I described how many Hasidic Jews consciously or unconsciously speak, write, and read in "Hasidic Yiddish" and "Hasidic English." I also noted that women and girls I met, in contrast to my analysis, only sometimes described their languages by the distinctive names they use—"Hasidic Yiddish" and "Yinglish." For Hasidic women and girls, the differences between the two languages seemed more relevant and less problematic than the nonstandard varieties of these languages that I have described. This chapter focuses on these differences. When the terms "Yiddish" and "English" are used, however, I mean to suggest that these are always the syncretic varieties of Hasidic Yiddish and Hasidic English described previously.

Hasidic girls today are more fluent in Yiddish than are their mothers and some of their grandmothers, many of whom were educated before the establishment of Hasidic schools for girls that use Yiddish for instruction and also teach Yiddish as a subject. Nevertheless, despite the explicit communal support for fluency in Yiddish, in first grade the Hasidic girls I observed gradually stopped speaking Yiddish and began to speak English as their everyday language—in contrast to Hasidic boys whose vernacular is Yiddish and who often have limited competence in English.

I puzzled over this paradox of language, gender, and religiosity: Why would Hasidic girls who participated in other forms of heightened stringency, such as increasingly modest clothing, reject Yiddish, especially given their fluency? The time I spent in homes and at Bnos Yisruel revealed that adult women were tacitly complicit in the girls' shift to English. Speaking Yiddish is one of the only areas where there is limited continuity across home and school. Mothers of first-graders, for example, who enforce school policy in all other areas, do not demand that girls use Yiddish at home, especially as they get older. This is partly because the school administration acknowledges that not all mothers are fluent in Yiddish. Even teachers at Bnos Yisruel, who *are* fluent in Hasidic Yiddish and who, at the administration's direction, frequently remind girls to speak Yiddish in class, speak Hasidic English among themselves at recess. They told me that they just feel more comfortable talking like their own mothers do, "in English."

More surprising was that after first grade Hasidic girls seem embarrassed to speak Yiddish, especially with adult women. Although they continue to use Yiddish in restricted contexts they increasingly describe Yiddish as unappealing, a _nebby_ 'nerdy' language, and English as _shtotty_ 'high-class or cosmopolitan', following American English pronunciation [ʃtody] (shtoddy).

When the Hasidic girls I observed rejected Yiddish as their vernacular, were they resisting the increasing religious stringency expected of Hasidic Jews today? Did these same girls want to be more modern by predominantly speaking English? Were they tempted by the English-speaking world around them?

I address these questions in this chapter by investigating what Kulick (1998) calls "associative networks"—the constellations of attributes that Hasidic girls begin to develop between Hasidic English and Hasidic Yiddish, their speakers, and the contexts in which these languages are used. In multilingual communities, a language may come to signify "social category of beings" and their particular activities (Agha 1998:178).[1] For example, Kulick has shown that in Gapun, New Guinea, the vernacular, Taiap, was increasingly associated with women, traditional life, indigenous religion, and aggression, whereas a newly introduced language, Tok Pisin, was associated with men, Christianity, wage labor, progress, and village cooperation. Women, who used the vernacular among themselves, unconsciously stopped speaking it to their children because of these negative associations. Associative networks linking gender, religion, and social change actually led to the unintentional loss of the vernacular among the next generation of speakers in Gapun (Kulick 1992, 1998).

The majority of scholarship on language and gender has focused on political economies, class, or ethnic identities, where a speaker's choice between languages is motivated by instrumental rationality and the assertion of individual autonomy in order to achieve progress, most often through material gain.[2] In a nonliberal religious community, like that of Hasidic Jews, the cultural beliefs about gender, power, and progress that shape language practices are different. God-given gendered responsibilities for Hasidic continuity are produced, in part, through men's and women's distinctive language competencies: Women must be fluent enough in the secular world so they can protect Torah-studying males from its distractions. Hasidic girls' shift to English is less about becoming more modern and more about learning to sound like the Hasidic women they have been taught to emulate, their mothers and grandmothers. Because of a moment in Hasidic women's educational histories, girls' participation in the heightened religiosity that defines Hasidic continuity today is, ironically, enacted through their loss of Yiddish fluency as they grow up. Speaking Hasidic English partly defines an adult, North American, Hasidic femininity. In contrast, Hasidic masculinity carries religious authority that is buttressed by fluency in Yiddish and a prestigious limited competence in English, both of which are linked to men's immersion in Torah study. The gendering of Yiddish and English represents a significant shift from prewar Eastern Europe, where Yiddish was especially associated with women and "uneducated" men who did not know loshn-koydesh.

Whereas Yiddish in prewar Europe united millions of Jews across a wide ideological spectrum, Yiddish now separates Hasidic Jews from other Jews in North America, most of whom no longer speak Yiddish. Among Hasidic women, Yiddish has come to mediate differences between Orthodox Jewish femininities. As noted in chapter 1, differences in stringency and style are apparent between the Hasidic circles, especially between Satmar and other Hasidic Jews. Women I met often contrasted those whom they called "the most/very Hasidish" from those Orthodox Jewish women they called more "modern." For women and girls, these differences are arbitrated by a repertoire of embodied signs that include the amount and variety of Yiddish or English that is spoken, style of modest dress, and education. Hasidic women and girls I worked with are ambivalent about "very Hasidic" women, whose English is marked by too much Yiddish interference; that is, they are not fluent enough in English to successfully navigate the secular world. They are also ambivalent, however, about the less stringently observant Jewish women whom they consider "too modern", too much like Gentiles, those whose English does not have enough Yiddish and loshn-koydesh in it to mark them as Orthodox Jews. The Bobover and similarly stringent Hasidic women and girls I spoke with strive to be what they call "with it," but not "modern." This distinctive Hasidic femininity is defined by the ability to participate selectively in the secular world in order to work toward religious progress, distinct from the notion of progress told in one narrative of Western secular modernity. Today's moderate Hasidic women and girls have new challenges to surmount in their efforts to reproduce the idealized and imagined femininity of past generations. Their interpretations of the present and the past, mediated through their use of language and other signifying practices, reveal a distinctive Hasidic femininity that is increasingly stringent and yet increasingly fluent in the secular world.

IMAGINING A LOST EASTERN EUROPEAN PAST

I spent a day visiting the Bobover camp for girls, a collection of wooden bungalows in the gentle Catskill Mountains of upstate New

York. A friend I was visiting, whose husband ran the camp, told me regretfully that I had just missed *alte haym* 'old home' (Eastern Europe) day. To remember how their great-grandmothers had lived, for a whole day all the campers wore black stockings, put their hair in two braids, and tried to talk only in Yiddish. There were even horse and buggy rides, like in the alte haym. It was not unusual to nostalgically remember life back then, when everyone's vernacular was Yiddish and girls still wore braids and black stockings. I had recently attended a "Chinese auction" (a women's function to raise money for a Jewish cause) with the theme "Once Upon a *Shtetl* 'Town' (a small Eastern European town)." The auction brochure had a drawing of some wooden houses and a horse-drawn carriage pulling two Jewish boys in Hasidic dress. Inside the hall where the auction was taking place, a slide show for children compared the lives of Jewish children in the shtetl to life in Boro Park and emphasized how easy life is for children today. The narrator intoned, "You take a bus to school; children in the shtetl took a horse and carriage." There were also horse-and-carriage rides for children down the streets of Boro Park, a veritable Hasidic Colonial "Villiamsboorg!"

Although the women I worked with often drew on biblical narratives to comment on the contemporary world, the most nostalgia was inspired by the more recent past, prewar Eastern Europe. Hasidic nostalgia echoes modern nostalgia for a rural community amid urban industrialization and anomie, yet it is distinctive; Hasidic nostalgia for the alte haym mourns the interruption of Jewish continuity—a legacy of the Holocaust when the transmitters of memory were killed.[3] Evocations of the alte haym gloss over the complicated specific histories of Eastern European empires and nations, along with any historical memory of the actual struggles among Jews back then over language, religion, and citizenship. Today grandparents, parents, teachers, counselors, and even children talk about the alte haym with reverence, imagining a romanticized, geographically unspecified alte haym: a simpler, better time and place when past generations of Hasidic Jews, especially women, had harder lives and were less materialistic, all evidence of their overall higher religious level than Jews today.

As the language of the alte haym, Yiddish, according to all the Hasidic women I met, signifies Hasidic continuity with a more moral generation of women. Hasidic women's beliefs about Yiddish, however, are complicated by real changes as a result of the history of educational institutions for Hasidic girls in North America. Recall, as discussed in chapter 1, that after the Holocaust and upon arriving in North America, few Hasidic leaders initially built private parochial schools for girls although these were immediately established for Hasidic boys.

Hasidic parents were legally obligated to send their daughters to school, however, and so they often sent them to the existing Beys Yaa-kov schools, the Orthodox schools for girls where the medium of in-struction is English and Hebrew (sometimes even Israeli Hebrew or *ivrit*). Girls did not learn Yiddish literacy in these schools. Any Yiddish they learned was acquired at home with family. In these schools Ha-sidic girls were often exposed to knowledge and standards of modesty that were inconsistent with the increasing levels of Hasidic stringency. In the 1970s, in order to provide more sheltered, Hasidic educational experiences for girls, a number of different rebbes began to establish schools for girls that teach Yiddish literacy and use Yiddish as the me-dium of instruction during the Jewish morning subjects. Because of this schooling history, at least one or two generations of women have some limited fluency in Yiddish. Despite schooling histories, of course, variations among women do exist, and I met some women in their thirties who are quite comfortable in Yiddish. However, the young girls I observed in Bnos Yisruel are now the most fluent female speak-ers of Yiddish in several generations, certainly more fluent than many of their mothers.

Women's limited competency in Yiddish, I believe, actually contrib-utes to women's sense that Yiddish is somehow outside of time or the mundane world. Many Hasidic women told me that Yiddish is a more *aydl* 'refined' language than English. A teacher told me that in Yiddish certain terms or ideas from "today's world" cannot even be articulated, meaning that Yiddish simply does not have the linguistic resources to express certain aspects of the contemporary world (such as the fashion-able color "peach"). An older woman's adult daughter asked her to say "I love you" in Yiddish rather than English, telling her mother that the Yiddish sounded more *aydl*. Her mother agreed. Some women's limited competency actually does make Yiddish something of a re-stricted language, one in which some Hasidic women cannot express themselves fluently. When I mentioned this theory to Rifky, she agreed. She compared the Hasidic women she knew in Boro Park to her "very Hasidic" cousins in Williamsburg, Brooklyn (Satmar Hasidim), who speak Yiddish far more fluently than many of the Bobover and other Hasidic women I met in Boro Park. Rifky told me that her Wil-liamsburg cousins "can say plenty of nasty things in Yiddish" because they are so fluent.

Paradoxically, Hasidic women who are not fluent in Yiddish claim that speaking Yiddish is an important way to maintain Jewish continu-ity over time and space, and also to keep Jews apart from Gentiles. When I asked Raizy, who is even less fluent than a Boro Parker because she grew up elsewhere, why Yiddish is important, she told me:

Why I think Yiddish is important? Well, that's how we, the Jewish people, keep ourselves separate from the rest of the world but keep together as a nation. We're doing what our parents did. We're not changing what our parents and grandparents did.

This response reveals a conflict for women and girls especially over how best to maintain Hasidic continuity. When Raizy, predominantly an English speaker, says, "We're not changing what our parents and grandparents did," she is accurate, at least for the women in her family. Her mother, and even most likely her grandmother, also mainly speak English. For Raizy and others like her, continuity occurs when girls reproduce the ways of their mothers, even when that means speaking English.

However, Raizy and other women of her generation can also claim to be reproducing the Yiddish of prewar Eastern Europe through their distinctive use of Hasidic Yiddish baby talk. All the mothers and teachers I worked with, most of whom did not speak Yiddish with one another, shared and were fluent in a baby-talk register of Hasidic Yiddish. These women ensure that the first language of very young children will be Yiddish, Hasidic Yiddish, with a great deal of influence from English baby talk, but Yiddish nevertheless. When I asked Rifky why *a yidish kind darf redn yidish* (a Jewish child needs to speak Yiddish), which another woman had told me, she responded, translating the Yiddish into Hasidic English (something women often do with Jews like me whose religious knowledge is shaky):

I think maybe the point is if *a yidish kind gayt es nisht redn*, if a Jewish child isn't going to speak it, then nobody will know it. It's with everything you know? It's up to the *yidishe kinder*, the Jewish children, to maintain everything. If *de yidish kind vet nisht redn yidish*, if the Jewish child won't speak Yiddish, there won't be anybody out there talking Yiddish.

Most likely, even women who did not attend Hasidic schools for girls heard and used a similar baby-talk register of Yiddish at home from their own parents and grandparents. Hasidic baby talk is proof that Hasidic women are not changing their own parents' childrearing practices or the language most appropriate for Jewish children, Yiddish.

Some families make a special effort to make Yiddish the language of the home, an issue usually discussed and decided during matchmaking (see chapter 7). Families that try to speak more Yiddish as part of their effort to be as close as possible to their perceptions of past European generations of Jews, are often called "European." Even in these families, however, women often speak English among themselves. An example is Morah Cohen, the kindergarten teacher whose son wanted shorter side curls. She told me that her husband, who is from Israel, was very *makpid* 'strict' and European. He required that the sleeves on her housecoat completely cover her arms, that she not listen to the radio or read magazines, and that she try to talk only in Yiddish with him and the children. Because she is from Montreal, where most Hasidic Jews speak Yiddish more fluently than in Brooklyn, she did not have too much trouble speaking Hasidic Yiddish at home with him and the children. She told me, however, that her husband had pointed out to her that when she talked to her mother on the phone, she quickly switched into English, which she herself was surprised to learn.

GENDER AND LANGUAGE AT HOME

In most families I met, as children around the age of three begin school, they are less frequently addressed in Hasidic Yiddish baby talk. After age three or four, girls and boys begin to speak, and are spoken to, in different languages. Mothers address their sons in Hasidic Yiddish and their daughters in Hasidic English, whereas men (from my more limited observations and women's reports) address both their sons and daughters in Hasidic Yiddish. As they get older, girls, like their mothers, alternate between Hasidic Yiddish and Hasidic English depending on the speaker's age and gender, making them, for a brief time, the most fluent bilingual speakers in the family. Boys, on the other hand, continue to speak exclusively in Hasidic Yiddish, with minimal competence in Hasidic English, at least until they are married, with children, and go to work. At that time their English competency often improves.

The relationship between age, gender, and language choice can be seen in the excerpt below of the Klein family playing Junior Monopoly, a version of Monopoly for younger children, one late afternoon before supper. Raizy Klein, a tall woman in a smooth, very dark shoulder-length wig, sat on the dining-room floor around the Monopoly board along with her three older children. She tried to keep up Yiddish baby talk with her younger children and Yiddish with her son, although she often lapsed into English. Her eldest, Yehudis (age seven), is the most fluent in Yiddish and English according to her mother and in my view as well, and it is she who mediates the choice of language for her brother Shimmy (age six) and her sister Malky (age four), who both predominantly use Yiddish:

(1) **Raizy** [to Malky]: <u>Ok</u>, <u>so</u> di darfst geybn ayn <u>dollar</u> (Ok, so you have to give one dollar).

(2) **Malky:** Vus? (What?)

(3) **Yehudis** [to Malky]: Geb ayn <u>dollar</u> (Give one dollar).

(4) **Raizy:** Ok, fine. Who's next? Yehudis.

(5) **Yehudis** [rolls dice]: Five. One, two, three, four, five.

(6) **Raizy:** Do you want to buy the paddle boats?

(7) **Yehudis:** Yeah!

(8) **Raizy:** Now, Shimmy, go next.

(9) **Yehudis:** Shimmy, gay (go). [He rolls and moves his piece.]

(10) **Raizy:** You have to put your house down over there. You have to give two dollars to the bank. Here's the bank.

(11) **Yehudis:** Shimmy, geb ayn <u>dollar</u> (Give one dollar) [meaning a two-dollar bill]. Ayn. Um, Shimmy, nem, nem ayns, tsvay (One, Um, Shimmy, take, take one, two).

Raizy attempts to talk to her daughter, Malky, in Yiddish (1), and Malky answers her in Yiddish (2). Yehudis repeats her mother's Yiddish instructions as well (3). However, Raizy is most comfortable in English, and after switching to English in her exchange with Yehudis (4–6), she also uses it with her son, Shimmy (8). Yehudis then translates her mother's English instructions into Yiddish for Shimmy (9 and 11). Yehudis's fluency in Yiddish, however, will most likely stall as she stops using it as a vernacular the older she gets.

Indeed, Rifky Katz told me that her two older daughters' levels of Yiddish are now similar to her own. When I first met them, at ages eight and nine, they were more fluent than their mother, but as they began to use English increasingly, their Yiddish fluency diminished until now, at eighteen and nineteen, their linguistic competencies resemble their mother's, which is still quite fluent. Similarly when Malky Klein, who now speaks mostly Yiddish, entered first grade, she began speaking English to her older sister, as well as to her mother. Shimmy, her six-year-old brother, however, will continue to use Yiddish with everyone in the family. Cultural conceptions of Yiddish as a language appropriate for addressing babies is linked to associative networks: Jewish continuity, moral purity, and the idealized generations of Eastern European Jews. In school, these associative networks are extended for older children and are gendered.

Gender and Language in School

Schools for boys and girls support the communal belief that there are specific and gendered forms of knowledge, language, and activities. In their separate preschool, which goes from ages three to five, boys and girls have women teachers who predominantly use Yiddish with the children. Most of the children respond in Yiddish as well. The only times that girls in kindergarten explicitly commented to me about language was when they asked me which language I liked more, Yiddish or English. Girls often asked me this question early on; most likely they were trying to place me, since I was so clearly not one of them. I either told them I liked both or that I liked to practice Yiddish. When I asked girls which language they liked more, some claimed to "only like to talk in English," although others said that they "liked both" or *bayde* 'both'. When children turn six, they enter first grade, at which point the gendering of languages and persons which had been a gradual process begins in earnest.

Boys' Religious Obligations and Yiddish

Although I had limited access to men and older boys, in my visits to families I was able to observe how mothers reinforced boys' Yiddish and the way some boys talked about Yiddish. As noted earlier, boys entering first grade spend the entire day in Yiddish-medium schools, taught by Hasidic men, acquiring oral fluency in Yiddish and literacy in loshn-koydesh and Yiddish. Becoming fluent in Yiddish is critical to boys' ability to study sacred texts. They do not receive instruction in English (literacy) or secular subjects (math and social studies) until second, sometimes even third grade. When non-Jewish subjects begin, they come at the end of a long day of study, and boys are often exhausted and restless. English literacy and secular learning are minimized and often trivialized. As Esty's nephew, eleven-year-old Benzion, commented about his English teacher, "*S'iz nisht kan teacher. S'iz a babysitter*" (That's not a teacher. That's a babysitter). Often the teachers chosen for secular instruction are Gentiles, since a Jewish male with expertise in secular subjects would present an undesirable alternative model for Jewish masculinity. With Gentile teachers, boys have even more license to ignore the authority of their English teachers. Israel Rubin (1997), who observed classes in a Satmar yeshiva in Williamsburg, for example, describes how boys sit silently and respectfully all day with their Yiddish teachers but sit in clusters, eating and chatting, with their back to their English teachers.

Beginning in second or third grade, according to the reports of their mothers, boys are taught that maintaining Yiddish at home is one of their gendered responsibilities, part of maintaining Jewish religious learning and tradition, which is exclusively male. It was not uncommon for young boys to assume the function of Yiddish watchdogs and ask their mothers to speak less English and more Yiddish. For example, Mindy (the mother who gave her son Yitsy a mitsve note in chapter 2) reported that her older son, Chaim (age nine), came home from school and said, "*Mommy, ikh beyt dikh, red nor yidish in de haym*" (Mommy, I beg you, only speak Yiddish at home). She was very proud that her son was taking his studies so seriously. She told him that he was right, and she would try to speak more Yiddish at home. Similarly, on a visit to Gitty's sister-in-law, she showed me a chart her son's teacher had sent home which asked her to keep track of how much Yiddish her son spoke, along with making sure he was fulfilling important mitsves such as honoring one's parents, making blessings over food, and so on. This reinforced the consistent message between home and school, where parents and teachers work together with shared goals for a child's emotional, academic, linguistic, and religious development.

These practices socialize boys and their mothers to require and expect boys to speak more Yiddish than girls. In addition to using Yiddish to address babies, Yiddish is definitive of Hasidic masculinity, appropriate for those who study Torah and preserve tradition through access to sacred texts. Again, although I had limited access to fathers and sons, from Hasidic women I heard that boys are taught at home and in school that they are the next generation of communal authorities by dint of their knowledge of sacred texts, which includes fluency in Yiddish and loshn-koydesh. Boys' Hasidic male teachers teach them their authoritative social positions, and, at home, their mothers and fathers reinforce it.

Yiddish and Girls' Restricted Religious Literacy

In contrast to boys' experience, administrators at the girls' school, Bnos Yisruel, do not enforce Yiddish outside the classroom. School administrators explicitly encourage girls to speak Yiddish, but they draw the line at demanding that mothers speak to their daughters exclusively in Yiddish. This contrasts with other realms of behavior where the school has no qualms requiring parents to sign a contract agreeing not to have a television at home, not to take their daughters to the public library, and to dress their daughters according to the modesty standards of the school. Reluctance to enforce Yiddish among girls at home is due, at least in part, to the fact that administrators are aware that many mothers are not fluent in Yiddish. When, for example, Mrs. Silver wanted to send home a chart where mothers had to keep an account of how often girls spoke in Yiddish, just as an account is kept for the boys, the principal vetoed the idea. She explained to Mrs. Silver, who explained to me, that some homes are English-speaking and that the school could not force mothers to speak Yiddish, although they do encourage it.

The organization of the school curriculum, moreover, had the (perhaps unintended) consequence of creating semiotic links between the restricted religious learning of girls, moral didacticism, and Yiddish. Dividing the day into Jewish and secular subjects, the former taught in Yiddish and the latter in English, socializes girls to use particular languages in particular contexts and with particular content areas. This is evident even in the school's library, which has separate sections for Yiddish and English books. Most of the Yiddish books are morally didactic. Even the picture books for very young children include a moral message. The English books, however, include (censored) mainstream English children's literature, as well as the *yidishe* 'Jewish' English fiction aimed at girls that is marketed as "fun and entertaining," in addition to being kosher and educational (see chapter 4).

For girls, Hasidic Yiddish, the medium for studying explicitly religious subjects, increasingly becomes most appropriate for its association with Hasidic nostalgia for a lost past, when Yiddish was the Jewish language for men and women. This nostalgia is particularly evident in Yiddish literacy lessons and texts, which explicitly instruct that knowledge of Yiddish prepares girls to study didactic texts appropriate for women. In a first-grade Yiddish reader, distributed by the school (Greenzweig 1990), the preface makes its agenda clear:

Mit de hartsige balernde maselekh vos zenen ungefilt mit yiras shemayim in mides toyvos, tsiyen mir de intires fin de kinder. Az de kinder veln derfiln dem zisn tam, veln zay alayn shoyn hobn groyse khayshk tsi laynen in yidish. Zay veln zan durshtig nokh mer tsi derkvikn zayere hertselekh in veln, mit der tsat, gayn vater in hekher. Zay veln, b'esras hashem, oukh zikh nemen tsi laynen mases veygn avosayni ve imosayni hakdoshem in dernentern zikh tsim gartn fin sifrey musar af yidish.

With these heartfelt instructive little stories which are filled with good values and awe of God, we draw the interest of the children. As children sense the sweet taste of Yiddish reading, they themselves will have a great desire to read in Yiddish. They will thirst to refresh their little hearts even more and will, with time, go higher and further. They will, with God's help, take to reading about our holy forefathers and foremothers and bring themselves closer to the garden of ethical writings in Yiddish.

The goal of the reader is to expose girls to Yiddish, so that the language nourishes their innate Jewish qualities and helps them bloom as good Jewish girls, and thus lead to the desire for more Jewish learning in Yiddish. As girls cannot study Torah, this learning refers to ethical writing (*musar*) in Yiddish, which Poll (1965) notes has been the traditional realm of study for those who are not allowed access to sacred texts, namely, uneducated men and women.

Each chapter of the Yiddish primer focuses on teaching a specific vowel through stories, while simultaneously imparting a moral lesson for girls. Teachers often use these readings as a springboard for discussions comparing life in the *alte haym*, 'old home' where women and girls spoke Yiddish, to the materialistic world of Boro Park, where women and girls speak English. The chapter on the Yiddish vowel ⁇ [aI] (ay), for example, presents the rhyming vocabulary *haym, fayn, klayd* 'home, nice, dress'; the story begins with a little girl's grandmother narrating a Yiddish story to her granddaughter about the simpler, less materialistic time when she grew up in the alte haym. The grandmother tells her granddaughter that when she was a little girl she had "one and only one" special dress, in honor of the Sabbath, and she was very happy with it. Even when the dress became worn out and had to be turned inside out and re-sewn, first once and then again, she was satisfied with her dress. In class, Mrs. Silver read the story aloud and then asked the girls if they would be satisfied with just one Sabbath dress. The girls clamored that they would. Their teacher responded skeptically as, in fact, a great deal of money and attention is spent on girls' fancy Sabbath dresses, which are made of velvet, satin, or silk and often sport layers of ruffled petticoats underneath:

I wish! *Ikh hof az indz volt geveyn tsifridn. Ober in de alte tsatn de mentshn zenen geveyn zayer tsifridn.*

I wish! I hope that you would be satisfied. But in the olden days, people were very satisfied.

This evocation of the "old days," when Yiddish-speaking grandmothers (by then, great-grandmothers) were less materialistic and vain than girls are today is essential to Hasidic nostalgia for an idealized lost Judaism that is defined today by poverty, hardship, and isolation from the temptations of Gentile life. This perception is probably exaggerated because, as noted, in fact, Eastern European Hasidic Jews often lived close to, and interacted with, not only Gentiles but also Jews who were bent on becoming more modern, that is, increasingly participating as European citizens.

GIRLS' FLUENT YIDDISH = NOT "WITH IT"

For girls, Yiddish is not only associated with an idealized lost past and Hasidic continuity. Girls have some unexpectedly negative associations with Yiddish that can be traced to their ambivalent feelings for the women and girls who are the most fluent female Yiddish speakers today: very Hasidic women and Hungarian women whose largest circle is Satmar.

Satmar women and girls speak Hasidic Yiddish as their vernacular because their own schooling histories included the early establishment of schools for girls in Hungary and the postwar United States. They also take the most isolationist stance of all Hasidic Jews to the secular world and its media. Many Hasidic women I worked with admired the religious rigor of Hungarian women, but at the same time they described Satmar women and girls in English as "backward," "primitive," and not "with it." Even their Yiddish, which is the most fluent of all Hasidic women, is often depicted by other Hasidic women as sounding "funny" or "ugly." Several different women told me about a younger sister or cousin who went to work in Hungarian bungalow colonies or went to Hungarian summer camp, and, much to their families' dismay, returned with the distinctive Hungarian accent (phonology) in their Yiddish. For example, when her younger sister returned from a summer at a Hungarian camp for girls, Esty told me her father said to her mother, "What happened? Why does she sound that way? Make her stop." Even men find Satmar women's fluent Yiddish unappealing.

Negative feelings toward Satmar girls go beyond their Yiddish fluency and accent. Older girls in Bnos Yisruel—middle and high school girls—use the term "_nebby_" to describe Hasidic girls who speak Yiddish, whose clothing is most stringently modest but also unfashionable, and who have more limited education in Jewish and secular subjects. The word nebby (or a "neb") is derived from the Yiddish word *nebekh*, an unfortunate person who inspires pity in others (Weinreich 1990). With an adjectival English "y" added to the Yiddish noun, nebby is a bivalent word, both Yiddish and English, and applies exclusively to Jewish women and girls. In Boro Park, the term connotes a girl who is not "with it," not in touch with what her peers or even more modern Jewish girls are wearing, reading, or how they speak. A colloquial English equivalent might be a "loser" or a "nerd." I heard the word neb used frequently by women and girls, so during one of our conversation classes in Yiddish, I asked Gitty to help me understand the term. She explained:

Like *nisht epes vus me kikt aruf tsi.* . . . *Lemushl if the* style is . . . az yeyde ayne trugt a <u>bob</u> [a short haircut], <u>*right?*</u> *In eymetse kimt aran trug yene in a <u>pony</u>,* so somebody might say she's <u>*nebby.*</u> Or if the teacher *hot, me hot <u>discussion and</u> eymetser haybt ouf ir hand in zugt epes* <u>silly</u> and it's a joke, but nobody laughs at it. Oh, what a *neb.* . . . *Shtayt alayn . . . di bist gurnisht, so* you're a *neb,* get it?

Like not something that you look up to. . . . For example, if the style is . . . that everybody wears a bob [a short haircut], right? And somebody comes in wearing a ponytail, so somebody might say she's nebby. Or if the teacher . . . you have a discussion and somebody raises her hand and says something silly and it's a joke but nobody laughs at it. Oh, what a neb. Standing alone . . . you're nothing, so you're a neb. Get it?

According to Gitty, a neb is a girl who is unfashionable (wearing her hair in a ponytail when everyone is wearing a bob) and unpopular (standing alone), evidenced by her jokes that no one finds funny. A neb is a loner, someone other girls do not like because she is not with it, up on what other girls are doing. Soon after this description, I heard that Yiddish had been described as nebby as well during an incident among the high school girls of Bnos Yisruel. Mrs. Silver told me during lunch that the day before there had been a big teachers' meeting about how to support Yiddish in school. What sparked the meeting, she said, was that monitors had been going around to each class and announcing the annual school play, which was to be in Yiddish. A teacher overheard a fourteen-year-old girl saying to her friend, "Oh, a play in Yiddish. That's so nebby." The principal was outraged by the remark. She called all the teachers together during recess and told them that they had to encourage positive attitudes toward Yiddish, acknowledging that many girls' had negative feelings about the language.

Around the same time, on our way to a local store to buy shoes for her children, Esty told me that she and Rifky had been talking about why the teenage girls that they knew, their sisters and cousins, described very Hasidic girls as the most nebby. One would think, Rifky said, that in this kind of community the most Hasidic girls, the most religiously stringent, the girls whose behavior was most closely modeled on their nostalgic imaginings of past generations of Hasidic women, would be the most admired. What, she wondered, made Yiddish and the opaque, seamed stockings of very Hasidic girls nebbier than the sheer stockings and the English of the girls she and I knew? When I asked a large group of teachers in Bnos Yisruel about Rifky's insight, they all strongly agreed that the most Hasidic girls were the nebbiest. In particular, and I return to this in the next chapter, the teachers explained that although the most Hasidic women and girls are so religiously stringent in their clothing and their use of Yiddish, their secular and religious education is not very rigorous compared to that of other Hasidic girls. Their limited education, a number of teachers suggested, makes them especially prone to materialism and shallowness. I suggest that, similarly, their limited fluency in English and their hyperbolically modest clothing make them unable to negotiate the secular world for their own Jewish purposes. Ironically, their religious stringency actually makes them less like their great-grandmothers in the alte haym, because they do not have the knowledge or skills necessary to protect themselves from the secular world by their very fluency in it.

In school and occasionally at home, teachers or mothers will sometimes attempt to change girls' associations between nebbiness and Yiddish. In these cases, like the lecture Mrs. Silver gave her students at the beginning of this chapter, mothers and teachers present Yiddish as a Jewish language and English as a Gentile language. This despite the emergence of Hasidic English described in the previous chapter, a linguistic variety that transforms English into a Jewish language for women. Hasidic mothers and teachers sometimes tell their daughters and their students that speaking Yiddish cultivates the refinement that is definitive of Hasidic femininity. One afternoon, for example, Mindy became angry with her daughter, Suri, a stocky six-year old with short brown hair. Suri had been chanting a rhyme in English to herself all afternoon: "Looking here, looking there, where's Mickey Mouse's underwear?" Suri, Mindy, and two-year-old Yitsy were in the kitchen. The children were looking for a ball that had rolled off somewhere. After addressing her brother in Yiddish about the ball, Suri switched to English to tease her mother and also to enlist her help in looking for the ball:

SURI: Hey. . . . where's Mickey Mouse's underwear, Mommy?
MINDY: Will you keep quiet? I don't like the way you are talking, Suri!
SURI: Ok, but where's that ball that we had?

Then Mindy switched into Yiddish and told her daughter to speak Yiddish, too. She told her that when she spoke Yiddish she did not say things like "Mickey Mouse's underwear." She said, "Ikh hob lib tse redn yidish. That's it . . . Ven di redst yidish, redsti nisht azoy" (I like to speak Yiddish. That's it . . . When you speak Yiddish, you don't speak like that). Suri responded to her mother in English, claiming that she did not know how to "talk Yiddish." Then she turned to her little brother and gave him directions for a game they were playing, speaking in fluent Yiddish. Mindy, who is not fluent in Yiddish herself, did not have much success in convincing Suri to use Yiddish with her. Suri simply refused to switch into Yiddish with her mother, although she continued to use it with her little brother. Eventually Mindy dropped the issue. Indeed, although a number of women told me that they respond to their daughter's English requests with, "*Ikh farshtay oukh yidish*" (I also understand Yiddish), girls continue to use English with adult women and peers, and their mothers rarely enforce Yiddish as they do with other aspects of Hasidic femininity (see chapter 6).

Teachers try more consistently to convince girls to speak Yiddish than their mothers do, because this is something the school administration, and ultimately the rebbe himself, wants. On one occasion Mrs. Silver invoked the pinnacle of religious authority, the rebbe, as proof that girls should be speaking Yiddish. She even suggested that girls should take on Yiddish as a religious obligation, a mitsve, regardless of what their mothers speak:

> *Zugst mikh oyb de ruv redt english mit de mentshn in shil. Zugst mikh,*
> *so oyb de ruv redt nisht english, oyb se volt geveyn a mitsve tse redn en-*
> *glish? . . . ken men indz zikh lernen fin deys, si'z nisht de rikhtike zakh tse*
> *tin. So fin hant in vater ken men gedenkn . . . afile oyb dan mame redt*
> *english, kensti beytn oyb di kenst redn yidish, in dan mame vet nisht zugn,*
> *"No way! Indz vil me redn nor de goyishe shprakh, loz nisht kan yidishe*
> *shprakh in inzer houz."*

Tell me if the rebbe speaks English with the men in synagogue. Tell me, so if the rebbe doesn't speak English, is it a commandment to speak English? Can we learn from this, that it's not the right thing to do? So from today on, you can remember, even if your mother speaks English, you can ask her if you can speak Yiddish. And your mother will not say, "No way! In this house we only speak the Gentile language. We don't allow any Jewish language in our house."

Mrs. Silver tried to frame Yiddish as the only legitimate Jewish language for Hasidic girls, and English as a Gentile language, although even she often speaks English outside class. If girls politely ask their mothers to take on the religious obligation of speaking Yiddish, their mothers, Mrs. Silver assures them, will gladly agree. In the end, however, the decision to speak Yiddish outside class is left to the girls.

Girls continue to speak English most likely because this allows them to participate in an adult Hasidic femininity that is "with it" and still Hasidic, savvy, and sophisticated, but never modern. Hasidic femininity is important to elaborations of a Hasidic alternative modernity, one where Hasidic women fluently negotiate the contemporary secular world to effectively transform it through a Jewish civilizing project. It is Hasidic English, not Hasidic Yiddish, that girls associate with this desirable Hasidic femininity.

ENGLISH AND FEMININITY

Teachers and mothers suggested to me that girls think English is "fancy, sophisticated, ladylike, and *shtotty* 'high-class or cosmopolitan',"concepts that are valued in terms of the elaboration of Hasidic adult femininity. This has a precedent in prewar European educational practice, where upper-class, observant Jewish women were often tutored in a Gentile language, usually Polish or German, as a sign of their refinement.[4] In Boro Park, outside the classroom, a number of mothers reported that as girls matured they frequently asked their mothers to speak and read to them only in English, rejecting Yiddish storybooks altogether.[5] I believe this is partly because reproducing a mother's religious practices in language, fashion, and ritual is expected and highly valued. Rifky theorized that when Hasidic girls hear their mothers and teachers speaking English among themselves, and hear their brothers and fathers speaking Yiddish at home, they begin to associate adult Hasidic femininity with speaking English and Hasidic masculinity with Yiddish. This seems accurate, because children experience gendered language at home and in school. I observed, for example, Mindy's 6-year-old daughter, Suri, who spoke Yiddish fluently, playing at being a mother and addressing an imaginary adult companion while pushing her doll in a stroller at home. Speaking in Hasidic English, she expertly mimicked a typical conversation between Boro Park mothers, "Oh Gitty, your baby is so cute. Where did you get his outfit?" Hasidic girls strive to emulate their mothers, so they speak English to their peers and women.

But the association between girls' mothers and Hasidic English is only part of the explanation. Just as girls have some negative associative networks with Yiddish and nebby Hungarian speakers, so, too, do Hasidic girls at Bnos Yisruel have positive associative networks with the more modern Jewish women who teach them secular subjects in the afternoons in English. For the secular afternoons, as noted earlier, the school administration hires more modern women because they have state certification, unlike Hasidic high school graduates who are generally hired to be Yiddish teachers only. A number of teachers told me that the presence of more modern, but still Orthodox, Jewish women is not considered especially threatening to the Hasidic girls.

Secular subjects are valued for girls much more than they are for boys, because girls will need reading, writing, and math skills when, for example, they pay their electric bills, read the restrictions on certain kinds of government programs, or even skim their daughters' books to make sure they are "kosher (i.e., untainted by immodest images or ideas)." A girl's academic success in both Yiddish and English subjects is considered desirable, a mark of intelligence and diligence, when matchmaking begins in the last year of high school (see chapter 7). In Bnos Yisruel, in contrast to the Yiddish mornings, English activities in the afternoons are not morally didactic. The orientation to knowledge in secular subjects is one of accumulation and repetition, rather than the moral conditioning teachers spoke about for Jewish subjects. English texts are public school readers that provide innocuous stories. For example, girls read a chapter in their English reader about a puppy who runs up and down a hill, with children chasing after him. In contrast to the Yiddish reader, neither the children nor their English teacher commented much on the text or connected the text to everyday Hasidic life.

On an exceptional occasion, a science reader presented Gentiles as normative North Americans, and this became an opportunity for their teacher to go beyond the differences between Jewish women to larger, more essential differences between Jews and Gentiles. During a science lesson that presented the idea that "all living things need food to live," the reader had a drawing of a family sitting down to dinner. The English teacher, Mrs. Nathan, an Orthodox, non-Hasidic teacher, asked the girls to look at the picture and report what the family was eating. She stopped short when she realized that the family was drinking milk and eating chicken, which is forbidden to Orthodox Jews who may not mix milk and meat as part of the Jewish dietary laws (*kashres*):

MRS. NATHAN: What are they drinking?
STUDENT 1: Milk.
MRS. NATHAN: [pause] Well, obviously they're not Jewish. Right? We don't eat chicken and milk together.
STUDENT 1: They're drinking and eating milk with their . . .
MRS. NATHAN: I know, but they're not Jewish, right? Are they wearing yarmulkes and *tsitses* 'ritual fringed garments'?
STUDENTS: No.

Mrs. Nathan's remarks encourage students to distinguish Jews from Gentiles by reading the male embodied signs (clothing), which are more immediately visible than signs of women's Orthodoxy. She presents Jews as a homogeneous category, all adhering to Orthodox religious practice. You can recognize a Gentile, Mrs. Nathan suggests to her students, by what they eat and what they wear. The activity of a secular science lesson actually became an opportunity for the teacher to remind them to read secular texts with a Jewish eye. When characters in the text deviate from Jewish Orthodox normative practices, Mrs. Nathan labels them non-Jews. This conversation, all in English in the context of secular afternoons, is not about language or science at all. Rather, the focus is on the visible, ritual practices that define Orthodox Jews (males) as different from Gentiles.

Secular studies in the afternoon are one of the most frequent occasions for Hasidic girls' exposure to more modern women like Mrs. Nathan, women who are Orthodox but less religiously stringent. More modern Jewish women often do not know much Yiddish, and their English is closer to Standard English. In fact, Mrs. Nathan was often exasperated by girls' Hasidic English, particularly their Yiddish calques (direct translations). Rolling her eyes, she often corrected girls who said, for example, "close the light" (*makh tsi de likht*) rather than "turn off the light." Many times I heard her tell a girl who had used Hasidic English, "That is not English," and offer corrections for a Standard English expression.

However, language is only one semiotic piece in defining a more modern Jewish Orthodox femininity. In addition to their fluent, Standard English, women like Mrs. Nathan are up on contemporary fashions. Because they are less religiously stringent, they have a bit more leeway in terms of their modest dress. They can, for example, wear long wigs without a hat (although in Bnos Yisruel the wig must be tied back in a pony), as well as shorter and tighter skirts and colored, sheer, or black stockings. In contrast, Hasidic girls in Bnos Yisruel who get married will most likely wear short wigs with hats, calf-length skirts, and opaque, seamed stockings. Because of their higher education, the more modern teachers also have a greater salary potential and sometimes even the secular prestige of a higher degree, most often in speech therapy.[6] I heard Bnos Yisruel girls, even first-graders, comment admiringly on the afternoon English teachers' clothing or wigs. As one first-grader said, "The English teachers are so shtotty this year!"

English, the language of more modern Jewish women, has an alternative covert prestige (Trudgill 1974), not as a rejection of tradition and continuity but as a less stringent form of Orthodox Jewish femininity. More modern Jewish women create ambivalence and ambiguity in the essential boundaries that, in the view of Hasidic women, separate them from Gentile women and the secular world. Many women and girls who deny that they want to be modern nevertheless admire the appearance and speech of more modern Jewish women and so they speak

English. There are even more subtle linguistic moves, however, for girls who want to be with it, but not modern.

SOUNDING HASIDIC OR SOUNDING MODERN

As Hasidic girls mature, they increasingly speak English as their vernacular language in order to be like their mothers, to sound like but remain distinct from more modern Jewish women, and to distinguish themselves from Hasidic men and boys who speak Yiddish. Within the two nonstandard varieties of Yiddish and English used in Boro Park, however, subtle variations in accent, intonation, and vocabulary create a continuum of syncretic language: At one end is the most Hasidic Yiddish and at the other is Standard English. On this continuum, Hasidic women can access the symbolic resources of varieties of Yiddish and English to serve specific goals of interaction (Hill and Hill 1986).

Modern Vowels in Yiddish/loshn-koydesh

Hasidic women and girls can negotiate hierarchies of Jewish piety, as well as their relationship to the secular world with its competing forms of prestige, by choosing vowels that sound more Hasidic or more modern. Although Hasidic women and young girls I met never said they wanted to be more modern, they do want to be shtotty. To achieve this, they must understand and be able to approximate their perception of prestigious forms of more modern Jewish women's English, clothing, and knowledge. As Rifky so insightfully put it:

> You don't say, "I want to sound like a goy." You want to sound like your sophisticated friend. And your sophisticated friend wants to look a little more like her modern [Jewish] neighbor, and her modern neighbor wants to look a little bit more like the lady in the magazine, and the lady in the magazine decided she is not proud of being a Jew. She'd rather be just an American citizen.

Sounding and looking more modern as an Orthodox Jewish woman is all about degrees of difference from an imagined Jew who has abandoned her faith and become "just an American citizen." Rifky invokes a continuum of religiosity that Hasidic women and girls negotiate, as well as the implicit danger that becoming too modern holds for Jews. When Hasidic women are enticed by the sophisticated sounds and look of more modern Jewish women, especially those they encounter in secular media such as magazines, they risk coming ever closer to being like a Gentile.

One day Esty contrasted my English and hers. She claimed her English was haymish because it had words that "kind of run into each other and are not so clear or perfect." As noted in the introduction, I was initially baffled, as women I met in Boro Park frequently asked me if I was from "out of town" because of my "accent." I had asked Esty about this, and she suggested that my English was "refined," clearly enunciated and educated. Initially I felt flattered, but as she went on I realized this was no compliment. "Refined English" was associated with higher education and immediately raised questions about my level of religiosity. If I were truly religious I would not have attended college, for example. My English, in contrast to Hasidic English, was marked as unfamiliar to Hasidic women. Most assumed I was either not from New York or that I was a bt, a returnee to the faith.

Refinement associated with higher education is a class marker that Hasidic women are conscious of and reject, because they are against most higher education for men and women. Simultaneously, however, some women and girls are ambivalent about the perceived sophistication of more modern women because they can obtain a more rigorous secular education. In their desire to be both Hasidic and to negotiate the secular world, some Hasidic women adjust their Hasidic English to be more or less Yiddish/Hasidic, depending on whom they are talking to. Esty explained how even Satmar girls, from whom Hasidic women I worked with try to distance themselves, code switch from their more Hasidic pronunciation of Yiddish/loshn-koydesh to what they perceive to be a more modern pronunciation, more generally a variant of Lithuanian pronunciation, when they interact with less Hasidic Jews. Esty explained:

> Satmar girls among themselves will say *paysekh* 'Passover', but as soon as they meet up with someone in a store, they say [in Hasidic English], "I want a *peysekh* outfit." They won't say, "I want a *paysekh* outfit."

These subtle distinctions in how a vowel is pronounced (peysekh vs. paysekh) marks differences in the religious practice and place of origin among observant Jewish women. Sounding more Hasidic means using a Central Yiddish dialect in Yiddish and loshn-koydesh. Central Yiddish contrasts to Lithuanian (Litvish) Yiddish, harkening back to nineteenth- and twentieth-century struggles between Hasidic Jews and Lithuanians Jews for religious authority. A number of Hasidic women I worked with said that Litvish Jewish Orthodoxy in postwar America has become "watered down" and is now understood as more modern.

When I asked further if Esty thought Satmar girls were embarrassed that they are so Hasidic, Esty did not see a conflict between being very Hasidic and wanting to negotiate the more modern world. She said:

> They [Satmar girls] don't want to have that backward, old-fashioned thing, and they're proud of their Hasidishness. They wouldn't give up those curly *peyes* 'sidecurls' for anything [i.e., they do not want their boys to look less Hasidic]. They're proud of their Hasidishness . . . but in the world at least, they want to appear that they're with it.

Esty claims that Satmar girls are proud of their religious stringency which they exhibit publicly in vowel use in Yiddish/loshn-koydesh and in their approval of boys' long side curls. Nevertheless, they still do not want to seem "backward or old-fashioned" when they are "in the world." According to Esty, even Satmar girls want to appear "with it" when they are in public places with other Orthodox Jews. Note that Esty, in her interaction with me, also uses a more Litvish pronunciation of the word for side curls, peyes—a more Hasidic pronunciation would be payes—perhaps evidence that Hasidic women are constantly assessing how Hasidic or modern an interlocutor is and trying to accommodate to that speaker. Esty concluded by emphasizing Hasidic women's desire to master secular knowledge and prestige without embracing it:

> It's that way with all of us. She's [the Satmar girl] like that to me, and me to somebody in a more modern school [where she teaches Hebrew Bible]. I'll also try to show that I'll know what you're talking about.

All Hasidic women, according to Esty, want to appear savvy to a Jewish woman who is a little more modern than they are. Esty told me that she felt embarrassed when it took her a few minutes to figure out what one of her more modern students meant when she told her she had just gone to "the Met" (the Metropolitan Museum of Art). As Esty said in Hasidic English to me—someone, perhaps, even beyond modern—"I'll also try to show that I'll know what you're talking about." This does not mean she would do anything that would actually make her less Hasidic and more modern, such as wearing more modern clothing or going to college. That would be considered "bummy," the local term for girls who actively are trying to become more modern, something that highlights the degrading implications of becoming less religiously stringent especially regarding one's clothing.[7] Instead, Esty and others try to be fluent in both Hasidic and more modern ways of talking by choosing to emphasize a vowel or using an English word, depending on whom she is talking with. This allows her to be fluent in the secular world but still reject being modern.

For children, boys and girls, any variation in their pronunciation of *loshn-koydesh* 'Hebrew-Aramaic' that deviates from family practice is the subject of adult scrutiny. According to Rifky, the loshn-koydesh of the Lithuanian-origin Orthodox Jews has fewer "Jewish-sounding" vowels. When a Litvish Jew, Rifky said, pronounces the Hebrew word for "holy" he says *kodesh* (with an [o] like the English /o/ of cone). A Hasidic Jew, Rifky pointed out, will say *koydesh* (with an [oy] like English /oy/ of boy). Rifky explained that the Hasidic pronunciation "sounds" much more Jewish, hypothesizing that, in postwar America, Litvish Jews were ashamed to sound too Jewish.

Some Hasidic children have even come to associate Litvish pronunciation with English. For example, Esty told me that, after her male cousin spent the summer in a Litvish camp, he asked his parents whether he could *davn* 'pray' in English. By this he meant that he wanted to say the Hebrew prayers using Litvish rather than Hasidic pronunciation. In young children, Hasidic adults find this vowel shifting amusing. However, adopting Litvish pronunciation is not amusing when children are older, as it offers insight into which kinds of Jews they are trying to emulate. Rifky told me that she knew many Hasidic girls in unaffiliated Hasidic schools who stopped saying *burikh* 'blessed' and began to say *borukh* instead once they entered high school. This was troubling, she suggested, because it meant that they were emulating more modern Jewish girls. She added that many Hasidic girls' schools now make explicit policy decisions about the kind of loshn-koydesh pronunciation they require, which tells potential families how modern they can expect the school to be, especially on the related issues of modesty and access to secular and religious knowledge.

Too Yiddish

When Hasidic women and girls cannot control how they speak—when they cannot fluently switch into more modern or more Hasidic Yiddish and English—they are called in English "backward," even "primitive." A joke I heard several times, told by more modern women, describes a Hungarian girl calquing a Yiddish word in the context of her attempts to speak English. Her limited knowledge of English, however, causes her to make a mistake. She translates *ayerneckhtn* 'the day before yesterday' as "egg-yesterday." The girl confused the separate words *ayer* 'egg' and *nekhtn* 'yesterday' with the word *ayernekhtn*. Similarly, Gitty made fun of how Satmar girls speak Hasidic English, suggesting that they could not control the influence of Yiddish in their English (phonological interference). She said, in the context of explaining how Hungarian girls are different from Bobover: "You know how Satmar talk, like [diz] (deez, meaning "this"), that's them." My tutor was remarking on her perception that Satmar girls cannot correctly pronounce English, because they have too much interference from Yiddish. They replace initial /th/ [ð] with [d] and lengthen the vowel (instead of /i/ of big, they use the /ee/ of feet). This makes them sound "funny" and "old-fashioned" and, I suggest, perhaps not like native-born North Americans. In contrast, third- and fourth-generation men and boys' Yiddish accents in English, as noted previously, are quite prestigious because their accent displays their absorption in the Jewish world of sacred learning.

In their attempts to be with it but not modern, teachers at Bnos Yisruel reject any attempts to speak Hasidic Yiddish in expanded contexts or speak a "purer" Yiddish, that is, without English influence. During recess among themselves the teachers generally spoke English, although they were encouraged by the vice principal to speak Yiddish. When some of the teachers in the upper grades attempted to speak Yiddish during recess, the lower-grade teachers were dismissive. One teacher sarcastically said, "Oh, those teachers on the floor above [the older grades], they're so special [a term that implies a voluntary heightened level of religious stringency]. They're speaking Yiddish." Similarly, when the "lunch lady" scolded Morah Chaya for using an English word in the context of speaking Hasidic Yiddish to her kindergarteners, the teacher grew annoyed. The lunch lady said to Morah Chaya, "You, from your family, say 'yummy-delicious'? You should say *geshmakt* 'delicious'." The teacher answered, "From my family, yes, we say 'yummy-delicious.'" References to Morah Chaya's family implied that they were "very Hasidish" for a Bobover family and should be using Yiddish without any English. Morah Chaya acknowledged her family's Hasidishness but denied that her Yiddish should be purged of any English; indeed, for Morah Chaya's family, religiosity is defined, in part, by the English fluency of the family's women and girls: they are with it, but not modern.

LEARNING HASIDIC FEMININITY

Hasidic girls' shift from Yiddish fluency is evidence of a divinely ordained gender hierarchy, where Hasidic male authority is tied to sacred study and Yiddish fluency, and women's role is to mediate the secular, English-speaking world for men. Hasidic men and boys comment on girls' use of language, complaining and teasing that it sounds, as one father said, "too American." Speaking English and sounding American locate Hasidic women and girls as less European, more distant than men from the idealized level of religiosity. Indeed, women and their involvement in the secular, material world are sometimes blamed by Hasidic religious leadership when hardships befall the community. For example, a young Orthodox teacher told me about the time a Hasidic child tragically died of an illness. The teacher attended a lecture soon after, where the influential rabbi delivering the lecture told his audience that the child's death had actually been caused by women's idle gossip (*loshn hure* 'evil talk') along with lax standards of modesty. The rabbi did not blame any particular person, but he suggested that women's general lack of vigilance led to this God-given punishment. I asked the teacher how the women around her responded. She said some women quietly grumbled that men always blamed them, but many also seemed to agree, saying that, in the future, they would be more vigilant over their bodies and words.

Hasidic women's involvement in the secular world makes it possible for men to study, but it also allows men to continuously assert the legitimacy of their authority because they more closely reproduce an imagined prewar European past. Again, this is somewhat ironic given the shift that has occurred among postwar Hasidim in North America: the Yiddish fluency that was associated especially with women in prewar Eastern Europe has today become symbolically associated with Hasidic males and their religious authenticity.

Hasidic women today often negatively assess men's English. When Hasidic women claim that their husbands can "barely speak English," however, they are not only laying claim to English as their own area of expertise, but they are also most likely emphasizing their own contributions to families in which the husband continues to study Torah, thanks to his wife's labor. Even girls' negative attitudes toward Yiddish-speaking, nebby Hasidic girls support, perhaps unintentionally, the authority of different Hasidic courts, each with its own standards for religious practice arbitrated by male leaders and practiced by male-headed households. When I brought up girls' rejection of Yiddish to mothers and teachers, they smiled, sighed, and often shrugged. Esty told me emphatically, "There's nothing wrong with English." Not only do women themselves share some of the girls' ambivalence to Yiddish as nebby, but the girls' shift ultimately, reproduces communal hierarchies of authority. When girls embrace English, they are reproducing how their own mothers talk, while giving truth to communal claims that their grandmothers were on a higher moral plane, as evidenced by their harder, less materialistic lives and their Yiddish fluency.

The distinctive Hasidic femininity of the women and girls I worked with offers a new way for them to reclaim the high moral level of past generations of Jewish women. By using language to exhibit fine-grained distinctions between observant Jewish women in North America, Hasidic women and girls suggest that they must become fluent in the secular world and its language in order to protect themselves from this North American generation's special challenges of comfort and economic success.[8] Hasidic girls and women transform some of the same criticisms that are often leveled at them by secular Jews and apply them to other Hasidic women and girls. They do not want to be like very Hasidic girls whom they consider "backward," "primitive," or "old-fashioned" because of how they sound and look. Nebby girls' lack of fluency in the secular world and its language ultimately limits and even embarrasses them when they interact with more modern observant Jewish women. And yet, although they admire more modern Jewish women, they still reject their religiosity as not stringent enough. They may speak like more modern women in some contexts and admire them for seeming sophisticated, but they would not wear the short, tighter skirts and long wigs that modern women do, nor would they consider, for example, getting a master's degree in speech therapy.

Earlier generations of Jewish immigrants were ashamed to sound like "greenhorns," just off the boat. They wanted to sound like Americans. In contrast, Hasidic women and girls I worked with want to be able to control how modern they sound when they interact with more modern women or even someone like me. This reveals a distinction between language and clothing, with language choice (between Yiddish and English and its varieties) a more problematic indicator of modern Jewish femininity than clothing or education. As Gitty told me, "There are plenty of *khushover* 'important' people who speak English," thus emphasizing that speaking English does not necessarily make a woman more modern. The emergence of Hasidic English as the language of Hasidic women and girls also complicates any direct link between English and being modern, making it increasingly acceptable for women and girls to speak English while at the same time reinscribing their positions in Hasidic hierarchies.

CHAPTER SIX

Ticket to Eden

A STORY GITTY ONCE TOLD ME about modesty (*tsnies*) reminded me that not all women think about the body and beauty, power and freedom, in the same way.[1] At age seventeen, Gitty told me, she went shopping with her mother and saw a beautiful matching skirt and top in gray and pink, her favorite color combination and one that complemented her dark hair and eyes. On closer inspection, however, she and her mother saw that the top had a low neckline that could not easily be altered. Her collarbone would have been exposed, which would have been immodest. Gitty remembered how much she had wanted that outfit, but she let her mother steer her to another rack to find something else. For Gitty, being modest meant having the discipline not to listen to her inclination for evil (*yaytser-hure*), the part of her that longed for the immodest outfit in the first place. Why, I wondered as I traveled home on the B train, would a young girl be willing to fight her inclination for evil when that evil was just a slight dip in a neckline? How could she see her own individualized struggle to be a more pious Jew in something so prosaic as choosing an outfit? And how had her mother brought her up to believe that subordinating her own tastes and desires to a set of religious rules was a worthy goal?

The focus of this chapter and the next is the everyday talk through which Hasidic girls learn to discipline their bodies, their voices, and their minds as they cross the threshold of girlhood to become modest Hasidic women. Hasidic adults spend a lot of energy teaching their daughters to be modest. In contrast to the ambivalent adult attention to girls' increasing use of Hasidic English after first grade, women are vigilant when girls pick up their skirts too high to jump rope, sneak a look at a forbidden secular book, or do not speak "nicely"—yelling or using "bad words"—regardless of which language they use. Communal authority figures, both men and women, engage in surveillance and gate-keeping practices to ensure that women and girls adhere to modesty standards or are severely sanctioned if they challenge them. In the high school homerooms of Bnos Yisruel, for example, every morning teachers walk up and down the aisles making sure that each girl is wearing appropriate stockings (no sheer or black stockings allowed). Repeatedly wearing the wrong stockings can be grounds for expulsion.

Modesty, however, goes beyond external surveillance and gate-keeping; Hasidic women's modesty has complex meanings not immediately apparent to outsiders.[2] Modesty practices are decidedly not about cultivating individual shyness or asceticism. The Hasidic women I met, for example, confounded my assumption that modesty included a particular temperament, such as passivity, although acting with restraint and what Rifky called "softness" is also valued as a quality of modesty. Nevertheless, many women, especially married women, were outgoing and assertive in their everyday lives, pushing to the front of lines, demanding service in stores. In fact, on our way out to go to the Bobover synagogue during a holiday, Mrs. Hirsch told Malky, her quiet teenage daughter, to help me push to the front of the women's section to see the rebbe because I did not seem "like a pusher." Sure enough, upon arriving, Malky aggressively shoved forward so that I got a glimpse of the rebbe amid the good-natured press of women.[3]

Dressing modestly also does not preclude being fashionable and attractive. For example, Hasidic wedding I attended, I looked around at the women dressed in pointy-toed high-heels and fitted, elegant black suits, some with lace or taffeta peeking out from hems. I was reminded then just how good modest Hasidic women could look. A Hasidic girl might be very *leybedik* 'lively', which is considered an inborn personality trait, dress in chic, expensive clothing, and still be very modest.

One meaning of modesty is an embodied language encompassing the body, dress, and language. As an interconnected set of signs and signifying practices, modesty includes clothing, especially stockings and skirt length; head-covering for married women, which are variations on hats, wigs, and kerchiefs (*tikhlekh*); comportment; speaking "nicely" in any language; and secular knowledge in books, magazines, and other media. Close communal attention to the seemingly mundane topics of, for example, whether a girl's stockings have a seam or whether a girl speaks in a modulated voice becomes part of the way girls perform where they and their families and their communities situate themselves in relation to Jewish Orthodoxy. When a girl calls too much attention to herself, by wearing a very bright color, for example, or wearing a skirt that is the wrong length, she may be perceived as challenging authority.

At the same time modesty is more than a text inscribed on bodies and read by other Jews for information about levels of religious stringency. Modesty is also a disciplinary practice that cultivates religious desires and protects against secular dreams. Modesty integrates language, material culture, and the body under a semiotic ideology, a cultural and religious belief about the nature of signs (Keane 2007);[4] as

I have argued, the sign for sacred languages like loshn-koydesh is not arbitrarily related to its referent but is God-given. This influences cultural beliefs about and opportunities for transforming other non-sacred languages such as Hasidic Yiddish and Hasidic English. Similarly I suggest here that the seemingly arbitrary embodied signs and practices that make up modesty are regularly transformed into divinely intended means for training pious Jewish bodies, language, and minds. The signs and practices of modesty teach girls that they need not reject much that is attractive from the secular world. Instead, the secular world can become part of the embodied repertoire that trains women and girls to discipline their wills and desires in order to participate in one particular version of North American Hasidic femininity.

This chapter discusses the ways in which Hasidic women attempt to teach girls to be *willing* to discipline individual desires that do not conform to modesty standards set by familial and communal authorities. Learning modesty goes beyond disciplining desires, however. The women and girls I met also talk about wanting to "look good," be "with it," and be literate both in their religious education and the secular world. These desires are not necessarily in conflict. A goal for this generation of Hasidic girls and their mothers is to successfully participate in the embodied discipline of modesty which, girls are taught, need not preclude being with it, looking good, and being knowledgeable about the world around them.

A central means by which girls come to desire to be modest and with it is through adults' characterizations of Gentiles, secular North Americans, and other Jewish Orthodox women.[5] In their everyday interactions, Hasidic women describe the innate, regal distinction of Jewish women compared to Gentiles. Women also show girls how to appropriate and give new meaning to "secular American" sensibilities of beauty, language, consumption, and realms of knowledge. Like other religious practices, moreover, modesty may have many legitimate interpretations, and so Hasidic girls I worked with must learn to negotiate hierarchies of Jewish piety. These women claimed that being with it and modest was the most appropriate femininity for the dangers surrounding them in contemporary Brooklyn.

The disciplining of Hasidic women's and girls' bodies and minds is important to their ongoing construction of an alternative religious modernity.[6] Hasidic women are engaged in an ethical struggle to change the meaning of secular materiality and consumption, a task that is the special responsibility of women. Their efforts to collapse distinctions between materiality and spirituality through the disciplines of modesty contrast with a modern (and underlying Protestant) semiotic ideology that Keane (2007:6) describes, where spirituality is achieved through a denial of materiality. The aim for Hasidic women and girls is to be able to discipline their bodies and desires, to use their moral autonomy to participate in and transform the material world. Vanity, adornment, consumption, and secular knowledge are not denied, but, as Rifky suggested earlier, must be "channeled," like the rest of the material world, and made to serve Hasidic goals of community building and redemption. In this way, authority, as Asad (1993:201) notes, is understood as a "predisposition of the embodied self" rather than ideologically justified coercion. Many women told me that their modesty is as important as men's study of Torah for bringing God's rewards in the afterlife. As Esty put it, "*Tsnies* is a woman's ticket to the Garden of Eden"—that is, Paradise.

Men's and Women's Modesty

The concept of modesty centers on constraining the body for men and women, adults and children. Modesty can be understood as part of the broader Hasidic project of sanctifying the material world by bracketing bodily functions within religious practice (see chapter 2). Tsnies for both males and females becomes increasingly important and mandatory as children reach the age of bar/bas-mitsve (age thirteen and twelve for boys and girls, respectively), when they become responsible by Jewish law for fulfilling all the Jewish commandments.

Male Modesty

Men's modesty practices focus on controlling and sacralizing bodily functions in order to keep the mind pure for Torah study. In the *Code of Jewish Law*[7] this includes, for example, wearing a sash (*gartl*) around the waist to separate the lower parts of the body from the upper parts (Ganzfried 1996:12), going to the bathroom and getting dressed in ways that do not expose the body or incite lustful thoughts that might somehow contaminate one during the study of Torah (ibid., 5–6), and purifying oneself in a ritual bath (*mikve*) (Heilman 2000). In order to minimize "sinful thoughts" in themselves or others, males are also instructed in the *Code of Jewish Law* to avoid, among other things, being alone with a woman, hearing a woman sing, and "flaunt[ing]" love between husband and wife (Ganzfried 1996:20–21).

A central way that Hasidic men's modesty is maintained is through distinctive dress codes. Historically most Jewish men have had distinctive dress from non-Jews. However, from the mid-nineteenth century, when many European Jews were offered citizenship, Jewish men's dress, excluding most Hasidim, began to be increasingly influenced by European dress. In some contexts, such as tsarist Russia, all Jewish men were legally forced to adopt more European clothing, whereas in Germany or Poland, for example, some Jews willingly began to dress more like Europeans. Hasidic Jews, in contrast, continued to wear clothing, where allowed, in order to distinguish themselves from other Jews and Europeans, investing their distinctive styles of clothing with mystical significance.

Similarly Hasidic men's clothing in Boro Park today publicly marks Hasidic males as different from those around them. A range of styles is seen in Hasidic male uniforms, with variations regarding jacket (*bekeshe*), white shirts, pants, socks, shoes, hat, beard, and side curls that generally indicate affiliation with a particular Hasidic circle (see Kamen 1985; Poll 1962:65–66). For example, Hungarian Hasidic men most often tuck their pants into white kneesocks and wear slip-on shoes (*vase zokn in shikh*). Most Hasidic men wear a large velvet yarmulke and, on weekdays, a brimmed hat of various shapes, such as a high flat velvet hat or a fedora that is "bent down" or "bent up" depending on the Hasidic circle. Hasidic men's clothing keeps men visible in diaspora and marks differences between them

Perhaps because they have a uniform of sorts, much less attention is paid to boys' modesty than to girls'. Based on my observations of the boys' nursery and kindergarten in Bnei Yisruel and in a number of Hasidic homes, I rarely heard talk about male modesty. Some boys even wear shorts and short-sleeved shirts until they reach bar-mitsve age, at which time they begin to wear clothing similar to that of their fathers. Girls' modesty is more regulated than boys', because, as a clerk in a Hasidic store explained, "they have so much more to worry about."

Female Modesty

In contrast to Hasidic men, Hasidic women and girls, since the nineteenth century, have worn European clothing with one stipulation: it must be appropriately modest.[8] Married Jewish women are obligated to cover their hair with a head-covering, a kerchief, hat or, since the eighteenth century, a wig. Rabbis initially rejected wigs as a "novelty" but later allowed them in the hopes that the innovative wig option would encourage married women to continue to cover their hair, something many were beginning to reject (Encyclopedia Judaica 1972, cited in Goldman Carrel 1999:167–168).

The textual basis for women's modesty is found in the *Code of Jewish Law,* but the laws are general and require rabbinic interpretation. The *Code* includes passages, for example, which note that a married woman's hair must be covered (Ganzfried 1996:11–12) and that a woman must keep covered "most of her body that is usually covered" (ibid., 11). Most observant Jews agree that the *ervah* 'erotic' parts include hair for married women, collarbones, elbows, shoulders, thighs, and knees. Also, most Hasidic women do not wear very bright colors so as not to draw attention.

Despite agreement over these general features of modesty, the exact length, material, or color of a skirt, and whether a woman covers her hair with a wig, kerchief, or a wig and a hat, or wears makeup— all are part of the broader and ongoing construction of male authority in families and in terms of rabbinic leadership. Concern over Hasidic women's modesty comes from the peak of communal power: the rebbe, who makes decrees regarding communal standards of female modesty and posts them on the streets of Brooklyn, to little girls who remind one another to sit modestly even at home on the sofa, simply by warning, "Tsnies!"

The greater scrutiny of Hasidic women's modesty is a feature of women's obligation to protect men who study Torah. I heard repeatedly that women have more control over their bodies and their desires than men. Many women told me that females' control over their physical desires was proof that they were inherently more "spiritual" than men. Because of this, women are obliged to protect men from the potential for arousal so that men can study Torah with pure hearts, which benefits the entire community. Gitty told me, for example, that it is her responsibility to cross the street or wait if she sees a young Torah scholar (*bukher*) walking down the same street. The streets, she told me, "belong to the men." It is up to her, Gitty explained, to make sure that the Torah scholar is not distracted by her passing him, or even, as he casts his eyes modestly down, by hearing the sound of her pumps as she goes by. The very click-clacking of a woman's heels on the pavement may be provocative to a sheltered Torah scholar.[9]

Signs of Modesty: Very Hasidic, Modern, and Everything In-Between

Modesty is a form of gendered social propriety where different Hasidic groups at different times and in different places create what they see as the most authentic set of modest signs and signifying practices. In the climate of heightened stringency that defines Hasidic Judaism today, I heard a number of Bobover little girls proudly tell their mothers that they had finally learned to wriggle into a fresh set of clothing underneath their nightgown without exposing their bodies at all. A goal for girls is never to show their naked bodies, even when it is just them and God behind a closed door. Similarly, girls' skirts have to be just the right length. Most Hasidic teachers at Bnos Yisruel and the students' mothers wear calf-length skirts. Mrs. Silver once told her students that, of course, skirts that are too short (exposing the knee) are immodest. Girls might then think that the longer the skirt, the more modest it is, but that is not the case. A skirt that is too long, Mrs. Silver told the girls, will make people stare, and looking conspicuous is never modest. Skirts, Mrs. Silver emphasized, must be a "normal" length, that is, a length that is approved by one's family and the wider community.

Standards for women's modesty are established by male religious leadership. The rebbe of each sect and his male advisers provide continual guidance to school administrators, teachers, and parents on every aspect of modesty. The continuity across home and school ensures that, as girls grow up, they hear a relatively coherent message about the expectations for modesty from both institutional authorities and their own families. For unaffiliated Hasidic Jews, families choose a girl's school partly by matching the family's level of religious stringency, including standards for modesty, with that of the school.

Material signs of modesty—stockings, hats, wigs, skirt length, and skirt material—are a semiotic language that locates for other observant Jews where a girl and her family and, if applicable, her Hasidic circle position themselves in terms of Orthodox religiosity. The "very Hasidic" (*zayer khsidish*) are at one end of a spectrum of Orthodoxy and the most modern, but still observant, are at the other. Many subtle variations are seen within these two extremes. Very Hasidic girls are most often Hungarian Hasidic Jews, considered by many to be the most stringently observant and isolated from North American life, and, as discussed earlier, who speak the most Hasidic Yiddish. These women have a clothing aesthetic that is most distinct from mainstream fashions. Other Hasidic women I met called this a "European look," again evoking an idealized prewar European past. Very Hasidic girls wear opaque, seamed stockings and slips, full A-line skirts of heavy material with matching vests or jackets, feminine blouses, gold or silver jewelry, and little or no makeup. At marriage, very Hasidic women shave their heads and wear a silk kerchief (*tikhl*) or a kerchief with a little false hair showing (*shpitsl* or a front) or a rolled-up piece of brown material, sometimes padded, tucked into the front of the kerchief to stand in for hair.[10]

More modern women, in contrast to the very Hasidic, have a different semiotic language of modesty. Generally, upon marriage, they wear a hat, a snood (a crocheted bag in which the hair is placed), or a kerchief that shows some of their own hair. Alternatively, they may wear expensive long, flowing wigs of real human hair. They also may wear kneesocks instead of stockings or colored and sheer stockings. Their skirts are either very long or tight and short (just grazing the knee) and may even have slits in them. These women do not shave their hair at marriage, although they always cover it, and they often wear makeup.

The language of modest signs is relative. Wigs, for example, have an incredible range, from short, synthetic styles to combinations of synthetic and human hair to long wigs of human hair (see also Goldman Carrel 1999). There is also a huge variety of hats and turbans either to cover wigs or to use instead of a wig, covering some or most of a woman's hair. Similarly, the seamless, opaque stockings that might seem more modern to a Hasidic woman in Williamsburg, Brooklyn, may look very Hasidic to a more modern woman in Flatbush, Brooklyn (a predominantly Litvish neighborhood).

Although Hasidic men make the official rulings on women's modest behavior and dress, Hasidic women interpret the possible variations in modesty by enforcing particular stances that a family or institution will take. Chani, a teacher in the Bobover boys' nursery school, for example, told me that her twelve-year-old daughter once modeled a denim skirt for her father, asking if he would allow her to wear it outside. He looked her over and said, "A nice dark skirt, long enough, sure, no problem." He was unaware, the teacher told me, laughing, that denim is considered modern because it is the material of the jeans Gentiles wear. When the young girl displayed her skirt for her mother, Chani told her emphatically that she was not allowed to wear the denim skirt. Her daughter said, defensively, "But _Totty_ 'Daddy' said it was all right," at which Chani explained to her husband that denim was too modern for their family. Once he understood he agreed with Chani, and their daughter did not wear the skirt.

In a family, a woman usually decides the appropriate way to dress modestly based on her husband's family's practices, which ideally should also match how she was brought up. At times, however, a husband weighs in on his wife's fashion choice, at which point his wife usually acquiesces. For example, when Esty bought a new pair of square, open-toed shoes with chunky heels, her husband asked her to return them. Esty showed me the shoes and asked my opinion. The shoes looked sexy to me, and I asked if they were immodest because her toes were exposed. Esty chuckled, and said no, her husband

A sample of wig styles. Beryl Goldberg, photographer. Reprinted with permission from Georgie's, Boro Park.

Hasidic women's hats to be worn on top of wigs. Beryl Goldberg, photographer. Reprinted with permission from The Blue Rose, Boro Park.

thought that the shoes were not feminine enough; many husbands were complaining that year about the current fashion of square-toed, chunky-heeled shoes, claiming it was hard to tell if the shoes were for men or women. Indeed, some Hasidic men, as noted, wear slip-on shoes that do resemble these women's shoes. Esty agreed with her husband and returned the shoes.

My own unfamiliarity with the ways that embodied signs of modesty were part of social and religious propriety made any exposure of my body feel improper, almost shameful. When I went swimming with Rifky in the country, I had to rethink my understanding of modesty. The bungalow colony where Rifky spent her summers had a pool with gender-segregated hours. I brought my swimsuit at her suggestion, and she gave me a long robe, bathing cap, and turban to wear on the way to the pool. Once there, however, despite the inviting water and her girls' screams of delight as they dived in, I had trouble taking off my robe. I had spent so much time with Hasidic women and girls anxiously trying to dress modestly, trying to look like other women and fit in, that I even had a recurring dream. In the dream I arrived in Boro Park only to realize that I had forgotten to wear my hat or had worn jeans. The thought of wearing a bathing suit, even my relatively modest one-piece suit, was horrifying to me. Then Rifky said, "Don't be so shy, Ayala. Come on in."

My own "shyness," I believe, was the result of not having any sense of the cultural propriety of modesty. Here at a pool for other modest Hasidic women and girls, it was culturally and religiously appropriate to be in a bathing suit as long as one's family's modesty practices were observed. At Rifky's pool there was a diversity of swimsuits though definitely no bikinis. A number of women and girls dressed in a *shvim-klayd* (a sleeveless, dropped-waist swim dress); others wore a bathing suit under a T-shirt; and still others wore one-piece suits. Married women wore bathing caps instead of their wigs and hats. I was the only one who had no sense of propriety about how exposed my body should be, because I was not attached to any group with whom I shared interpretations of modesty. Eventually I did get over my shyness and enjoyed a swim.

BEING SPECIAL VERSUS BEING HORRIBLE

To their daughters, Hasidic women defined becoming a "big girl" as having an increasingly autonomous desire to fit into the family's modesty conventions. These include not only material signs but also modest comportment, language, and exposure to secular knowledge. Girls who tried to participate in adult forms of modesty, especially by individual choice, were publicly praised as "special," whereas girls who did not put modesty first were scolded and labeled "horrible" or "crazy." One day a first-grader with short brown hair and big brown eyes, Shayndie, raised her hand and shyly told Mrs. Silver that she had asked her mother if she could wear tights that summer instead of kneesocks. Her family's practice was to allow girls to wear kneesocks in the summer (to be cooler) until they were in second grade, at which time they would have to wear tights year-round. Shayndie's mother had happily agreed and bought her daughter new tights. Mrs. Silver told the class, "Wow! That is such a special story that I'm going to share it with the principal." She retold the story to the class, as Shayndie, a quiet girl, beamed from her seat. "Special," as I noted, has an idiomatic Hasidic meaning: an unusual and admirable willingness to take on additional levels of observance. In publicly praising Shayndie's desire to go beyond the dispensation that her age allowed according to her family (wearing kneesocks instead of tights), Mrs. Silver linked individual choice and responsibility for disciplining the body with being "special." Shayndie was "special," because she had chosen to take on a level of modesty that she was not yet obliged to follow. She had also asked her mother "nicely" if she could wear tights. Changing practices of modesty without getting permission from an authority, as I discuss later, is considered selfish and immature.

When girls comport themselves in an immodest way, they are quickly disciplined by an adult who often expresses shock and anger at the behavior. During recess, for example, first-graders often played a jump-rope game called Ching-Chang, where they progressively raised the rope higher and higher each turn, to the "first floor, second floor," and so on. To avoid getting caught in the rope, a number of girls held their skirts up around their knees. Mrs. Silver saw this one day, stopped the game, and chastised the girls:

> *S'iz du a* _style_ *ven men shpilt Ching-Chang, me haybt ouf de klayd biz* _on_ _top_, *me halt es azoy in me* _jump_. *Val oyb nisht, vert men* _out_. *S'iz nisht emes . . . val de Ching-Chang iz* _all the way by de floor._

There's a style when you play Ching-Chang. You pick up your skirt to the top, you hold it like this and jump. Because if not, you'll be out. That's not true . . . because the Ching-Chang is on the floor.

The students interrupted Mrs. Silver and contradicted her: "*Ober _by second and third floor, ya_!*" (But by second and third floor, yes!). They meant that when the rope was lifted higher, a girl's skirt actually could get caught in the rope if she did not pick it up. Mrs. Silver became angry:

So by second floor, in by third floor both nisht, ok? In oyb ya, kenst nisht shpiln yene game val s'iz nishdu kan ayn excuse ouftsehaybn a klayd biz azoy [putting her hand on her thighs]. *Terrible! . . . Horrible! . . . S'iz a mishegas, s'iz a mishegas, s'iz a mishegas . . . Dus iz nisht shayn . . . Se makht nisht kan sense. Se miz indz zan tsniesdik ven me shpilt, ven me zitst, ven me gayt, ven me loyft, ale mul miz men gedenkn . . . in afile ven ikh zey nisht, afile ven ets iz in de country, s'iz nishtu aza zakh az me haybt ouf de klayd.*

So at the second floor and the third floor, both not, ok? And if yes, then you can't play that game because there is no excuse for picking your skirt up to here [putting her hand on her thighs.] Terrible! . . . Horrible! . . . It's crazy, it's crazy, it's crazy . . . It's not nice . . . It doesn't make sense. You have to be modest when you play, when you sit, when you walk, when you run. You always have to remember . . . and even if I don't see you, even when you're in the country, there's no such thing as picking up your skirt.

Mrs. Silver's outraged reaction to the girls' game reiterates the meanings and practice of modesty. Effectively, girls have to sacrifice a game if it requires them to behave immodestly. Mrs. Silver describes immodest behavior as "crazy, horrible, terrible, senseless, and not nice." She emphasizes that modest behavior is the responsibility of each individual girl who has to have the "sense" for putting modesty above all other personal desires. Even when Mrs. Silver is not there to watch the girls, it is up to them to be modest, because God is always watching. This is similar to the message that Mrs. Silver and other teachers told girls about prayer, "You don't pray to the teacher. You pray to God, and God is everywhere."

In contrast to school, where immodest behavior is constantly commented upon, at home modest comportment can be a little more relaxed. Some teachers told me, for example, that they wore kneesocks at home or in the country. One afternoon at the Klein's house, the oldest daughter, Yehudis, who was seven, sat on a chair with her legs drawn up beneath her. She was wearing thigh-highs, a compromise between tights and kneesocks for the warmer months common among Bobover girls, so her underwear was on display to her mother, Raizy, and to me. Her mother tried to pull her skirt over her knees, and said, "Yehudis, tsnies," but then she laughed, as did Yehudis, and allowed her to stay as she was. Raizy turned to me and said, "I was just like her when I was a girl. A tomboy. But somehow when I turned seventeen, I just changed." In contrast to North American evocations of the tomboy who desires boys as playmates, as well as the clothing and activities which are culturally the realm of boys, a Hasidic tomboy is a girl who is not very concerned with modesty in contexts where it is permissible to be more lax. As girls grow up, however, they must prepare themselves to put the discipline of modesty above any other desires.

Fulfillment of modesty practices is a process, and girls are given some latitude for ignorance, errors, forgetfulness, or defiance, especially at home. Teaching young girls to be modest is similar to the training that Hasidic girls receive in other areas of religious practice. As a mother told me, "Keep them doing it until it becomes second nature." From a very young age, mothers pull their daughters' dresses over their knees when they sit down, teachers remind girls not to sit too *bakveym* 'comfortably' (i.e., sprawled out) at their desks, and older girls constantly remind their sisters not to let their skirts ride up as they relax by saying, reprovingly, "Tsnies!" In addition to the rote training in modesty that occurs starting at age three, Hasidic women elaborate for girls how Jews are different from Gentiles, creating the desire to be a Jewish woman and the fear of resembling an uncontrolled Gentile.

Jews and Gentiles

Anthropologist Tamar El-Or (1994:145) suggests that, for Ger Hasidic women in Israel, Gentiles are outside the sphere of Jewish social responsibility and can effectively be ignored as irrelevant. In North America, however, Gentiles cannot be ignored. In some ways Gentiles and their immodest ways sustain and enable Hasidic women's claims to superiority and truth. Gentiles—their bodies, behavior, and ways of speaking—are a continual warning of how *not* to be (Kulick and Schieffelin 2004). Gentiles and the fear they inspire, particularly in children, can be a powerful way to socialize the desire to be different. The embodied practices of modesty provide a public display of that difference in the diversity of New York City.

One day, while reminding her students about the importance of being modest, Mrs. Silver illustrated with a story, translated here from her Hasidic Yiddish: She had seen a Jewish man studying Torah on the subway. The door opened and a group of girls came in. "Jewish?" A student interrupted. "He couldn't tell," Mrs. Silver responded. The girls had long hair "just like a goy." "Loose hair?" Another student asked. Mrs. Silver replied, "Yes, loose hair, and they were screaming just like a goy." The Jewish man "couldn't tell the difference" (i.e., if the girls were Jewish or Gentile). Mrs. Silver reminded her students, "We always have to be careful. We always have to remember that we are Jews."

In Mrs. Silver's story, the ultimate authority, the Torah-studying male, was unable to distinguish if the girls on the train were Jewish; their signs (hair) and signifying practices (the embodied act of speech, as well as their implicit use of English) were not marked as Jewish enough. As Mrs. Silver reminded the girls, "We always have to be careful." Implicit in this statement is the warning that girls who do not act or talk with a certain refinement may breach, or at least brush up against, the defining boundary between Jews and Gentiles.

Comportment

Observing, imagining, and theorizing about what defines Gentile bodies and comportment by comparison defines modest Jewish behavior for girls. For example, when preschool girls in Bnos Yisruel were taught the biblical story of Jacob and Esau, their teacher, Morah Chaya, presented the narrative as an allegory for two kinds of people, the "Jacob type" and the "Esau type," that is, Jews and Gentiles. Morah Chaya told them that because Esau was greedy and impatient, he lost his inheritance to his wise younger brother, Jacob. An arts-and-crafts project followed. The girls were told to draw Jacob and Esau based on the teacher's descriptions of them, that Jacob is a pious, Torah-loving Jew and Esau is a wild man covered in curly red hair. Inevitably the girls all drew the same images: Jacob was depicted as a Hasidic male, complete with long side curls, black and white clothing, and a tall black hat, and Esau resembled a monkey-like figure, unclothed and covered with red fur.

Hasidic perceptions of Gentiles, as noted, draw on religious beliefs in a hierarchy of peoples, a distinctive Jewish soul, and racist discourse. Hasidic children observe their Gentile neighbors carefully, even, as the Gross children once did, running to their balcony to observe a Gentile couple arguing in the neighboring backyard below. "Come see," the children cried, "The goyim are fighting!" Another time eight-year-old Chaim Gross leaned over the railing of his balcony, eyeing his Gentile neighbor in her garden. Why, he wondered, did she have such a nice *yidish punim* 'Jewish face'? Although he was unable to explain further when I asked, Chaim seemed to be suggesting that a Jewish soul actually shapes physiognomy, a merging of North American notions of racialized biology and religious belief in the soul. He was puzzled, as are other Hasidic children when they cannot tell by a face or behavior who is a Jew and who a Gentile, as they have learned that the physical body is a diagnostic of the Jewish soul. When I questioned Rifky about this, she said that in public, she too, always tries to ascertain who "looks *yidish*" 'Jewish.' Whenever she sees a girl who dresses or talks "nicely," she wonders if perhaps she had a Jewish relative unbeknownst to her or if she is just one of the "good goyim." Embodied signs of Jewishness in a Gentile need to be explained, because, for Hasidic children and women, race and religion, body and soul, shape each other. Rifky even admitted, unapologetically, that Jews and their ideas about being God's chosen nation is "a little racist." She continued: "But the fact is that the Jewish *neshume* 'soul' is just different [from the Gentile soul]."

The Jewish soul and its distinction are on display for many Hasidic women and children on the streets of Brooklyn. On a visit at Rifky's house, when I asked her about differences between Jews and Gentiles, she gestured out the window to the local public junior high school across the street.

> Take a look at dismissal. I mean, it's like animals out of the zoo. I mean, so vulgar and so crass and so violent and so cracked up and so nutty. The language that you hear, and the way these boys and girls are carrying on, little *shtinkers* 'stinkers'. I can't imagine my daughter [acting like that]. And they're busy, this one's dissing that one and that one's dissing that one, and they're breaking up, and they're hanging out with dirty language and everything. So us being fine and nice, makes us so much more, what's the word? So much better, so much more decent, so much more lofty, I mean this [a Gentile child] is like an animal by extension.

Despite claims such as Rifky's, that Gentiles are more like animals and are not as "decent" or "lofty" as Jews, I want to emphasize that these differences are not only the result of an innate Jewish soul. Rather, Jews' willingness to discipline and nurture that soul through religious practice creates the embodied differences between Jews and Gentiles. Rifky, on another occasion, emphasized distinctive Hasidic ideas about race, religion, and discipline:

> What differentiates creatures from each other is the level of self-control and of niceness. When you're finer, you're better bred, and if you're vulgar, you're more animalistic. So there is such a thing that a Jewish boy or a Jewish girl is like a *ben-meylekh* 'son of a king' or the chosen nation. We're better than the goyim . . . You're more aristocratic. It's about decency. It's about being a mentsh more than the goyim.

In issues of modesty, Hasidic women tell girls, Gentiles just cannot muster the strength to control their immodest desires, even if they want to. For example, in the context of reminding girls that no matter the weather they had to dress modestly, Mrs. Silver imagined Gentiles' reactions, their English comments, to seeing modest Hasidic girls on the streets of Boro Park.

> Oh, who are those girls? They look so special! *Goyim zeyen oukh. Afile zay visn az zay tien epes vus iz nisht azoy shayn. Vil zayer yaytser-hure redn tse zay, "Oh, ti es, far vus darfsti tin mitsves? Far vus darfsti zan tsniesdik?"*

> Oh, who are those girls? They look so special! Gentiles see too. Even they know that they are doing something that isn't nice. Their evil inclination speaks to them, "Oh, do it. What do you need to follow the commandments for? What do you need to be modest for?"

Gentiles are a frightening, ever-present reminder of the consequences for those who do not fight against their inclination for evil, who do not exercise self-control and cultivate their Jewish souls. Jewish girls have the Torah, reminded Mrs. Silver, which gives them the strength to fight against their evil inclination. Similarly anthropologist Jerome Mintz (1968:65) describes a Hasidic man who tells his son to follow ritual behavior or "he is a goy." The Hasid continued: "That's the worst thing in the world. His [son's] worst fear is he's going to be goy."

The disciplined behavior of Hasidic women and girls in a community of like-minded Jews nurtures and protects the innate Jewish soul, creating the definitive features of Hasidic femininity: refinement (*aydl-kayt*) and "niceness." Rifky describes being refined as "a softness, a purity, an innocence." Refinement comes out of being protected from what so many women described, pejoratively, as "today's world." The notion of refinement is also, I believe, related to evocations of life in prewar Eastern Europe as a simpler, purer time when women and girls especially were not tempted as they are today by materialism and wealth. The refined behavior of Jewish women and girls emphasizes their continuity with an imagined past.

Refinement also refers to the way that many Hasidic women portray themselves as royalty, not the mainstream, self-critical term "Jewish American Princesses," but real princesses who inherit royalty through bloodlines and who willingly discipline themselves to look and behave regally. In Morah Chaya's kindergarten class, an arts-and-crafts project had preschoolers making paper crowns with the words *tsnies iz man kroyn* (modesty is my crown), stenciled across the front. Morah Chaya told the girls that their Jewish souls made them royal, and she reminded them to always walk as if they had crowns on their heads to remind the world that they are the real princesses.

Speaking Nicely

Hasidic women compare Jewish and Gentile ways of speaking, just as they compare Jewish and Gentiles' bodies and comportment.[11] Speech in this context is understood as a bodily act, part of a broader repertoire of embodied modesty. As discussed in the previous chapter, Hasidic Yiddish is considered a more refined, nicer language, although most women and girls use Hasidic English. But no matter what language is used, Rifky told me, part of Jewish upbringing includes teaching boys and girls that the *way* they speak—word choice, volume, tone, and politeness—is what makes them distinct as Jews:

> And speech is a form of action, really, it goes into the category of being a good Jew and being a mentsh, a human being . . . You know, understanding you don't use certain language, you don't yell like that, you don't etc, etc. . . . But more or less it's part of the whole thing of khinekh, Jewish education, khinekh of children and of self that, it's a certain sense of refinement, just like you refine your speech, you refine your action, you're more caring, considerate, good, etc, etc. . . . You'll see different people that they'll talk differently, and you see that it reflects their inside.

Just as learning to discipline the body produces particular forms of Hasidic femininity, girls must learn to understand that the way they speak reflects and cultivates their Jewish souls. The concepts of niceness and refinement, valued in boys and girls, but especially girls, include the importance of self-control, restraint, softness, and discretion in everyday talk. Caregivers contrast refined speech with "street language," the language of Gentiles. Street language is *grobe* 'vulgar' language that includes expletives and expressions that might hurt the feelings of others, and also coarse expressive behavior such as screaming or yelling. This kind of speech would not be found in a Hasidic home, a number of women told me.

Mothers and teachers draw attention to the ways that Gentiles speak in the shared space of the neighborhood in order to clarify how Jews are different. For example, one summer day in a Boro Park playground Raizy and her son, Shimmy, overheard a boy yell at another child, "You're stupid. I hate you. Shut up. You're not my friend." The boy was in his bathing suit and not wearing a yarmulke, and so, by

Boro Park standards, it could be assumed that he was a Gentile. Shimmy did not know what to make of this. He looked at his mother and smiled uncomfortably. His mother quickly responded, "Is that nice? *Azoy me redt? S'iz shayn tse redn azoy?*" (Is that how you talk? Is it nice to talk like that?). Shimmy stopped smiling and shook his head. Raizy used the Gentile boy's speech as a living example of how not to behave as a Jew.

Hasidic adults find certain words particularly objectionable because of their idiomatic Hasidic meaning, which children playing in peer groups can use as provocative attention getters. Two common examples include potty talk like "tushy" and the more serious *meshigene* 'crazy' or *tsedrayte* 'warped', both implying a mental deficiency. If someone in a family is a *meshigener*, or "not all there," that person casts suspicion on the entire genetic line of the family, discussed further in the next chapter. At the Klein's house one day Shimmy was playing with a group of boys and girls from his building, ages three to eight. He repeatedly said "tushy" and "meshigene," which made all the children laugh, but within a few minutes his older sister Yehudis, who had been laughing, too, left to tell her mother, who put a quick stop to their playing. Similarly, one of the first-graders told me that mishigene was a *miese vort* 'ugly word' after another student had used it. Mothers and teachers ask boys and girls to rephrase their language and say what they want to say in a *shayne veyg* 'nice way'. Rifky explained how she reminds and instructs her young daughters to speak nicely:

> At a young age it's really reminder and drilling in, *me redt nisht azoy, di kenst es zugn in a shayne veyg*? (We don't talk like that. Can you say it in a nice way?) There's no reason why not. *Di kenst zugn* this way. (You can say it this way.) Why do you have to say it like that? And it's really constant repetition, and I think as they'll get older they'll have that certain discretion of why this, yes, and this not.

Of course, parents of many different backgrounds chastise their children if they curse or are rude, scream or hurt others' feelings. Children's bad language can negatively reflect on themselves, their parents, and their upbringing. For Hasidic women, however, language is a reflection of more than that; it reflects the soul and actually helps inherent Jewish traits to blossom, such as compassion, charity, and a desire to follow the commandments.

Hasidic mothers remind their sons and daughters of this if children use language they associate with Gentiles. Raizy told me that one day she heard her son Shimmy say a bad word. When I pressed her to explain, she told me he had said the "f-word." Raizy was shocked but saw that Shimmy thought it merely meant stupid or silly. She asked where he had learned it, and he said that when he and his friend had been playing the game *shaygets* (young Gentile male), his friend had used the word. This game is similar to the North American game of cops and robbers, but here the scenario is Gentiles versus Jews. The *shaygets*, an iconic evil figure, must be beaten by Jews even in child's play.

Raizy remarked that Shimmy's friend must live on the outskirts of Boro Park, because that kind of language comes from playing in "the street," not the Jewish streets of Boro Park but on the city streets dominated by Gentiles. She told her son, "Just like we have to watch what we put in our mouths when we eat, we have to watch what comes out of our mouths [when we speak]. That is why *hashem* 'God' gave us two closings for our mouths, the lips and the teeth. We have to be very careful not to use ekhy, yucky, language. It's not who we are." Shimmy pointed out that we only have one covering on our eyes. "That's right," she said, "we can close our eyes and that's enough. But talking is very important because we can really hurt someone by what we say."

Disciplining Secular Materialism and Knowledge

A key task for Hasidic girls, as I pointed out, is to discipline their minds, their language, and their bodies so as to be able to engage with knowledge and material culture from the secular sphere, while rejecting anything that cannot be made to serve Hasidic goals. This is socialized early on as mothers, teachers, and relatives teach girls how to transform secular media, objects, and forms of consumption for Hasidic purposes. Hasidic adults also censor secular objects or media in order to protect girls' minds until they can protect themselves.

Jewish Princesses and Secular Fashion

Viewpoints vary as to how Jewish women should most appropriately participate in secular forms of consumption and fashion. The refinement (*aydlkayt*) attributed to Jewish women, as noted, compares Jewish women to royalty. Some Hasidic women suggested to me that Jewish women's "royal souls" require or seek out expensive finery. These souls potentially can transform materialistic desires into an appropriate form of adornment for a Jewish woman. When I asked Rifky why so many Hasidic women emphasize "looking good," she said, "I think my mother would say we're *faynshmekers* 'connoisseurs', you know, we have a certain fineness in our *neshume* 'soul' so we drift to the finer things in this world." Jewish women, according to this theory, are drawn to expensive clothes and jewelry because their very souls demand it.

Goldman Carrel (1993:92) calls this a "discourse of royalty" evident in the advertisements for women's clothing and wigs in Boro Park, including, for example, a picture of a Hasidic bride who is "crowned with royalty" in the ad copy of the "The Royal Bride." Similarly, in a lecture I attended for brides, the speaker reminded the audience that Jewish women's bodies are holy. She compared the girls' bodies to Torahs, the scrolls of sacred texts which, when not being used for prayer, are "dressed" in velvet and ornamented with silver and jewels. When you are disrobed with your husbands, the speaker said, you are fulfilling your holy God-given purpose of procreation. Like a Torah, a Jewish girl, in other situations, should be adorned in a way that befits her holy, royal Jewish nature.

This discourse of royalty is especially evident in the ways that Hasidic women transform mass-produced clothing into communally approved modest dress, as Goldman Carrel described (1993). Alterations to mass-produced clothing are, Goldman Carrel suggests, a "Hasidification" of clothing, a way to appropriate North American fashion in order to provide modest Jewish women and girls with the beauty their souls crave (1993:92–93). Women use commonly accepted practices to extend the length of a sleeve, for example, or sew up a slit in a skirt. Stores in Boro Park even order extra material to match certain clothing, which is then sold to customers along with an outfit needing modification. Similarly, dickeys or removable collars can make an immodest neckline suddenly modest.

In contrast to Hasidic women's need for beautiful, expensive clothing, some women suggested—especially to little girls—that Jewish women need no adornment because the beauty of their souls shines out and makes their bodies and faces beautiful naturally. Hasidic mothers and teachers try to counter the bourgeois tendencies that define Boro Park by distinguishing between the simple, authentic beauty of Jewish women and the superficial materialism of Gentile femininity (see also Kranzler 1995; Rubin 1997). When Mrs. Silver told her class the story of Purim, for example, the carnivalesque spring holiday, she provided an allegory for feminine beauty, materialism, and the embodied differences between Jews and Gentiles. In describing a beauty contest that the King of Persia held to choose a new queen, Mrs. Silver ascribed the negative qualities of vanity, materialism, and greed to Gentile girls. The Jewish Esther, on the other hand, who had been forced to participate in the contest, was presented as a paragon of modesty, obedience, and simplicity. Mrs. Silver emphasized that Esther refused to wear fancy clothing, jewelry, or makeup, asking only that she be allowed to keep the Sabbath. Esther's authentic beauty eclipsed all the "fancy" Gentile girls. The king had eyes only for Esther, and he made her his queen.

Similarly, an English book written for Orthodox Jewish girls, *Fit for a Princess* (Rotman 2008), takes the Disney princess fairy-tale genre and uses it to criticize the temptations of materialism represented by non-Jewish women. The author describes a Jewish Princess's dilemma over what to wear while she does her royal good works about her castle. Her conventional princess clothing of a pink, puffy dress and golden crown is getting in her way. The author tells us that the princess needs new clothes but they must be "graceful and dignified, beautiful and neat," because wherever she goes, she "wants to look like the daughter of a king." After being presented with alternative costumes from "advisers" from the four corners of the earth, she realizes that the modest dress typical of a Brooklyn schoolgirl, a pleated skirt and blouse, is "exactly what is fit for a princess." On the last page, written on a picture of parchment set beside a golden crown and scepter, and adorned with flowers, are the words, "Dear Jewish Daughter, We can be proud to dress in our own unique way, because we are all daughters of *Hashem* 'God', our King."

Nevertheless, despite adult efforts to emphasize simplicity as beauty, the topics of consumption and fashion interest many Hasidic women and girls today, as evidenced by the shopping mecca that Boro Park has become. Even during the celebration of Purim, where many little girls dress up as Queen Esther, they do not dress simply; they wear long dresses, high-heels, makeup, and sparkling costume jewelry.[12] Most of the women and girls I worked with lived with this tension of wanting to be appropriately modest *and* at the same time living up to North American aesthetic ideals, such as being tall and slim, with straight blond hair, and fashionably dressed. Esty once told me, laughingly, that with their wigs and hats, Hasidic women today look even more elegant than women in Manhattan. She meant that, although Hasidic women wear wigs and hats to fulfill God's commandments, they end up actually looking even better than sophisticated Manhattanites. By transforming adornment from a form of vanity into culturally and religiously appropriate signs for Jewish distinction, modesty channels the material world and sustains a workable tension between the material and the spiritual.

Very Hasidic mother and daughter entering an elegant clothing store, Boro Park.

Secular Knowledge

Living in New York, English-language books and magazines are readily available to Hasidic girls, who, unlike boys whose school schedules are intense, have more time for reading as an individual, leisure activity. Girls' reading of English *goyishe mases* 'Gentile stories' is carefully monitored by adults in and out of school. Goyishe mases are contrasted to Jewish *ekhte mases* 'real stories', the uplifting true stories from the Torah and its commentaries that are told to girls. Goyishe mases often implicitly impart secular liberal values and can potentially contaminate and pollute the pure souls of Jewish children, in much the same way that nonkosher food will physically degrade a Jewish person's body, mind, and soul.

In Bnos Yisruel English-language books in the school library are generally older books from the 1950s, which, Hasidic women told me, was a "more decent time," even for Gentiles. Censorship practices are mandated from the administration in much the same way that Alan Peshkin (1986) describes censorship in a fundamentalist Christian school. Texts with inappropriate displays of the body are simply blacked out, or entire series of books are forbidden. The school is especially vigilant about English books portraying romance between men and women. When, for example, a student brought in a story of Cinderella (based on the animated Disney movie) for her kindergarten teacher to read, the teacher first consulted the principal. She then decided not to read the book to the girls, explaining that there was not enough time. I imagined that Cinderella's immodest gown had been the problem, but she told me later that the real issue was that Cinderella dances with the prince and kisses him in front of others. This, she told me, will not be these girls' lives, so why should they be exposed?

The school also attempts to monitor its students' leisure reading practices at home. Recently the administration forbade its students from visiting the public library, an example of increasing levels of religious stringency, as most of the girls' mothers had gone to the library as children. When the school administration learned that some families were still going to the public library, they ordered spot-checks of girls' schoolbags, confiscated any library cards found, and ripped them up. The Kleins, despite the ban, continued to go to the library, as did many families. But when Raizy Klein sent her children to the library, she always had an older child accompanying them to check that each book borrowed was "kosher." Similarly, when Raizy accidentally ordered a book which she later discovered featured a child whose parents were divorced, she returned the book unread, much to the disappointment of her older daughter, Yehudis. Although the book had looked "exciting" to her daughter, she told me that she did not want Yehudis exposed to the idea of divorce at such a young age.

Girls sometimes do explore forbidden books. A young Hasidic teacher told me that when she had gone to Bnos Yisruel, girls were secretly circulating books from the Sweet Valley Twins series by Francine Pascal. These books follow the lives of non-Jewish middle school and high school girls, especially their dating exploits. Somehow the administration discovered that girls were passing the books back and forth. They checked every girl's bag, confiscated books, and sent warning notes home to parents.

Part of growing up is to learn to take over the censorship that parents and schools have provided. This involves disciplining one's mind and eyes so as to minimize exposure to "nonkosher" images or texts. Esty described a lapse in her own self-censorship that had serious consequences. On a long airplane flight from Israel to New York, although she had not put on the headset, she could not help but glance over at the in-flight movie. Later, some of the romantic images from the film popped into her head while she was praying. She felt terrible and told me she had resolved never again to look at a movie on a plane. Similarly Gitty told me that she had accidentally looked at a Calvin Klein advertisement on the side of a bus that featured a buff man in briefs. She would remember never to look at the sides of buses again, she told me, in order not to expose herself to that image again. A woman who is disciplined only to take what she wants from the secular world provides a model for other Jewish women and even Gentiles.

When women do not discipline their minds and their desires in their interactions with the secular world, they and their children may suffer. Among Hasidic parents, higher secular education and the pursuit of wealth are often used to explain a lapse in Hasidic continuity. Rifky's husband told me at the Sabbath table that "culture" in institutions of higher learning was one of the most serious threats to North American Hasidic communities today. Many Jews were lost, he said, once they went to universities to study art, science, or literature. Rifky told me on another occasion that some Hasidic Jews went "off the path" and stopped being observant, because they wanted to reach a certain level of material success unhampered by religious restrictions such as the prohibition to work on the Sabbath.

Hasidic women frequently tell one another stories in quiet moments as a reminder of the importance to continually discipline oneself, especially in the face of the bourgeois materialism of Boro Park. Mrs. Mandel told a group of teachers about a Hasidic mother with mixed-up priorities: she kept her home so organized that each sheet and towel in her linen closet was tied with a color-coded ribbon, but she sent her children to the pizza shop for supper most nights.

The teachers all agreed that feeding your children a homemade supper was far more important than maintaining a beautiful, organized home. Esty told me about a married woman who could not or would not stop taking dancing lessons and eventually ran off with her Gentile teacher. The dancing, she told me, led her off the path. A mother's ability to discipline her interactions with the secular world and its very real allures of vanity or materialism can affect the survival of the next generation.

Hierarchies of Pious Modesty

Jewish women and girls with different modesty practices are a problem, particularly for children, because, unlike Gentiles, other Jews cannot be dismissed outright as inferior. Every Jew, Hasidic women suggested, no matter how ignorant, has a Jewish soul and a Jewish heart and potentially can return to a religious life. One of the nursery school teachers once told me that I had a Jewish heart "no matter what" (referring, I suppose, to my Reform Jewish background). My Jewish heart, she told me, was what made me such an "*aydl* 'refined' girl," implying a gentle personality.

Girls as young as four and five are aware of distinctions of religiosity between Jews. One day a kindergartner, Layele, told me about a wedding she had attended. The groom was "a little Litvish, a little modern," she said, because he had not worn a *shtraml* (the big round fur hat worn by Hasidic married men on holidays and the Sabbath). When I told her teacher, Morah Chaya, she grew annoyed and said that Layele had made a mistake; just because a Jew does not wear a *shtraml* does not mean he is more modern. Yet because their children are taught to look for signs of Jewish difference, Hasidic teachers and mothers must address these differences as they are experienced in their own neighborhoods and even commonly in their own extended families.

Jews who were not very observant were described to girls as ignorant.[13] "What happens," Mrs. Silver asked the girls one day, "if you see a Jewish girl dressed in a red, short-sleeved T-shirt, and she is your friend?" "A Jew?" one student asked. "Of course," the teacher responded, "we don't care about a Gentile girl (*af a goyte indz care me nisht*). A Jew is dressed like that. A girl who goes to another school and who is your friend, and all of a sudden you see that she is not dressed modestly?" Another student responded, "You should teach her." "Excellent!" said Mrs. Silver. She then told the students that it was most important that they never shame the girl. They should never scream, Mrs. Silver imitated, "You go to that school? They don't teach you how to dress? That's not tsnies! Your mother doesn't know how to buy clothing for you? " (*Di gayst tse dey* school? *Zay lernen nisht zikh untsetin? Deys iz nisht tsniesdik. Dan mame vayst nisht vi azoy tse koyfn klayder far dikh?*). They may, however, tell the girl what they have learned in school about modesty and suggest that it is not "nice" to be dressed immodestly. If the more modern girl wants to change, that would be wonderful. If not, "you don't have to say anything else. You are not her policeman. You aren't her mommy." Mrs. Silver reminded her students that parents are the ultimate authority figures, even Jewish parents who do not teach their daughters the "proper" way to dress. The appropriate response, then, to more modern or even *fray* 'free' (unobservant) Jewish girls, is pity and efforts to educate.

Observant Jewish girls who are just a little more modern, in contrast, are sources of ambivalent admiration for more Hasidic girls, as discussed previously. More modern girls who, perhaps, go to a Litvish Beys Yaakov school are considered more *shtotty* 'sophisticated' and exciting than Hasidic girls who attend a school like Bnos Yisruel. A Bnos Yisruel girl would never dress or even act like these more modern girls; however, more modern girls are regularly integrated into a Hasidic context in order to liven up the experience for everyone. More modern girls are often more outgoing and loud than Hasidic girls. Once, when visiting the Bnos Yisruel camp, I attended a morning rally held in a large wooden building that housed the cafeteria. A teacher I was sitting with told me that the camp administration always paired the Hasidic head counselor with a more modern girl. When I asked why, she gestured to the more modern head counselor who was leading the campers in a series of cheers. "Take a look at her," she said. To me the girl did not look very different from the other counselor; she was modestly dressed in a pleated navy skirt and blouse, and her shoulder-length brown hair was pulled back in a ponytail. Her behavior, however, was completely different from the Hasidic head counselor at her side who was quietly chanting. The more modern girl was dancing on a table, yelling the cheers at the top of her lungs and exhorting the girls to give it their all. When I visited a Satmar camp the next day, this perception was confirmed by the director. She told me that she had a hard time competing with the more modern camps, as they were more "exciting" to girls. Indeed, compared to the Bnos Yisruel camp, the Satmar camp was run down, and the girls I saw were sitting, sewing, and talking quietly, evidence of Bobov's greater wealth and interest in offering recreational activities that drew on more modern camp experiences.

Although very Hasidic girls are admired for their levels of piety, they are also sometimes criticized by women I worked with for their narrowness and inability to transform the secular world in order to strengthen their own communities. The very Hasidic are considered too sheltered from the world and not able to negotiate being modest, fashionable, and knowledgeable; they were described to me as lacking the necessary knowledge to protect themselves adequately from to-day's moral challenges, particularly materialism and vanity. There is even a term, _yunchy_, for girls who fail both at being modest and with it.[14] When I asked Rifky's eleven-year-old daughter to define the term, she suggested "ugly." However, Rifky, who telephoned her sister-in-law and sisters in Williamsburg to confirm this definition, proposed that _yunchy_ clothing or hair styles are modest but do not follow the current standards for fashion and beauty in a woman's community.

Further, the limited education of very Hasidic girls leaves them few resources for the inspirational learning that the women I worked with generally sought. Raizy, for example, told me that when she had a question, she wanted to be able to "look into a _sayfer_ 'a religious book' and find the answer herself without having to bother her husband all the time. Rifky, who has a number of relatives in Williamsburg, noted that the most stringent modesty is too often enforced by fear rather than knowledge:

> There are not many encouraging _shiers_ 'inspirational lectures' in Williamsburg. When they do have them they are always about that your sleeves have to be down to here [pointing to her wrists] or God forbid, _khas-veshulem_, terrible things will happen. This leads to emptiness.

Gitty similarly remarked that Satmar girls' limited education makes them especially prone to materialism:

> _Zay lernen zayer vaynik_ (They learn very little), right? They learn, ex-cuse me, just enough to know. They don't learn to be intelligent . . . A _Satmere_ girl is not an intelligent person. I'm not embarrassed to say . . . She's not interested in intelligence. _Zay glaybn de maydlekh darfn vern ofgetsoygn trugn tsep, in me darf gayn tsigedekt, in visn tse kokhn, tse bakn, tse laynen, tse davnen, tse esn_ . . . (They believe that girls should be brought up to wear braids, and you have to go cov-ered [a headscarf at marriage] and to know how to bake, to read, to pray, to eat) . . . that's it but they don't believe in using their brain. They're very into _gashmiesdike zakhn_ 'materialistic things'. It should be nice and fancy.

In the same vein a teacher at Bnos Yisruel remarked to me, "You always know Satmar, they're the ones wearing Ferragamos (very expensive Italian shoes)." Another told me that a Satmar woman is always the most stringently modest. She wears a kerchief instead of a wig, but that kerchief is almost always a designer Chanel scarf. These criticisms of very Hasidic women and girls, however, are also ambivalent, tinged with respect for the heightened stringency of these women and girls.

Hasidic women I met contrasted their standards of modesty to those of the very Hasidic and the more modern. In their critiques of other Orthodox Jewish women, they claim to be best prepared to mediate the secular world, with today's special trials including wealth and opportunities for participation in North American cultural life. Women I worked with suggested that they are best able to fulfill God's commandments because they are both with it and modest. They are fashionable, beautiful, and well-educated, but never too well-educated. They are never like Gentiles or like men.

GIRLS' CHALLENGES TO MODESTY

During the time I spent in Boro Park I did not hear girls ask why they had to be modest, although they may have done so when I was not around. Girls certainly did not always comply with their families' standards of modesty. Indeed, little girls were often lax in covering up, speaking nicely, or sitting modestly, just as they were with other ritual obligations. Even teenagers can choose to satisfy other desires rather than behave modestly. During my visit to the Bnos Yisruel girls' summer camp, for example, some girls, despite the rules, did not put on their long robes when they got out of the camp swimming pool because they wanted to tan their whole body. Their *rukhnies* 'spirituality' counselor chastised them at a camp meeting, emphatically telling them that robes and stockings had to be worn on top of bathing suits whenever a girl was not in the pool.

Occasionally I heard girls disagreeing with women authorities about the most appropriate ways to be modest. I heard about high school girls who challenged their school's interpretation of what met the standards of modesty. Malky, Mrs. Hirsch's daughter—the one who had pushed me to the front of the women's section in the synagogue—complained to me about her principal's extreme standards for modesty. She and some friends were involved in a fund-raising drive for the school, and they advertised the event by posting signs in the school with photos of themselves holding umbrellas with drawings of dollar bills raining down on them. The principal made them remove the posters, saying it was immodest to publicly display photos of themselves. Miriam angrily complained to me and her family (who seemed sympathetic, as they are not very Hasidic), but she had to comply or risk expulsion.

Another young woman told me about a friend who was angry because the principal of her school forced her to pay a modesty fine of $5.00 for wearing a hooded sweater rather than a blouse to school. The principal felt that although the sweater covered all the right areas, the hood made it too "informal" to be appropriately modest. The girl, it should be noted, was from out of town and was living with relatives in order to attend a Hasidic high school. She argued with the principal, telling her that the sweater was very expensive, reasoning that because it was expensive, the sweater could not be informal. Despite cost, however, casual clothing, like a hooded sweater, is considered less modest because of its associations with North American dress more generally, such as jeans, hooded sweatshirts, and sneakers. Indeed, formal dress is one of the defining features of Hasidic femininity; thus girls who dress less formally by wearing a long jean skirt or Doc Marten boots, for example, are seen as becoming more modern—or "bummy" —with the implication that they may be going off the path of observance.

THE SACRIFICES AND REWARDS OF MODESTY

As girls get ready to make a marriage match, they may be asked to raise their level of modesty from what they were brought up with in exchange for an increase in social status and special treatment from God. This change is described as a "personal sacrifice" that girls may make for their family and themselves, revealing much about the dynamics of Hasidic women's modesty. An example is Chaya Rosenbaum's engagement to the Goldman family, as told to me by her neighbor and peer, Esty.

In the negotiations with a potential groom's family that are involved in the matchmaking process, decisions about how the new couple will live are all made explicit. As with other religious practice (even which language will dominate the home), the two families decide together how a girl will cover her head and what kind of stockings she will wear. Chaya Rosenbaum agreed to become much more Hasidic in her modesty in order to marry into a particular family. Chaya Rosenbaum comes from a family with a prestigious genealogical lineage, a very "nice" family, Esty told me, and she continued: "This family has a father, grandfather, great-grandfather, all sides. On all sides she's special, uncles, everyone doing something," meaning that they provided religious services to the community through a range of activities. The Rosenbaum's are unaffiliated Hasidim but not "that" Hasidic. For example, before the match Chaya's mother wore a short wig without a hat, and her husband did not wear a *shtraml* (high fur hat worn on the Sabbath and holidays). None of the Rosenbaum women wore seamed stockings, and the girls all spoke English to one another. After high school Chaya had even spent a year at the Teachers' Seminary for Hasidic girls in Boro Park.

The Goldmans, on the other hand, were a much bigger name in the community based on Mr. Goldman's following as a *rov,* a rabbi who interprets Jewish law for the community. Esty told me he was a big *poysek* (interpreter of Jewish law) in Boro Park, although he was a "self-made" man and did not come from such a "distinguished" background. He and his family, however, were very Hasidic. All the women in the family "go *gebindn*" (completely covered with a headscarf instead of a wig or a covered wig) and wear seamed stockings. Of course, Mr. Goldman wears a shtraml. They also all speak Hasidic Yiddish at home. When the Goldman match was proposed to the Rosenbaum parents, they could hardly believe their luck—to marry into one of the biggest names in Boro Park! The Goldmans were interested in the match because of the Rosenbaum's prestigious lineage. However, the Goldmans did demand that the Rosenbaum girl, Chaya, accommodate to their level of modesty by "going gebindn" and wearing seamed stockings. Goldman's concession was even to consider a girl who had attended a year at the Teacher's Seminary, as the very Hasidic are opposed to higher education for girls.

Chaya Rosenbaum was eighteen years old at the time and at sleep-away camp. Esty shared a bunk with her and told me how "the parents put it into her lap." Esty said, "I imagine that she felt she had her hands tied. Because her parents put it down like, for us, for them it was like such a jump up. You know? And it happens often that you have a family who is being proposed this great match and they can't believe their luck and then they'll look away at something big." In this case the "something big" was the heightened level of modesty to which Chaya would have to conform. However much she felt constrained to say yes, the family waited until Chaya officially agreed to the match. The Goldmans compromised a bit and let her wear a *tikhl* with a *shpitsl* (a headscarf with a roll of nylon at her hairline which imitated hair exposed at the front, rather than only a headscarf), because Chaya had not been raised with the expectation of making this kind of sacrifice.

After both families agreed to the match, Chaya's parents went up one more level in observance: her mother put a hat on her wig and her father wore a shtraml for holidays and Shabbes. It would have been inappropriate to have their daughter suddenly assume a very Hasidic position without also changing their own level of stringency. After the match, the Rosenbaums' status rose considerably, and they were suddenly privy to a whole new set of possible matches as people who thought they were not Hasidic enough suddenly saw that they were willing to actually become more Hasidic. The heightened prestige for the family helped the rest of their children make matches that previously would have been out of their league.

Coincidentally, I happened to be visiting with Chaya's sister, Frimmy, a second-grade teacher at Bnos Yisruel, when she was browsing through her family photo albums. Frimmy pointed out her sister and her kerchief in a family photo and told me admiringly that her sister had had to make a big sacrifice. She elaborated that a woman does not look very nice with all of her hair covered under a kerchief. Frimmy said she was grateful that she herself did not have to make such a sacrifice and could wear a short wig with a beret. Then Frimmy showed me pictures of her sister's children, who were very blond and lovely, and told me that God had given her especially beautiful children as a reward for her modesty. Frimmy, and many other women, told me that a woman's ability to sacrifice her own vanity to help her family or husband merits rewards from God. Chaya's acceptance of the match was understood by the two women who narrated the episode as a responsibility she did not want but that was thrust upon her, and she accepted it.

A noteworthy point is that the more modest head covering is considered a sacrifice and not innately or more authentically beautiful. Women I spoke with openly talked about how much worse a woman looks in a kerchief than a wig. This contrasts to other kinds of expressive religious culture that is considered "gorgeous," such as men's loud prayers in the synagogue, women's wedding dances (to me exceedingly repetitive), and the rebbe's barely audible singing. Why is wearing a headscarf and seams considered unattractive, a sacrifice, rather than inherently beautiful because of its stringency? A possible answer returns to some Hasidic women and girls' ambivalence toward the most Hasidic girls whom they see as not "with it," as "backward and primitive" because they are unable to control their participation in the secular world. When a Bobover or an unaffiliated Hasidic girl agrees to dress like a Hungarian girl, everyone understands that it is an admirable sacrifice rewarded by God, but nevertheless a personal loss of a girl's beauty. The ideal for the Hasidic women and girls I worked with is to find the perfect balance where a woman can be with it, without sacrificing her modesty. This is similar to the discussion in the previous chapter regarding language, where the women and girls I worked with wanted to sound with it, but not modern. This balance is different for every Hasidic group, and even from family to family and across generations, so that it must be constantly assessed, policed, and debated.

Hasidic women could decide (given a web of obligations) for themselves if they were ready to rise to a new level of modesty proposed by authority figures. More unusual was when a woman initiated a change herself, although it did happen, especially if a woman was trying to resolve a problem or make amends for a breached commandment. For example, Gitty, my Yiddish tutor, who was dealing with issues of infertility, told her husband that she wanted to wear only a kerchief instead of her wig and hat. She told me she "felt ready" to go to a new level of modesty. Her husband initially rejected the proposal, claiming that she could not look more observant than his own mother and that he did not like how she looked in a kerchief. She told me sadly that she had to put her husband's wishes before her own, and she agreed to keep wearing her wig and hat. When I saw her years later (happily, with three children in tow), she was wearing the kerchief, but with a small front of artificial hair showing. When I questioned her, first she told me that she looked better in a brightly colored kerchief than she had in a dark hat and wig. I suspected that this was not the whole story and asked if there was a religious reason for the shift. She nodded and told me she had finally said to her husband, "C'mon. You know it's the right thing to do," and he ultimately agreed. Perhaps her reward had indeed been her children whom she openly told me had been conceived using fertility treatments.[15] Perhaps she had effectively bargained with God, her biology, and her husband by putting on that kerchief.

DISCIPLINE AND MODESTY

Hasidic girls' religious desires are formed through their experiences and perceptions of the secular world. In a very different context, Talal Asad (1993:141) has described how new monks in twelfth-century Europe, who had had extensive experience with the secular world often as knights, were recruited for monastic communities. How, he asks, were "obedient wills created" from these worldly adults? Asad suggests that the new monks' resocialization did not repress novices' secular experiences of freedom, but rather formed religious desires out of them through religious rituals (165). I share Asad's interest in the formation of "obedient wills," although I suggest that, for young girls, obedient wills are formed not only through religious ritual. My focus on cultural and religious beliefs about modesty and signifying practices suggests that obedient wills in girls are produced through the everyday embodied practices of comportment, talk, dress, and literacy. Just as English becomes a resource for Jewish ways of speaking, consumption or reading secular books, for example, may become the means for cultivating Jewish virtues. The embodied practices of modesty redeem secular signs and practices, so that women and girls can cultivate the interior royal nature of their souls.

Returning to Foucault's discussion of ethics (chapters 2 and 3), the discipline of modesty can be understood as another technology of the self, a means for producing ethical individuals who are willing to live by moral norms. When Hasidic caregivers tell their daughters and students that being modest is about refinement, unchanging Jewish practices, maturity, and divine rewards, they present a moral basis (to borrow a term from Abu-Lughod 1986) for differentiating themselves from secular North Americans, Gentiles, more modern Jewish women, and even very Hasidic women. A goal for Jewish women, as Rifky said, is to "take their body along for a ride with their soul."

Hasidic girls' willingness to participate in the disciplines of modesty complicates notions of women's agency in nonliberal religious movements: women and girls must be able to subordinate their own desires if they are inappropriate and reconcile their desires with the requirements of communal authority figures. However, they can also use the disciplines of modesty to affect their everyday lives by enjoying, in culturally and religiously appropriate ways, the pleasures of secular consumption, bodily adornment, and literacy. They even claim that it is part of their royal, Jewish nature to seek out the highest-quality clothing or jewelry, legitimizing their taste for expensive goods. Simultaneously they know that their embodied discipline fulfills God's will, helps their families, and brings rewards in the afterlife. Webb Keane (2007:57) has suggested that discipline, with its orientation of the self toward an outside agent, forms an important alternative to liberal models of agency.[16] For Hasidic women, the embodied discipline of modesty is part of a broader effort to collapse distinctions that are often assumed to be oppositional. The discipline modesty entails accommodates both the desire to look good according to secular North American standards and the desire to be pious Jewish women. These desires complement each other, challenging the liberal belief that the sacred and the secular, the spiritual and the material, the body and the soul, need be oppositions at all.

CHAPTER SEVEN

Becoming Hasidic Wives

THE HIRSCH FAMILY sat around their long dining room table one Sabbath evening. They are a lively, loud Bobover family with nine children ranging from toddlers to married adults with children of their own. Mrs. Hirsch, a teacher at Bnos Yisruel, had invited me, and dinnertime was filled with laughter and good-natured teasing. In between the fish course and the soup, Mrs. Hirsch's daughter-in-law, Perele, told the gathering about a girl who had gotten engaged. A small explosion of exclamations erupted. Mrs. Hirsch quickly asked, "To whom?" This was, of course, the critical question. Perele said, "To Cohen [the family name]." "That's so nice," "I'm so happy," was repeated again and again. Then Mrs. Hirsch announced that she knew a boy, Weissman, who was looking for a "top" girl. Another daughter-in-law, Sheyndie, called out that she knew a top girl, Yiffy Klein. She thought for a minute and added that maybe she was not "Hasidish enough" for Weissman. High school–aged Miriam Hirsch said she knew Yiffy from school and that she was willing to "put on beige." Trying to follow the rapid-fire conversation, I asked, "Beige, as in stockings?" "Yes," said Miriam. Thick, beige, seamed stockings, as noted, are for the very Hasidic or the most stringent in religious observance, especially tsnies. Heskie Hirsch, engaged himself, said that he knew Weissman and confirmed that he was a top boy. Mr. Hirsch turned to me with a smile, and asked, "You see how it all works?"

Everyday talk about matchmaking, engagement, and marriage is an important way that girls on the brink of adulthood (ages eighteen to twenty-one) learn to become modest Hasidic wives, ultimately responsible for bringing up the next generation of believers. In this chapter I extend the discussion of modesty from the previous chapter to the arranged marriages made by all Hasidic Jews. Hasidic mothers and teachers prepare young brides, who have had little interaction with boys, for the new forms of modesty necessary as they begin to talk about and participate in previously forbidden topics of love, romance, and sexuality.

At the heart of arranged marriages is a Hasidic critique of their perception of Gentile and secular families. This critique focuses on what Hasidic women suggest is an immature belief that marriage is about individuals rather than family status, about the selfish fulfillment of passions rather than the commitment to building real love through religious discipline. Hasidic women tell an alternative story of the family, which is made explicit in talk about matchmaking and women's efforts to prepare Hasidic brides to take on their new responsibilities as wives.

In matchmaking practices women and girls search out their *basherte* 'predestined mate' (by God). However, only a small window of opportunity exists to find one's basherte because, by the age of twenty-five or twenty-six, boys and girls who are still unmarried are often considered problematic. In their search for God's choice of a partner, families pragmatically evaluate other families based on the Hasidic concept of social class. Families, in addition to assuring their children's happiness by finding the partner God has chosen just for them, at the same time aim to maintain or increase their social status in making a match. The concept of social class is distinctive among Hasidic Jews in that it makes materialism and religiosity complementary rather than opposed by understanding wealth as the potential to help other Jews.[1] When a couple becomes engaged, secular consumption is channeled into religious obligation as the two families outfit the new couple with a full Jewish home and arrange an elaborate wedding.

As the wedding nears, girls attend formal classes for brides. Here they are taught that true Jewish love comes from a girl's ability to discipline her own body and desires as she assumes her new religious responsibilities for the laws of family purity (*tahares-hamishpukhe*), which regulate conjugal intimacy based on the woman's menstrual cycle. Hasidic teachers consistently compare observant Jewish marriage to caricatures of Gentile and secular marriages. Hasidic girls are promised that their modesty and innate Jewish refinement will bring them the rewards elaborated in secular discourses of romance and love, but Hasidic young women will gain even more; they will enjoy an intimacy and friendship with their husbands that Gentiles and the secular cannot even imagine. Hasidic girls' willingness to discipline their hearts and bodies by submitting to religious authority not only fulfills their sacred obligation to the Jewish people and God, but it will also make all their dreams come true.

JEWISH KINSHIP

Jewish identity is matrilineal, but Jewish marriage ties are traced patrilaterally. When women marry, they take their husband's name as their own, as do any children they have. In fact, many of my Hasidic women friends were distressed to hear that I was not planning to take my husband's name at marriage. They considered it an insult to my husband and his family. Nevertheless, women's family names before marriage continue to be important as Jewish kinship is cognatic, that is, children have ties and obligations to both the mother's and the father's sides of the family. Whenever I identified a woman by her married name, I would be asked, "What was her name as a girl?" which meant before she married and became a "lady" or a "mommy." This helps not only identify the woman as originating in a certain family, it also provides alliance information about which families made a match.

Many Hasidic women I worked with easily reeled off names of families that were related through marriage both locally and abroad. When I expressed amazement, for example, that Gitty knew so many families and their marriage histories, she explained that she knew no more than most women, which turned out to be true. She just knew the "basics," she told me, which included "Bobov, the Pupa crowd, the Bobover camp crowd, a little bit of Satmar, a little bit of Belz, a little Beys Sure [a nonaffiliated Hasidic girls' school], a little modern type."

Marriage ties map out a Hasidic geography that is a guide to diasporic communities across time and space. Marriages are often brokered across national boundaries, reinforcing and building social and economic networks transnationally. When Mr. Silber, a Bobover Hasid from Boro Park, married Chaya, an Israeli Bobover girl, they spent many of the Jewish holidays in Boro Park (up to two months at a time), living with Mr. Silber's parents. While there, Chaya and her husband worked in her father-in-law's hat store, sewing on brims and selling to customers. Today, now that the couple has a large family, Mr. Silber's parents spend half the year living in Israel with them. Others I knew made matches between Boro Park and Argentina, Belgium, Canada, or Australia. Because the Bobover Hasidic community is so large, it is now possible for Bobover to try to marry other Bobover exclusively. On many occasions, however, different Hasidic sects intermarry. The critical factor, discussed below, is that the families share a level of religiosity and that the potential partners share a certain "lifestyle."

Just as families are linked across space through marriage ties, families also span time through remembered family histories. Families are traced back to the *alte haym* 'old home' in Eastern Europe. Today's generation of Hasidic Jews know how observant, rich, and well-known certain families were in Europe, how they fared in the war, and how they rebuilt their lives in New York. This information, along with knowledge about a family's current position, is critical to the matchmaking process.

Marriage ties increase the size and strength of families. The most often used English term, "related," can signify a relationship either by blood or marriage, and various qualifying terms account for different ways families can be connected. Although marriage ties are not always considered "really related" or are clarified as related "by marriage," in practice relations by marriage are also important for building families. The litmus test for relatedness is a guest list for a wedding, which commonly includes up to five hundred people. A wedding becomes a site where a family's strength and alliances are displayed publicly and reinforced through the exchange of money or gifts.

Blood kinship is considered more binding than marriage ties, although it, too, may be qualified according to concepts of closeness. For example, relatives who are not directly descended from a rebbe, but are rather related indirectly, are called "not straight." However, blood ties to illustrious families can prove prestigious, no matter how distant the reckoning. Gitty once told me that one of her sisters-in-law, Rokhl, was the rebbe's granddaughter. When I expressed confusion, she explained that she was not related "straight" but only through a distant relative. This relationship allowed her to claim some prestige when it came time for her own marriage negotiations. In fact, Rokhl's distant relationship to the rebbe was very important for her because her parents were divorced and her brother was not "100 hundred percent," meaning that he had some kind of psychological or social problem. The divorce and the brother's problem are black marks in the matchmaking market. Rokhl's tie to the rebbe, as well as her own personal qualities—she was popular, had good grades, and was a blond-haired beauty—all helped her to ultimately make a respectable match.

Kin terms in everyday practice tend to get pared down to their most basic form, although everyone seems aware of actual distances between relations when I questioned the specifics. My head would spin, for example, as Esty explained to me how she was related to Rifky through several family connections: a second cousin through a shared relative, but through marriage a third cousin. Women in Boro Park often told me that the relationships themselves were not so complicated; instead, the complications arose because there were so many ties, especially through marriage, that were claimed as family. These ties can be called, in shorthand, simply "relatives," because most people in this small community know the histories of specific families.

HASIDIC SOCIAL CLASS: DESCENT, MONEY, AND RELIGIOSITY

Hasidic women elaborate a notion of marriage as an alliance between families that are *pasik* 'fitting' or 'appropriate'. What makes one family appropriate for another is based on a particular notion of social class that draws on inherited family histories going back generations, as well as contemporary status based on wealth, religious learning, piety, involvement in Hasidic community life, and personal characteristics. Women I spoke with claimed that wealth among Hasidic Jews—in contrast to Gentiles and the secular world—is valued not only for its material pleasures but, more important, as a resource for helping one's family and community through charity and good works. Even if a man is convicted of illegal business dealings and serves time in jail for a white-collar crime, which was quite common during my research, his family's reputation in the community will not be sullied if the money he made illegally helps the Hasidic community through, for example, donations to charity. Federal and state laws are trumped by the ability to help other Hasidic Jews through wealth acquired in the secular world.

Hasidic women I spoke with described familial status using Yiddish and English categories and terms in a syncretic system of distinction that integrates different forms of capital that are complementary: economic and cultural, religious and secular, past and present, male and female, inherited and self-made. Yiddish categories are generally about religious learning, family lineage, and social position among male Hasidic Jews based on involvement in Hasidic male court politics and community life. English categories refer more to the realms of Hasidic women and are about lifestyle choices, particularly forms of consumption, personal traits such as popularity, and a certain bourgeois aesthetic sensibility for how a household is managed. English-language qualifiers create a continuum within the Yiddish categories that allow for more subtle gradations of social class.

Based on interviews with four different Hasidic women and confirmed by others, I observed six different Yiddish categories of families. These familial categories are based on *yikhes* 'lineage', wealth, occupation (which includes Jewish learning), and visible involvement in the Jewish public sphere, the public religious life of the community. The rebbe, for example, has a bureaucracy of males who help him run his office, and closeness to the rebbe is an important aspect of male prestige. Although other categories are involved in matchmaking, the six I discuss here are apparently the most common among the Hasidic women I worked with and reveal important distinctions between families (table 7.1).

Families are officially defined by male realms of value and activity. Women's social status and marriage options in a family are generally based on males' social positions, although a woman's individual traits are also important considerations in a match. Women's work outside the home, however, does not seem to affect social status. Their work

TABLE 7.1
Categories of Hasidic Families

Category	Rebish	Rabunish	Shayne	Balebatish	Yeshivish	Farshlept
Family background	dynastic	illustrious	respectable	businessmen	dedicated to study	unsuccessful
Wealth	wealthy	possibly wealthy	comfortable income	"middle-class"	frugal life-style by choice	difficulty making ends meet
Occupation	community spiritual leaders	community scholars and leaders	providers of a religious service to the community	involved in business but use wealth for charity and communal purposes	involved in a community organized around a yeshiva	unable to give to the community

is not devalued; on the contrary, it is recognized as allowing husbands to spend more time studying Torah. However, women's work, unlike men's, does not have the potential to raise a family's social status. This is because their work does not allow them to participate in the public religious life of the community, which revolves around a rebbe or yeshiva. Hasidic men's involvement in the Jewish public sphere potentially provides them with a certain fame, as well as a means of making money. There are, of course, exceptions such as Esty's mother, a very successful businesswoman who owns her own shop. Generally, however, women add to the prestige of their families through their individual accomplishments in school (good grades and popularity), their skills as a potential homemaker ("being *geshikt*" 'efficient'), and their physical charms which seem to count a great deal.

The most elite families, in the sense of exclusivity, are *rebishe* families that descended from a charismatic Hasidic spiritual leader, a rebbe. A rebishe family can trace its connection to a rebbe over time through their genealogy. Simply by saying a family's name, Hasidic Jews can recognize who is rebish. Metaphors of royalty are often used to describe rebbishe families, including terms like "dynasty" and the rebbe's "court" (his advisers). Many Hasidic homes display framed genealogies of famous rebbes that trace bloodlines in much the same way that monarchs might display their family tree. Wealth is another feature of rebishe families, and finances or the need to earn a living do not seem to concern them. As community leaders, their livelihoods are taken care of and they live amid plenty, and often luxuriously. Although a rebishe lineage is passed through bloodlines, it can become "diluted" if, as Rifky told me, "rebish identity isn't retained after a number of generations and people forget." Community memory and individual actions, then, can maintain or jeopardize a rebishe family.

Rebishe families usually marry into other rebishe families in order to maintain the bloodlines. This means that first-cousin marriages are not uncommon among rebishe families because, as Gitty noted, "*Azoy me blabt in de mishpukhe*" (That's how you keep it in the family). However, even though rebish is in some ways at the pinnacle of Hasidic status based on blood, piety, and power over generations, a rebishe match is not always the most desirable, especially for girls. Gitty told me about a Hasidic rebbe who chose sons-in-law from important (*khushever*) families but not rebishe ones. As Gitty suggested, the rebbe probably wanted his sons-in-law to study Torah, be relaxed, and be available for their wives and families. When the rebbe married off his son, however, he chose a rebishe girl in order to maintain the succession of the lineage.

Although non-rebishe Hasidim often prefer to marry within the same Hasidic group, rebishe families often marry outside their *hasidus*, their Hasidic court. Gitty suggested that rebishe families were "aiming for the heavens, so they don't care which hasidus as long as the family is rebish." As Rifky explained, "*A rebishe shidekh* 'a rebbishe match', is like elite, it's royal, but you know it's not within anyone's reach." The royalty of rebishe families was made especially clear to me when the Bobover rebbe married off his granddaughter in a ceremony that the Klein family and I observed by craning our necks out their fourth-floor apartment window. The wedding took place at dusk on a newly erected wooden stage in the middle of the street, blocked off from traffic by police barricades lining Fourteenth Avenue. The long, wide avenue was swirling with men in black coats and fur hats who watched the actual reproduction of the next link of an important Hasidic dynasty. After the ceremony, the entire community was invited for a sit-down dinner to celebrate. For an evening, an alternative religious monarchy controlled the streets of Brooklyn.

Khushever, or important families, are usually *rabunish*: families who are well known in the religious life of the community but do not trace their genealogy to a rebbe. The category of rabunish can be traced to social organization in prewar Europe. A rebbe was distinguished from a *rov* 'a rabbi' in terms of lineage and occupation. Both the rebbe and the rov had *smikhe* (rabbinic certification upon completion of yeshiva), as do all Hasidic young men who graduate from yeshiva. The rebbe was the spiritual leader of the community and the founder of the Hasidic court or group, providing spiritual inspiration to his followers.

The *rov*, in contrast, interpreted religious law on a daily basis. The division of labor regarding religious guidance and leadership of the Hasidic community is split along a material and spiritual plane. A rov's children are called rabunish. Although being rabunish is not passed on through bloodlines as rebish is, as Rifky said, "It turns out that a rov wasn't either Tom, Dick, or Harry. It was someone who learned, and aspired, and achieved." Thus, although a rov's children also had to learn enough to be able to *paskn* 'adjudicate' matters of Jewish law over time, the honor of having a rov in the family elevated that family's status to rabunish. Rabunish generally means that the family had a famous rov in Europe, but a man can become a rov through his own efforts. If his children followed in his footsteps and were also "successful" rabunim—that is, they had a following of other Jews—their children would be considered rabunish. Rabunishe families, then, gain their status from either a prestigious relative in the past or by recent individual effort and striving.

I heard mixed information about wealth among rabunishe families. Rifky told me that rabunish, especially if the status is based on a rov in the family's European past, is usually not very wealthy. However, Esty told me that a successful rov today who has a big following is never lacking for funds. I suspect that wealth varies among rabunishe families that gain their high prestige from distinguished relatives, a high level of scholarship, and authority in religious matters. A rabunishe match is highly valued and only slightly more accessible than a rebishe match. As Rifky suggested, "A rabunishe shidekh there's more class, or more whatever than a regular shidekh."

The third category is one step below rabunish, the *shayne mishpukhe* (the nice or beautiful family, implying spiritual, not physical, characteristics). Shayne mishpukhes are those that are involved in communal religious life but are not rabunim (i.e., people do not go to them for interpretation of Jewish law). Occupations for a shayne mishpukhe might be a ritual slaughterer (a *shoykhet*) or a learned Torah scholar (*talmed-khukhem*). Critical to being a shayne mishpukhe is a certain level of community respect for the family's piety, involvement, and dedication to community religious life. A shayne mishpukhe, however, can easily deteriorate and cease being shayn. Rifky told me about someone her mother-in-law knew in Europe whose status changed when he came to North America; in Europe he was a well-respected Torah scholar, but during World War II he lost his family and remarried although not very well. Today his grandchildren are "no great shakes," and all because he made a "junky" match. The war and coming to America are clearly important turning points for families that either continue to build on past prestige, go downhill and lose prestige, or build themselves anew based on *yikhes atsmoy*, one's own individual efforts.

The most common familial category, *balebatish* (literally, home-owning) is based on occupation, income, and what Rifky called "decency." I define balebatish as "bourgeois." Balebatish families often use their success and business acumen to help build up the community and thus gain social recognition. Rifky defined balebatish as "middle-class, well-off, decent earning, not ridiculously rich or showy, but better." Rifky suggested that balebatish families are upright and respectable. The ability to support themselves comfortably is a sign that the family is productive and capable. Balebatish families are strictly observant and still Hasidic, but men's learning competes for time with business activities that often bring them into contact with the non-Hasidic world. Their involvement in the Hasidic religious community generally consists of contributions to charities and other good works projects. In the last generation or so, balebatish families often used their money to support a newlywed son-in-law for a year or more, so that he can devote himself to Torah study. Balebatish, then, is not necessarily less prestigious; rather, it is an orientation to work, family, and religiosity. Esty told me that her father was the type of person who just would not feel comfortable if he did not provide for his family adequately by working. She seemed proud that her father supported them well.

In contrast, some Hasidic and non-Hasidic but equally Orthodox yeshivish families are so committed to studying Torah that it compromises a family's income. The yeshivish families are usually associated with, or participants in, a yeshiva around which communal life revolves, whereas Hasidic married men study in a kollel, a yeshiva exclusively for them. For Hasidic families where the man devotes himself to Torah study, the families try to maintain a balebatish lifestyle as best they can and participate in the Hasidic bourgeoisie more generally (but see the next section for exceptions). Being yeshivish for males indicates piety. A yeshivish label for women, in contrast, implies an informal and frugal style of dress and homemaking. Esty told me that girls from yeshivishe families would probably dress very casually, perhaps in a denim skirt and oversized, long-sleeved T-shirt. They would serve their families inexpensive, uncomplicated meals. The yeshivish frugal lifestyle and rejection of appearances is acceptable to Hasidim in a boy because of the commitment to study, but is less desirable to Hasidim in a girl. When I asked Rifky if she would make a match between her children and a yeshivishe family, she thought not. Was it because yeshivish families were not observant enough? "No," said Rifky, "Because it is just a different culture, a different lifestyle. Let's say if they're going to serve spaghetti every night, my son would be miserable . . ." Yeshivish has come to be associated with an ideology of piety through frugality, which is more appealing in a prospective husband than a wife, the actual homemaker.

Less elaborated or discussed are the non-prestigious families that are sometimes called "plain" as opposed to "fancy," or the *farshlept* 'the downtrodden'. These families have a hard time making ends meet financially. Undistinguished by male piety, earning power, or lineage, one woman suggested that fate decrees that these families will never gain much prestige. Private charitable organizations among Hasidic Jews provide help to these families.

English Qualifiers of Hasidic Social Class

In addition to Yiddish categories of families, women use English qualifiers to make the categories more subtle and to address what many call "lifestyle issues." For example, Rifky described her family in this way:

> My husband's family is definitely considered balebatish. My father is a little bit balebatish-yeshivish. My mother's family is very balebatish, and my mother's family is very similar to my mother-in-law's family. My father was a little rabunish you could say, his grandfather was in Europe a poysek, an interpreter of Jewish law. But also the war cut it off.

"A little" and "real" or "very" balebatish refer to degrees of wealth, and "a little rabunish" might refer to having a distinguished relative in Europe. English qualifiers reveal that family hierarchies are not clear-cut, so when Rifky said that her father is "a little bit balebatish-yeshivish," she is making a subtle negotiation that can accommodate a high level of piety and commitment to Jewish learning, along with a commitment to earning a living.

In addition to the types of social status that focus on family histories and contemporary financial success, families are also tagged with more general English terms. These categories address issues of social class through lifestyle in the postwar diaspora. An important word is "nice." This is often paired with the word "normal," in the idiomatic Hasidic sense of fitting in to cultural expectations. The English term is so vague that I had trouble pinning it down. I asked Gitty to explain the meaning of "nice," and she gave me the example of a family that owns a Hasidic camp for girls, suggesting that they were a nice family and people "know who they are." From this and similar conversations with other women, I gather that a nice family is well known and well regarded in the community by their good social standing. "Nice" can apply to any rung of the status hierarchy.

Even little girls are aware of the importance of marrying into a nice family. When I began my fieldwork, I had just become engaged and the wedding was set for late spring. One day in February I was visiting the Fine family, and Chumie, the Fines' six-year-old daughter whom I knew from Bnos Yisruel, questioned me about my impending marriage. She asked me the date of the wedding and if she could come. Then she asked me, "Who is the boy?" I told her his full name. "Is he from a nice family?" she asked. After months of fieldwork, I knew she was not asking if his parents were kind people. She already knew that some families were nice and the importance of marrying into them. He is, I told her, from a very nice family.

Another English-language category includes a set of oppositional terms, "simple" and "fancy," that focus on lifestyle, piety, and orientation to material wealth and its display. "Fancy" implies not only wealth but the manner of consumption, which includes a lavish lifestyle. "Simple" connotes restraint in the display of wealth, rather than a commentary on wealth itself. At the wedding of the Bobover rebbe's granddaughter, Chaya, an older Hasidic woman, pointed out to me that the bride's mother was not even wearing a wig; her head was completely covered by a white kerchief. Chaya was impressed that such a high-status woman from a royal family, who could afford the finest wig and hat, would choose to cover her head in such a "simple" way. She made sure to explain to me that her head covering was evidence of the bride's mother's piety, as she willingly sacrificed fancy displays of her family's wealth and rebish position.

When people ask about recent matches, "fancy" characterizes a bride, a groom, or a whole family on issues of money, not religious practice. In the teachers' room, for example, I overheard Mrs. Silver ask about a girl who had gotten engaged to a Klausenberger Hasidic boy. Mrs. Silver asked another teacher what kind of girl the bride was: "Hasidish? Litvish? Fancy?" The other teacher confirmed that the girl was fancy. Mrs. Silver responded, "I thought so because he is a super boy, but they are very rich and fancy." The other teacher clarified that the bride's family was more simple but that the bride herself was fancy. A "super boy" usually implies a high level of Torah study and seriousness, and "fancy" often indicates greater involvement in the materialistic world and interest in displaying and enjoying one's wealth. Family hierarchies (in Yiddish) reproduce historical categories of difference in male occupation, piety, and wealth. The English adjectives "nice" and "fancy" allow commentary on women's participation in these categories and other lifestyle choices, particular to the most recent experience of the diaspora in Brooklyn.

Families usually make matches with those in a similar social position. As Rifky said, "Rebish takes rebish, rabunish takes rabunish, and the plain-Janes take the plain-Janes." Within these categories, there are additional hierarchies that evaluate family histories as well as contemporary lifestyles. The English language qualifier "top-tier" indicates a ranking system within familial categories. For example, when Esty's sister was getting married, her parents, who are balebatish, sought out other balebatishe families for a potential match. Their goal, however, was to find a top-tier match from among all the balebatish families. A top-tier family has no black marks in its history, such as divorce or diseases, and is well respected in the community. After waiting quite some time and rejecting many potential matches, Esty's sister did indeed find a top-tier match. Occasionally a "regular" person may make a rabunishe match, or a rabunishe family may make a rebishe match. In both cases the regular family and the rabunishe family must have something special to offer in exchange for raising their status: *yikhes* 'lineage', a good name, money, or heightened observance. As illustration, Rifky suggested that when there is a very special rov, really someone who is "more than just a rov," he might be recognized by a rebbe who would join the families in marriage.

Wealth can also give a family unexpected marriage opportunities and choices. Wealth as a form of exchange in marriage does not necessarily dilute religiosity. Rifky told me about one such match that she called a "real *knok shidekh*" 'explosive match', because two very different families joined in order to raise the status of both. The bride, Rifky said, comes from a "real" rabunishe but not very wealthy family; her great-uncle is a famous rov. Her mother's side is also an illustrious rabunishe family. The groom's family is "real" balebatish; they own a thriving business and are extremely wealthy. They did not have a very distinguished lineage, however; so when the match was made—a very wealthy family without much yikhes married into a very illustrious family without much money—both families benefited greatly. The new couple's children can have the benefits of wealth and the rabunishe status when it is their turn to make matches. This example shows that financial success in business and technology through participation in national and global economies cannot be easily categorized as secular. Rather, this kind of success becomes a bargaining chip for a family that wants to raise its position in a Hasidic class structure that also greatly values lineage and male piety. The business acumen of the groom's family created the possibility for alignment with a family whose prestige comes from religious learning and lineage, strengthening the religious and financial positions of both families within the community, as well as their future matchmaking abilities.

REDN A SHIDEKH 'MAKING A MATCH'

When Hasidic girls are in high school, they take "the test," which is not about math, English, or Jewish law. It is for Tay-Sachs disease and three other genetic diseases that occur most commonly among Ashkenazic Jews. The test is administered by Dor Yesharim 'Straight Generation', an Orthodox Jewish organization established in the 1980s, with worldwide contacts. Before parties are approached for a match, the matchmaker or the family calls Dor Yesharim. If neither or only one member of the couple is a carrier of one of the diseases, then a match may be considered. If both are carriers of the gene, the match would not go forward, as the couple would have a one in four chance of having a child with one of the genetic diseases. Neither the boy nor the girl nor the families ever know the results of the test. Thanks to Dor Yesharim's efforts, incidences of Jewish genetic diseases have plummeted among Hasidic Jews. Genetic testing is one more way that Hasidic Jews engage with the secular world in order to have it serve the Hasidic goal of remaking an ethical, religious society. As a representative from Dor Yesharim noted, "We want to adapt the world to what we are doing, not the reverse."

The test is only the beginning of the matchmaking process. As noted, Hasidim believe that there is one basherte for every person, pre-chosen by God. Trying to help those destined mates reach each other is everyone's concern. There are professional *shadkhunim/shadkhntes* 'matchmakers' (male and female) who are paid when a match is made, as well as individuals who jump at the chance to claim credit for making a match because it is considered a mitsve.[2] Despite this belief in destiny, the goal of matchmaking is to search for a compatible mate as well as for a *pasik* 'fitting' family. In contrast to other Orthodox Jews, before a boy and girl even meet Hasidic parents determine if they are suited by intensive investigation and data gathering. The kinds of questions asked about potential mates reveal Hasidic notions about men and women and their critique of romantic love as a basis for marriage. Hasidic Jews do not "date-out," as it is called in Hasidic English. The information-gathering phase precludes any contact between the pair, and matches are often rejected by parents or the bride or groom upon learning certain negative facts about the possible mate or the family. During this gathering of information, relatives are especially valued in providing honest insight into the character of the prospective mate. When I expressed surprise that people would be willing to provide personal information over the phone about a boy or a girl, Esty explained that if a relative called her, she wanted to be honest and tell all that she knew so as to help make a good match. Relatives who have one's interest at heart are important, because both the prospective *khusn* 'bridegroom' and *kale* 'bride' will try to emphasize the good and hide any bad or undesirable qualities from the other side. As Gitty commented, "By *shidikhim* 'matches' you always say the *males fin a mentsh* (the virtues of a person), right? You try to cover up the *khesroynes* 'drawbacks'." Rather than admit a problem, a family will try to cover up any mental or physical complications by asserting that the problem has passed or never existed at all.

In addition to relatives, everybody and anybody can, and is, telephoned and questioned. When a match was proposed for Hesky Hirsch, for example, not only did his family call relatives, friends, classmates, and teachers to ask about the girl and her family, they even called the local butcher to ask about the family's consumption patterns. The more one asks, Esty pointed out, the clearer the picture. Sometimes one gets contradictory information. This can be a tip-off that further questioning is necessary or that someone is not being completely honest. Hasidic women told me that by the time they actually meet the prospective bridegroom, they already have extensive knowledge about the kind of scholar, son, brother, and friend he is.

The questions asked about the potential bride are different, of course, than those asked about the groom. Questions frequently asked about the bride, according to Gitty, include: What does she look like? How did she do in school? Who are her friends? Was she loud or over-loud? Was she a big mouth? Was she smart? How does she dress? Is she *geshikt* 'organized' 'efficient', or is she slow? Is she outgoing, or is she quiet and shy?" Questions about girls focus on appearance, popularity and peer group, efficiency and organization skills (especially valued traits), intelligence, and personality such as being outgoing or shy. Certain characteristics are always desirable in a homemaker, for example, efficiency, organization, and neatness. A girl's character profile is also matched to the boy's in hopes of a compatible fit. A girl who is very quiet, for example, might not be very happy with a gregarious boy. Further, as the homemaker, a girl must share a sense of aesthetics and lifestyle with the family she is marrying into. Rifky told me that in-laws must feel comfortable in their daughter-in-law's house, be able to eat her food, and not be "embarrassed" by how she raises their grandchildren. In this way the girl has to live up to her in-laws' standard of living, economically, aesthetically, and religiously.

I was generally exposed to less information about questions boys were asked, but I know that much effort goes into investigating a boy's level of Torah scholarship and religious practice. An especially important source of information is his *khevrise* 'study partner', as boys study Torah in groups of two, in addition to studying as a class with a teacher. Parents ask these questions not merely to assess "appropriate" religious feeling, commitment to study, and level of intelligence, but also to ensure that the bride will be able to count on her mate as a companion who is not always lost in prayer or study. Esty explained some of the motivations behind asking about a boy's prayer habits:

> When you ask about *davening* 'praying', for example, you want to know if he davens so much. That's not so good because then you will be waiting for him a whole day. But not too fast either. You want someone normal.

The local category of "normal," as mentioned earlier, implies a certain conformity to desirable Hasidic norms of behavior. Someone who is "not normal" is either a nonconformist or has a psychological problem.

At times, however, even extensive questioning does not reveal well-hidden problems. Sometimes this may lead to divorce, as in the example Gitty offered:

> There are a lot of divorces today . . . someone got married. She's a beauty, she's a beauty. She might not be the brightest at school but she's a beauty, *azoy geshikt*, so efficient. And she saw that her husband just . . . there's no real love. He just indulges in her and that's it. *Shoyn* 'just' after three months, he picked up a hand, hit her. Abuse. And they found out that he takes pills for nerves. She never, ever knew. She left, she was scared . . . She still keeps up with the *shver, shviger*, in-laws, whatever. Yeah, but he does not want to get a divorce . . . He's not 100 percent. He wants her back and that's it. He likes her.

Somebody had to have known before the wedding, I suggested. Gitty agreed. Somebody must have known he was taking medication, but no one revealed it. As Gitty put it: "They figured that he's a little funny and she's a little slow—perfect match. They didn't know [about the] abuse." In this case the drawbacks of each marriage candidate seemed to match the other, and so information was withheld because the match seemed fitting. In fact, over the past two decades there has been an increasing awareness of domestic abuse and little tolerance for it in the community. Notices posted in the bathrooms of a prominent synagogue give hotline numbers for abused women. However, Jewish law holds, even with domestic abuse, that a woman has to wait to be granted a divorce by her husband. In this case the woman's husband is not granting the divorce, and so the woman must wait until he does to remarry, if she wishes. Pressure can be brought to bear on the husband by the girls' parents, or even by a rebbe who may send out some of his men to physically threaten a reluctant husband.

If both families and the boy and girl agree that the prospective mate seems appropriate, the girl's parents arrange a meeting with the boy. If they approve of him, there is usually a *beshou* (a meeting between the boy and girl). Hasidim "sit in," which means that the boy usually comes to visit the girl and the two are allowed to be alone together in a room with the door open for an hour or less. The two families also meet at this time. The beshou can be anxiety-provoking for boys and girls who have been strictly kept apart since beginning school. Gitty described her first meeting with her husband as "very scary"; she felt terribly shy and could barely talk. He read a brief passage from the Torah and then explained it to demonstrate his level of learning. She told me he mumbled, and she could hardly hear him. Perhaps this is because, as Mordkhe Schaechter suggested, some Hasidic males find it prestigious to speak quickly and unclearly, as it has come to connote a level of religious fluency.[3] Unsure that he was the right one, she asked to meet again, which is acceptable. The second meeting was better, because both felt a bit more comfortable. When Gitty's parents asked her what she thought, she told them he was the one. Her future husband felt the same way, so they got engaged, and a few months later they were married. A girl or boy can, however, refuse the match and ask to meet other prospective mates.

On the other hand, the beshou can also be an exciting time when both boy and girl are satisfied that they are making the right choice. A pretty, blond young bride, Zisi, whom I met in bride class, told me that by the time she met her intended, her father had asked so much about him, that she was pretty sure he was right for her. Her mother, however, did not want to push her and told her that she did not have to decide right after the first meeting. For some Hasidim it is a *mineg* 'custom' to avoid eye contact with the opposite sex out of modesty. Zisi's mother told her, however, that when Zisi walked into the room, her intended smiled; in a typical practical solution, he had a mirror on the table and could see her reflection without looking into her eyes. Zisi was all aflutter that her intended was happy with her appearance. Their first meeting was also satisfactory, because he talked honestly about his father's death two years earlier. The loss of a parent is considered a drawback in a match because the family is not complete. In fact, orphans have a much harder time finding matches. It was important, Zisi told me, that he talked about "real" things right away, such as his family situation. Although they met again, Zisi knew after the first meeting that they would get married.

It is rare, but occasionally the boy and girl will not meet until the wedding itself. I heard about a girl whose father was a famous rov, and after her father investigated the boy and proposed the match to her, she immediately agreed. Her classmates asked her how she could agree without meeting him. (In fact, she did see a photo of him.) She said that if important people trusted her father to interpret difficult questions about Jewish law, she could trust her father's choice for a bridegroom. Most girls were awed by this trust in and respect for a father.

If both parties agree to the engagement after the beshou, the two families drink a *lekhayim* 'toast' together that includes a ceremonial breaking of a plate, a piece of which is often set in gold and presented as a necklace to the bride. Then, the *tnoyim* 'engagement' terms are drawn up, specifying the exchange of goods between the families in the forms of gifts to the bride and groom before the wedding, as well as who will pay to *upshtufirn* 'outfit' the new couple. The gifts given to the bride and groom begin the process of their transformation into adulthood, culminating in the provisioning of a Jewish home complete with furniture and appropriately attired husband and wife. A husband, for example, will need a *shtraml*, the expensive beaver fur hat worn by married men on holidays, and certain kinds of coats, vests, and jackets. A wife will need at least two wigs and two hats or kerchiefs, one for everyday use and one for the Sabbath and holidays. She will also need many new "outfits" for the seven days of parties that follow the wedding, and new nightgowns and underwear (as part of keeping the laws of family purity). The cost of the wedding itself also is negotiated. The goal is to have the cost to both families balance out, so that, for example, if the bride's family pays for the wedding meal and the bride's gown, the groom pays for the wedding liquor and, perhaps, the music, typically in the form of a one-man band on a synthesizer. Finally, the young couple is usually supported by the bride's family for the first year of marriage if the boy continues to study Torah, as is now common. Marriage for Hasidic Jews is explicitly a financial and social proposition that supports Jews' sacred duty to have children and build up the community.

The consumption involved in marriage is made to serve the Hasidic goals of provisioning a new Jewish home and inspiring feelings of love between a bride and groom. At every Jewish holiday during the en-

gagement period, for example, gifts are exchanged. Girls typically receive religious books, such as prayer books, which they display publicly when they go to synagogue. They also receive jewelry appropriate
for an adult married woman: a diamond ring, earrings, a bracelet, a
watch, and pearls. Boys receive a complete religious library and religious articles for the home, for example, a large silver Hanukah meno-
rah worth, minimally, hundreds of dollars. Under the guise of practic-
ing Yiddish, Gitty, who had just gotten married, actually questioned
me just as carefully as I was questioning her about marriage and love.
When I expressed surprise that Hasidic brides received so much jewelry during the engagement period, Gitty asked me what people in my
"circles" give to the bride, although it was never clear exactly what my
circle was. She was shocked to learn that most of my friends had not
received any gifts from the groom's family before the wedding. Gitty
compared my practices to hers:

> You see, *by dikh* 'with you' you know him longer. You're going out.
> There's a certain *libshaft* 'love' that it's not depending on anything
> because you're going out for years. By us, we meet once . . . when
> he meets her [at the wedding] she has to be fully adorned. She has
> to strike . . . Oy, what we get!

The engagement, wedding, and the first year of marriage require a
tremendous amount of money from both families, especially since Hasidic families are so large and so many weddings have to be brokered.
Some families go into debt, taking out loans, and others try to limit
spending to the basics. The Bobover rebbe and other rebbes have encouraged people to spend less money on engagement presents and
make arrangements with wedding halls that will give just the basics
for the wedding at a lower cost. Gitty told me that for families who
cannot afford to "make *khasene*" (put on a wedding), the families agree
to write out *takunes*, or a plan for limited spending by both sides of the
family. Many families have responded to the rebbe's plea for greater
simplicity and have done away with giving the groom an expensive
khusn-zayger, a wrist-watch traditionally given to a groom. However,
familial differences in wealth and its display continue to be touchy
subjects. When, for example, Yitty Fine's "fancy" future in-laws (whose
son, to everyone's surprise, had asked for the khusn-zayger) brought
over an expensive silver basket filled with candies wrapped in silver
foil for the exchange of treats (*shalekh-munes*) during the holiday of
Purim while I was visiting, Mrs. Fine told her husband that she felt
embarrassed. They had only given the future in-laws a huge wicker
basket filled with wine, dried fruit, pastries, and candies. "Listen," Mr.

Fine told his wife, "if they [the in-laws] feel they have to do that, that's their problem. There's nothing to be embarrassed about. We didn't do it for any of the others [their other married children]."

The Hasidic women I spoke with were confident about the matchmaking process and its efficacy in building strong marital relationships. Frequently citing the high rate of divorce in North America, they claimed that their marriages are stronger and built on mutual interest and similar personalities, rather than fleeting passion. Dating without help from family is evidence to Hasidic women of the breakdown of the modern family, something that other nonliberal religious groups such as Evangelical Christians in North America also posit (e.g., Ammerman 1987). In our Yiddish tutorials, Gitty persistently asked me about dating because she had trouble understanding how a girl could trust a boy whom her parents had not checked out. She wondered about parents who would not "care" enough to do that checking. According to Gitty, anybody can be on good behavior for a date. She suggested that by questioning people from all facets of a boy's life, the matchmaking process actually produced more accurate information. Gitty seemed especially interested to hear about my own experience, perhaps because, although I represented a Jew she probably pitied, we had become friends. When I told her that my parents had liked my boyfriend but allowed me to make my own decisions, she suggested, to my irritation, that they had shirked their responsibility. To her, lack of parental involvement meant lack of interest and commitment to the children. She brushed aside my attempts to explain that, in my opinion, my parents had trusted my judgment. Matchmaking practices, then, offer a direct counterpoint to Hasidic notions about Gentile marriages and the high divorce rate in North America. With familial support and help, Hasidic women argue, they are actually making sure that their children will have happier, more stable marriages than nonbelievers have.

KALE 'BRIDE' CLASS

Once a match is made, young men and women must begin to prepare for the physical, emotional, and religious responsibilities of marriage. This includes learning how to talk modestly about topics considered private and, before the engagement, not mentioned. Socialization for these new forms of modest comportment and talk happens most often in group or individual classes for brides and grooms, *kale* and *khusn* classes, respectively. These gender-segregated classes provide communally approved ways of teaching young people about to enter another stage of life how to live a Jewish marriage and build a Jewish home. The classes are also used to legitimize the superiority of Hasidic marriage practices to girls who, despite censorship, seem to have absorbed some North American ideas about romantic love.[4] As the wedding day nears, parents choose a kale-teacher. Bride classes can be one-on-one tutorials, especially popular today, small groups of girls and a teacher, or a large group of up to fifty girls. The classes generally meet for about eight sessions and can cost from $100 to $600. Khusn classes, in contrast, are usually one-one-one with a rabbi, last only a few days, and are just before the wedding. Before these classes, young women generally know little about what to expect when they go home with their new partner after the wedding, and little about the intricate laws of family purity or *tahares-hamishpukhe*, which regulate conjugal intimacy, although some have older siblings who share information with them. Parents and teachers told me that before an engagement there was no need for boys and girls to be exposed to knowledge about sexuality and reproduction; knowledge not put to use was considered potentially harmful and distracting.

In kale class Hasidic parents expect their daughters to enter a controlled environment where they will learn what are considered private and sensitive aspects of Jewish religious practice. I had already attended several inspirational lectures for Hasidic brides in Boro Park, as well as a Hasidic refresher class for married women, also in Boro Park. The refresher course was open to anyone, because married women are not as protected from those who are different in the same way as brides. When I tried to join a small Hasidic kale class as a bride myself, however, parents of the others in the class did not tolerate my presence. I had met the kale teacher in an inspirational lecture and told her about my research, as well as my upcoming marriage. She reluctantly agreed to let me into the class, on the condition that I would not interact in the classroom. She felt that with my different background I would not be well served by the class. She also told me that the girls in the class were very young and innocent, and she did not think they should be exposed to my different experience. When I promised only to observe the class, she graciously told me I would be welcome. But a few days later she called to say that the other girls' parents had asked to see a class list and did not want an unknown, non-Hasidic girl to participate. The parents, the teacher explained, did not want their daughters exposed to different kinds of girls who might confuse or distract their daughters.

On the advice of Malky, the Litvish woman whose home I shared when I stayed overnight in Boro Park, I decided, instead, to enroll in a larger kale class where "all kinds of girls" went—Hasidic Boro Park girls, Litvish, Sephardic, and more modern types. The class met in Flatbush, a more modern neighborhood in Brooklyn. I enrolled by phone and on the first day, when we were asked to fill out index cards about ourselves (the school we attended, the date of the wedding, and so on), I indicated that I was a graduate student doing research on Hasidic Yiddish and childrearing. Much to my relief, I was admitted, no questions asked, although I was not allowed to tape-record the classes; the teacher, Rebbetsin Cohen, explicitly asked girls not to tape-record because the materials she would be teaching were "sensitive."[5] The classes I attended were, perhaps, not what very Hasidic girls might hear. Because she was teaching a mixed crowd, Rebbetsin Cohen had to address a wider range of expectations and experiences. For example, when she taught the brides about the laws of family purity, she always qualified which laws were for families that were more stringent and which were for the less stringent. However, a number of mothers told me that these classes were not very different from any other, and a number of Bobover teachers told me they had attended these same classes.

The classes were lectures that took place in Rebbetsin Cohen's finished basement. Girls took notes and were able to ask questions, but there was little discussion. Before and after the class, girls chatted. They talked mainly about their preparations for the wedding and married life. Girls compared their decisions regarding, for example, choice of furniture for the new apartment, type of gown or headpiece, the shape of their diamonds, and the choice of wedding halls. There was also much discussion of plans for after the wedding: Would the couple move to Israel or stay in Boro Park? Would the bride work while her husband continued to study Torah? I heard no explicit discussion of the class materials except for the frequent commiseration about how overwhelming all these new responsibilities were. Many of the girls seemed to know one another either from school or because of a family connection. Girls generally ignored me, except for one outgoing girl with whom I shared a car service one night (Zisi), perhaps because I looked and sounded significantly different, older, and with strange, not-quite-right modest clothing. Many may have assumed I was a returnee to the faith.

The Laws of Family Purity: Creating Modest Women

Kale class balances instruction in the laws of family purity that regulate physical relations between a husband and wife, with *hashgukhe* 'outlook' (guiding principles for everyday life). Girls study the laws and how modesty should shape this new relationship. Rebbetsin Cohen, by day a Hebrew Bible teacher in a Litvish girls' high school, was a compelling and thorough teacher. In her lectures, she tempered the complicated Jewish laws with stories, always reminding the girls that the laws would elevate their lives, bringing them "serenity, *kedishe* 'holiness', and joy." Rebbetsin Cohen began the class by emphasizing the unique and serious nature of the laws of family purity. Among Jews there are three central sins, she said: idol worship, murder, and adultery. A woman who does not go to the ritual bath (*mikve*) is seen as an adulterer. Further, the Jewish community values a mikve at the same level as a yeshiva. Sages tell us, she said, that if a Jewish community only has enough money to build a synagogue, buy a Torah, or build a mikve, the community should build the mikve. Rebbetsin Cohen suggested that a mikve deals with the seeds of the Jewish nation, and a yeshiva, the male study house, develops its roots. She repeated an oft-evoked Hasidic belief about divinely intended gender complementarity, where men and women have their separate responsibilities and rewards for the reproduction of Jewish life. Because of the private nature of the laws of family purity, however, children never see their parents following them, unlike most of the other commandments. "In our world," Rebbetsin Cohen suggested, "we hear almost nothing about the marital relationship or the laws that shape it. What's a girl to think?" she asked. The purpose of bride class is to initiate girls into this more private set of commandments.

The laws of family purity set the rhythm for conjugal life. Sacred text and rabbinic commentary provide detailed ritual practices revolving around a woman's menstrual cycle. Brides must learn how to monitor their bodies during their monthly periods. When the period begins, intimacy between husband and wife ceases. A woman is called a *nide* (Hebrew, 'impure woman'), so characterized when blood comes out of the uterus. Rebbetsin Cohen discussed the translation of the Hebrew term nide, suggesting that all the Standard English translations were inadequate: unclean, unwell, or impure, although this last one she considered the most accurate. She warned, however, that the word "impure" implies sin, and this is not accurate. A woman who is nide has not sinned. On the contrary, her body is working as it should, and she is remaining separated from her husband as she should. The best strategy, she suggested, was not to translate the term at all, because Hebrew, the most modest language, was also the most accurate.

In order to prevent intimacy while they are nide, brides learn about the most minute, everyday physical and verbal interactions that are forbidden during their periods. These include, for example, touching, sleeping in the same bed, pouring a drink for each other, or a wife making a husband's bed. Joking and laughing are also discouraged during this time of separation. All these actions are considered intimate and familiar, with the possibility of tempting couples toward further intimacy, which is strictly forbidden. When Rebbetsin Cohen was explaining the laws of separation to the girls, she told them about all the prohibitions that only apply to husbands. When she is menstruating, for example, a wife can eat from her husband's leftovers, but her husband cannot eat from hers. A man's body will respond much more quickly than a woman's, explained Rebbetsin Cohen, and women have to protect their husband's *makhsheyve* 'thoughts'. While males are authority figures in the family, they are also more at the mercy of their bodies. Wives have an obligation, then, not only to obey their husbands but also to protect them. Wives monitor their bleeding until there is absolutely no blood for several days. When a woman is "clean," she is immersed in the ritual bath, which sanctifies her for resuming full relations with her husband.

A central theme of the class was preparing girls who had been taught to dress, behave, and speak modestly to continue to be modest in a new set of circumstances. Very early on Rebbetsin Cohen briefly explained the mechanics of intercourse to the brides in clinical, matter-of-fact terms. She then acknowledged that it was probably shocking for a girl to hear this the first time, "a girl who has learned to cover up." Indeed, although, as I suggested, some sisters, cousins, or peers sometimes do share knowledge with girls before they are brides themselves, there are stories of girls fainting the first time they hear about intercourse. Then Rebbetsin Cohen reminded the girls that modesty does not mean shame but rather appropriateness. During marriage, she said, the "cherished and precious" human body is used for the purpose for which it was created by God. In this way, Rebbetsin Cohen framed sexuality as holy.

The brides also learned cultural and religious expectations for how to comport themselves and how to speak modestly with their new husbands in public and in private. For example, in the first class, girls learned to refer to intercourse and genitals by their loshn-koydesh names after translating them one time only from the clinical terms. Rebbetsin Cohen cited the sage Maimonedes, whose claim that Hebrew was the most modest language made it most appropriate for talking about private, intimate matters. Girls learned to use this vocabulary themselves in order to refer to subjects that were generally not spoken of in the community. In public, Rebbetsin Cohen told the girls, husband and wife should be like brother and sister. She compared Jewish romantic love, which is private, sacred, and controlled, to Gentile lust, which is indiscriminately flaunted on the streets. In the ritual bath (particularly in the waiting room), girls have to be discreet and private. Going to the mikve means that you will be having "relations" with your husband that evening. It is therefore immodest to tell anyone that you are going or to talk to other women once you are in the waiting room. Girls should be proud to be there as Orthodox wives, but they should be discreet. Being in a mikve waiting room, said Rebbetsin Cohen, "we cross the sea of time," meaning girls carry on a tradition that began with their Jewish foremother, Sarah. In order to honor that tradition, girls should watch their words; they should not gossip in the waiting room, nor should they tell someone else whom they saw there. This form of modesty, said Rebbetsin Cohen, protects a Jewish woman's honor (*kuved*).

The brides were also taught how to express their physical desires in a modest way, using a range of English euphemisms for intercourse. Girls learned that "in the bedroom" modesty must determine talk and thought. For example, wives should be enthusiastic about their "husband's affections," but they must always maintain an appropriate level of restraint in expressing that enthusiasm. Wives may not verbally ask for intercourse; they should, instead, ask with their hearts, instructed Rebbetsin Cohen. Brides also were taught that Gentiles might talk about politics or art during relations. "Phooey, Jews only speak words of love," said Rebbetsin Cohen. Hasidic females are taught that modesty during intimacy transforms sexuality from the physical plane to the spiritual. She even suggested that girls try to think about holy sages during relations or intimacy with their husbands. The strength to control their thoughts has the potential to sanctify the act itself and also to sanctify children that may be conceived.

Although the laws of family purity were new to the class, Rebbetsin Cohen and other teachers of brides framed them as part of the familiar Jewish endeavor of disciplining the physical, material world in order to have it reach the level of the soul, erasing distinctions between spirituality and materiality. On the first day, for example, Rebbetsin Cohen drew on an explanation that girls had been hearing since they were very young. She told the brides to imagine that they were back at Mt. Sinai where the Jews pledged, "*naseh venishma*" (Hebrew, 'we will do and we will listen'). As with all Jewish commandments, girls were assured that once they were following the commandments, they would understand the laws' true beauty. I have suggested that girls, from a very young age, are taught that they must use their autonomy to fulfill God's commandments so that when their teacher leaves the room, for example, they do not stop praying as they are "praying to God, not a teacher." Similarly, in their transformation from girls to wives, brides are told that they must take responsibility for disciplining themselves as they observe these new laws. "No one checks on you," Rebbetsin Cohen told the brides, "This is between you and God."

Pleasures of Discipline

Despite the requirement that girls participate in the laws regardless of their understanding or desire, many of the bride classes were devoted to explaining all the benefits girls would accrue when they disciplined their individual bodies and minds to be modest with their husbands. In Chapter 6, I discussed the ways modesty mediates the complicated desires of Hasidic women to be with it, but not modern. This inflection of Hasidic femininity was elaborated, in part, by the rejection of other Orthodox Jewish femininities. However, distinctions between Orthodox Jewish women were muted in bride classes. Instead, bride teachers' lectures addressed all girls' desires to participate in the pleasures of romantic love. However, bride teachers tell girls that authentic romantic love is achieved through ritual practice, differentiating Jewish romantic love from their perceptions of Gentile and secular romantic love. In a one-day lecture for brides with a different teacher, for example, the instructor began by asking the brides to raise their hands if they felt they were in love with their intended. All the girls, giggling, raised their hands. The teacher, an older woman, snorted and told them that they did not know what love was all about. Love, she told them, is about building a life together over time. Love is not instant. It comes about through shared experiences raising a Jewish family.

In their marriages, bride teachers said that girls would be able to go beyond the emptiness of individual fulfillment and lust, the realm of Gentiles. The discipline that Hasidic brides must acquire, which in some cases means they sacrifice their own individual desires, will lead to material and spiritual rewards, their teachers promised. The commandment of family purity would give them all that the secular world promised and much more: love, romance, beautiful children, fulfillment of God's will, and rewards in the afterlife.

Rebbetsin Cohen presented the laws of family purity as a civilizing discourse that disrupted the liberal oppositions of nature and culture, the primitive and the civilized. She told the girls that the laws are the most natural way to help them follow the rhythm of their own bodies (i.e., their menstrual cycles). The laws regulating Hasidic conjugal intimacy leads to refinement of the body and the soul because they are God's design. Jewish ritual—the laws of family purity in this case—gives Jewish couples the discipline to live as God intended, ensuring that romantic love is tempered by periods of platonic love. One girl questioned whether the laws of family purity were "like a prison" because of the separation between husband and wife during menstruation. When another girl expressed her fear that the laws were "cold and depressing," Rebbestin Cohen elaborated a metaphor of married life she called "mountains and valleys" to show the brides that the laws, although difficult to observe at first, actually lead to a much deeper relationship with their husbands than Gentiles and the secular can even imagine. When a girl is under the wedding canopy, Rebbetsin Cohen asked, does she want love and passion or friendship and peace? She really wants both. Rebbetsin Cohen compared love and passion to being on top of a mountain: the air is crisp and fresh, but a person who is always high up loses the ability to see the view; a valley is quieter, a place of rest. When a person who has been in a valley comes to the top of the next mountain, the view is fresh and beautiful all over again. Valleys are not inferior to mountains. They are just different.

Distance or closeness to a husband matches the "mountains and valleys" of women's physical bodies. So, although the laws may initially seem like a burden and, perhaps, frightening to young brides, they have built-in rewards. Not only are girls fulfilling God's commandments when they follow the laws, but they attain a closeness to and respect from their husbands, which those who have no such laws cannot conceive of. Gentiles, suggested Rebbetsin Cohen, rely on the easy way of communicating—through physical love and passion. Look on the street, she advised, to see that it means nothing. During their time apart, Jewish husbands and wives have to develop a whole other dimension of communication. They say to each other, "I remember why I chose you." What is always available is not always appreciated, explained Rebbetsin Cohen. Distance enhances a relationship. She concluded that the laws tell us what "women's lib" only discovered in the 1960s: a woman is not just a body. A man can forget this, but Jewish husbands always appreciate their wives.

In order to show the brides how "warped" "American society" is compared to the Jewish Orthodox world, Rebbetsin Cohen divided North America into "Hollywood" and "Christianity." In Hollywood, she stated, no one is married. More generally a large percentage of the American population is divorced, drug addicted, and suicidal, she said, and added that "they [secular Americans] can't criticize Jewish marriage. They can't take it seriously." The other voice of America is the message of Christianity, because "America is a Christian country." The message of Christianity, she said, is that "sex" is a dirty word. The holiest person, the priest, does not even get married. Note here that "Christian" is being glossed as Catholic. The married state by default is impure. "Christianity," said Rebbetsin Cohen, "is just as *shmitsik* 'dirty' and perverted as Hollywood." Both think that the sexual act is an animalistic act. In contrast, she claimed, Jews see that sex is a human act and also a mitsve, thus conflating holiness and humanity. Rebbetsin Cohen imitated an imaginary Gentile, complete with her version of African American English, to show how "animals copulate and Jews love each other":

> Poor Jew. I feels sorry for the poor Jew-man . . . I wants my woman, I takes my woman. [Brides laugh.] But we say poor goy . . . The whole thing is beautiful. The laws of tahares-hamishpukhe keep it from deteriorating. We are on the opposite pole from Hollywood. We pity Gentiles because it [sex] remains a physical act for them. For Jews, marriage brings us up . . . children complete us . . . the whole thing is beautiful.

The discipline necessary to be a pious Jew produces civilized, ethical humans. It is those who only inhabit the sphere of the material body who are like animals.

Throughout the class, Rebbetsin Cohen used a discourse of truth and beauty to define Jewish marriage. Jews know "real" beauty, she claimed, because they have the sensitivity to appreciate the more subtle ways that love, made holy through the discipline of ritual, infuses everyday life. For example, she suggested that Gentiles are not "refined" enough to perceive how much love everyday activities express. After going to the mikve, when a woman is again allowed to pour juice for her husband, a Gentile will never see the special romantic glance that passes between a Jewish husband and wife as she hands him the glass. Gentiles can never understand the most romantic words in a Jewish marriage: "Today I was *toyvled* 'immersed' in the mikve." The discipline required in a Jewish marriage leads to a holier, more refined humanity and a deeper conjugal relationship based on respect and shared aims for transcendence.

Although Gentiles were constantly held up to brides as examples of how *not* to behave, Rebbetsin Cohen also marshaled Gentiles' acknowledgment of the superiority of Jewish marriages. Rebbetsin Cohen told the girls that a New York University doctor, an "expert," said that there must be magic in the waters of the mikve because the insides of all Jewish women look so supple and healthy. The approbation of a doctor, someone with secular social prestige, was used as unbiased proof that the Jewish way of life is the healthiest and the most "natural." This example is similar to Esty's suggestion, noted in chapter 6, that Hasidic women's wigs and hats, their religious stringency, also happen to make them even more elegant than women in Manhattan. Gentiles' acknowledgment of Jewish superiority further supports Jewish women's claims to distinction, as well as, perhaps, assuring Hasidic girls that they are not missing anything by not fully participating in North American life.

General Hasidic beliefs about modesty, as already discussed, include the belief that "looking good" and being modest are complementary, not contradictory. Similarly, in bride class girls heard that women's obligation to look good for their husbands transforms adornment and consumption into a religious requirement. Rebbetsin Cohen advised the girls to choose beautiful things for their new conjugal bedrooms, to always be "sweet-smelling" and look good. "Take a shower," she said, "throw out those ratty slippers, and always have clean night clothing." It is a wife's responsibility to make herself desirable to her husband and to show him that she loves being with him. However, as Rebbetsin Cohen warned, "a woman should always look beautiful, but she can never lose by being more modest." Rebbetsin Cohen told the girls that marital relations are not only a commandment but also a "*simkhe* 'a joy' and a pleasure." Buying new clothes, making their bedrooms beautiful, being stringently modest, fulfilling commandments, experiencing joy and pleasure all support one another in defining the Hasidic woman. Combining aesthetics, religiosity, and consumption, Hasidic women explode the perceived limitations in the secular distinctions between the material and the spiritual, the secular and the religious, asceticism and sensuality. This allows them to participate in a disciplined way of life that will bring true individual happiness through the fulfillment of religious obligation.

Nevertheless, noted Rebbetsin Cohen, in certain situations a Jewish wife will have to choose between external appearance and the proper observation of the laws of family purity. She instructed girls who might confront this situation to sacrifice outer beauty in order to attain true spiritual beauty. For example, a girl may have to decide between going to the mikve and looking good; if a woman immerses herself in the mikve just before the Sabbath begins, she may not have time to put on makeup, for doing so would be "working" during the Sabbath, which is forbidden. For the entire Sabbath period, then, she would be without makeup. Rebbetsin Cohen was certain, she told the girls, that husbands would prefer that their wives go to the mikve rather than wear makeup. "A woman looks so beautiful to her husband after the mikve," she went on, "and that's who it's a mitsve to look beautiful for." Drawing on her own personal experience, she told the girls that often when she comes home from the mikve, she looks terrible: her hair is wet, she is wearing only a kerchief and not a wig— wet hair stretches a wig, she warned the girls—and she might not be wearing any makeup. Her husband's face, nevertheless, lights up when he sees her, and he looks at her the same way he did under the wedding canopy after so many years of marriage. Girls must be prepared at times to discipline themselves in order to make the right choice between religious obligation to God and their husband and their own vanity.

In an effort to move brides emotionally and encourage them in their transformation into Jewish wives, Rebbetsin Cohen often related inspirational stories of women who made personal sacrifices to follow the laws of family purity and the rewards they received. She once told the girls about a woman who convinced her nonreligious husband to observe the laws of family purity and how happy she became. She also described a disabled Orthodox woman who made a tremendous effort to get to the mikve in the middle of winter, only to discover there was no hot water. She immersed herself anyway, and nine months later she gave birth to a beautiful baby. The girls are reminded that sometimes personal sacrifices are needed to achieve real happiness.

Disciplined modesty requires that each girl recognize and submit to new male authority figures, her husband and his rebbe. Modest behavior is a wife's responsibility, but judgments about modesty are not hers to make. Girls were told repeatedly that regardless of what they learned in class, they were to follow their husband and his rebbe in all areas of *rukhnies* 'spirituality'. For example, Rebbetsin Cohen said that it was most appropriate and modest to have intercourse during the night, but a wife has to trust her husband to decide: "A husband needs a wife to be a wife, not a *mashgiekh* 'interpreter of Jewish law' in the bedroom." All the bride teachers I observed stressed that when wives let their husbands be the leaders in matters of spirituality, *shulem-bayes* 'peace at home' reined. Shulem-bayes and how to attain it were, in fact, one of the most frequent and popular lectures for women in Boro Park. These lectures most often advised women that when they supported their husbands as the spiritual leaders, their own needs would be met or they would change and become better wives.

Through stories about wives who attempted to interpret the laws of family purity themselves, teachers warned girls not to overstep their authority. For example, wives monitor the end of their period by judging when they are finished bleeding, but often the color on the cloth used to check for blood is ambiguous. If they are unsure whether their period is over, girls should show the cloth to their husband's rebbe who would *paskn* the *shayle* ('resolve the question' by proclaiming on an unclear area of the law) and thus determine if a wife is ready to go to the mikve. Rebbetsin Cohen suggested that a girl might feel it is immodest to show a rabbi a cloth that had been in her body. You might, she said, think to yourself that you will just tell your husband that you checked and your period was not yet over. That, Rebbetsin Cohen said, is not being frum, and she recounted cases where women interpreted the color themselves and for three months told their husbands they were impure; finally, the husband insisted that she consult a rabbi, who glanced at the cloth and said it was fine. "The frum thing to do is to ask [an authority figure]," said Rebbetsin Cohen. The message was that frum wives allow familial or communal authority figures to make the final decisions on questions of appropriate religious practice. This stance to questioning and authority is part of the broader cultivation of Hasidic women who willingly submit to Hasidic male authority (see chapter 3).

The emphasis on teaching girls to allow their husbands to be religious authorities is perhaps an attempt to prevent wives from using the mikve as a way to control sex, and thus their husbands. Marmon (1999), for example, documents how many Orthodox women, including some Hasidic women, use the mikve as their own realm of authority and control in the conjugal relationship. Ginsburg (1987) similarly shows how women in an Orthodox Syrian Jewish community used the mikve to make claims on their husbands and assert their own demands. In my own research, women did not speak of this, but perhaps it would have been considered inappropriate, given my own uncertain religious orientation and social role as a bride and then as a new wife.

AN ALTERNATIVE PATH TO TRUE LOVE

Although romantic love is almost certainly a universal human characteristic, culture and history shape its specific manifestations (Ahearn 2001). One form of romantic love that emerged as a cultural ideal in nineteenth-century Europe is, according to some scholars, associated with Western secular modernity.[6] Despite its historical imbrication with the Industrial Revolution and the rise of capitalism, modern romantic love and the nuclear family in North America is imagined to be a haven from the market.[7] Hasidic girls, even though they are protected against much of the media through censorship, also express their desires for romantic love.[8] They also build families they hope to protect; they engage the modern narrative of love and marriage but learn to make different claims: true love only comes with self-discipline, and the real modern danger from which they must protect their families is Gentile and secular culture, not the market. Hasidic women reject the idea that individual choice leads to real love and happy families; instead, it is religious discipline and submission to familial and religious male authority that brings a deeper, more mature, personal satisfaction. In this alternative narrative of religious modernity, personal fulfillment, religious discipline, and redemption are complementary, not at odds.

In their everyday talk about matchmaking and marriage, Hasidic women distinguish Hasidic consumption from Gentile materialism, which is consumption for its own sake or for the superficial satisfaction of individual desires. Arranged marriages create sites for negotiating social class among observant Jews which redefines wealth and consumption as a religious obligation. The consumption required by huge Hasidic weddings and outfitting the new couple, for example, is the religious duty of the families. Hasidic families, in contrast to Gentiles, care enough to search out the mate God created just for each person. Bride-preparation classes caricature the love and marriage of Gentiles and the secular. Women tell girls that not only will they enjoy the gratifications that Gentiles have, but they will reach heights of intimacy and spirituality with their husbands and with God that Gentiles will never know. Hasidic women told me that no matter how materialistic they might become or how many modern innovations might slip in, their community is still more ethical, warmer, and family-oriented than the Gentile or the secular world. Stereotyping non-Hasidic life as immoral, cold, and anti-family is a discursive strategy for reinforcing the idea that Hasidic lives have a monopoly on truth.

My own presence, however, sometimes complicated these stereotypes, as do relationships with less observant Jews more generally. Although I was clearly not one of them, neither was I completely other. This is evident in the conversation I had with one of the kindergarten teachers, Morah Margolis, a few days after her son's wedding, to which I had been invited. She told me it was a shame that I had not been able to stay for the *mitsve-tants* 'commandment dance'. This is the only time at the wedding that the bride and groom dance in public, touching. Indeed, this is the only time they will ever touch publicly in their married lives together. The dance occurs at the end of the wedding, at around 4:00 AM, after the bride has danced with all her male relatives, holding a handkerchief or a sash between them in order to be modest. Then she finally dances with her husband, holding hands. I had seen the mitsve-tants at Gitty's wedding, which had indeed been very moving. Gitty cried and trembled, and at one point had to be supported by female relatives as she almost fainted. Actually, I had assumed at the time that she was overcome with bittersweet feelings at the life change that marriage entails, but she told me later that she had simply been terrified. Morah Margolis told me that at her son's wedding the mitsve-tants had been an especially emotional experience, with the *badkhn*, a cross between a jester and an emcee, telling the guests that the souls of her recently departed parents were rejoicing with them at the wedding.

I had just gotten married a few weeks before so I told her about my wedding, which had also been very emotional, with lots of weepy toasts, kissing, and hugging. I showed her pictures. She was really surprised, saying, "I thought by those kinds of weddings . . ." Then she stopped herself and said, "But you're not like them. They're so cold, like you see in the movies." She made a face of disgust, implying that "they" have weddings that are all for show, involving no real familial feelings.[9] My encounter with nonliberal Jewish brides as a liberal Jewish bride myself, who is also an anthropologist, remained ambiguous for all. Despite our shared familiarity with the narrative of romantic love, the dreams Hasidic brides and I had at marriage differed dramatically—all North American Jewish women but with distinct beliefs and feelings about love and family, the secular and the religious, freedom and discipline.

Coda

Recently, I received an unexpected e-mail from a rabbi in California whom I did not know. He wrote:

Hi Ms. Fader,
Having been born and raised in a Chasidic household in Boro Park, I enjoyed the write-up on your research [in the Fordham Faculty Newsletter] . . . You nailed it pretty good. I look forward to your future book and articles. By the way, where would I google to find your published article? . . . Also, the word we use is Yinglish.
Sincerely,
Shlomo

How, I wondered, could this Shlomo from California possibly have read an article about my research published the previous month in an obscure newsletter for the faculty at Fordham University? I e-mailed him back to ask. "You've been officially blogged," he responded, "by the most Orthodox blog out of Boro Park." Another Boro Parker had sent him the link, which he forwarded on to me. I clicked on the link and ended up at *Vuz iz Neias*, translated on the blog as "What's News," the self-proclaimed "Voice of the New York Orthodox Jewish Community." The slogan on top of the blog read, "Today's Neias 'news' is Tomorrow's News. If you don't see it here, it's not Neias."[1] The blog had excerpted part of the Fordham article. Underneath was a thread that gave me pause: people had posted their reactions to my research and also to me as a Jewish woman. I include some of these here verbatim in Hasidic English:

May 1, 2007 3:14 PM, Anonymous said . . . Who really cares what these people write? they cannot possibly understand our way of life so they write what is their perception and/or snippets of information they pick up on the street.

May 1, 2007 6:44 PM, O. Gevald said . . .
Is this Ayala Fader really a Frum girl who only pretended to "penetrate" the Orthodox Jewish community but all the while grew up in

one as well??? Just wondering. "Fader" is a *heimishe* [a communal spelling of *haymishe*] name.

May 1, 2007 11:33 PM, Anonymous said . . .
The name "ayala" is generally either heimish, israeli, or religious Zionist . . . in no way an outsider.

At May 2, 2007 12:14 PM, Anonymous said . . .
A number of women pursue advanced degrees in order to become more accomplished teachers, and they are required to write dissertations, etc. Better that they should fulfill requirements by researching and writing about some element of their own community rather than go chasing after information about goyish culture. I think it's interesting to see these studies from time to time; we just have to remember that they represent a "school project" rather than emes 'truth'.

This instance of "blogging the anthropologist" is one implication of working with a group of nonliberal Jews who, in their everyday lives, are formulating an alternative religious modernity. Their concern with their representation is part of their broader engagement with what they call the "secular" and "Gentile world," an engagement that is the basis of their cultural critique. Despite differences between Hasidic circles and across denominational divides, the Hasidic narrative of religious modernity described in this book takes particular issue with secular liberal versions of knowledge, truth, and freedom. As the posted comments suggest, academic knowledge, with its secular prestige, is, after all, a form of what many Hasidic women call *goyim-nakhes* 'Gentile rewards' (superficial rewards that have no real Jewish meaning). Those seeking secular knowledge, the blogger suggests, can never truly understand Jewish *emes* 'truth', because they do not live by the discipline of Jewish law as interpreted by contemporary Hasidic and other ultra-Orthodox Jews.

In this book I have described how Hasidic women elaborate nonliberal understandings of the person, language, knowledge, and the body. This is a broader epistemological project that aims, ultimately, at messianic redemption and yet depends on participation in and knowledge of secular modernity. The specifics of the Hasidic case have broader implications for anthropological conversations about alternative modernities, for both theory and methods. There are also implications for the discipline of anthropology when an ethnographic encounter between the anthropologist and those with whom she works is characterized by a contested struggle for truth(s).

ALTERNATIVE MODERNITIES AND NONLIBERAL
RELIGIOUS MOVEMENTS

Hasidic women's construction of an alternative religious modernity points to the value of ethnographically studying narratives of modernity thriving here at home. My approach contributes to the growing literature on what are variously called parallel modernities, alternative modernities, and multiple modernities.[2] This literature examines the encounter between the West and its others, often depicting a singular Western modernity against which non-Western others in postcolonial contexts react. One of the critiques of this literature has been that it essentializes Western modernity.[3] The experiences of Hasidic women and girls provide a corrective, a case of one alternative narrative of Western modernity thriving within the heart of cosmopolitan New York City. Hasidic Jews' historical and contemporary participation in European and North American forms of modernity complicates the analytic category of the West itself.

In some ways, the alternative religious modernity that Hasidic women and girls live is a very modern, North American story. Arriving after persecution, they have flourished in a climate of religious pluralism and tolerance. Fluent in the language of liberal democracy, Hasidic women use this language for their own nonliberal religious purposes; they have especially adapted the North American emphasis on the freedom to be different, on self-improvement, ingenuity, and self-transformation, to complement their Jewish religious beliefs that a person can achieve perfection through discipline, whether through controlling the inclination for evil, speaking in Hasidic English, or sewing up a slit in a skirt. Hasidic women even call themselves *amerikaner yidn* 'American Jews' in contrast to Jews in other global contexts. And yet, ultimately, Hasidic Jews roundly reject North American goals of tolerance and pluralism, or even, as noted in the introduction, neighborhood building across ethnic and religious lines. Rifky, for example, told me that in North America Hasidic Jews can "respect others, you know, live and let live," meaning that Jews and Gentiles can live side by side peacefully. However, she added:

> We don't raise our kids that this is ok, this is ok. We're lucky that we were born into this family ... and we have such an education, and we have an obligation to continue in that way, and it's not a matter of choice, and it's not a matter of acceptance and tolerance.

Hasidic Jews tolerate others as long as they do not interfere with their way of life. Tolerance, however, goes no further. "It has," as Rifky said, "no bearing on our life." The Hasidic interpretation of the North American concept of tolerance reveals broader tensions in the contemporary United States and elsewhere, where liberal politics of tolerance compete with the ever growing violence over difference, be it race, religion, gender, or ethnicity.

An aim of this book has been to include the experiences of Hasidic women and girls in Brooklyn within the body of scholarship that explores narratives of modernity as they are told in nonliberal religious communities. In particular, nonliberal women's piety expressed in unexpected ways and places continues to require social scientists to rethink notions about gender and power, public and private, the traditional and the modern, the secular and the religious. Consider, for example, the Shi'i Muslim women studied by anthropologist Lara Deeb (2006:23–28) in Lebanon. These middle-class women, called "fundamentalist" by some, have become committed to public piety. They define their inflection of Islam as "modern," in contrast to the "traditional" Islam of their grandmothers or the uneducated poor. Their modern Islam, these women claim, leads to spiritual progress, something the West lacks, despite its modernization.

Hasidic women's elaboration of an alternative Western religious modernity contrasts significantly because of Jews' long and complicated relationship to Euro-American forms of modernity. Hasidic women explain their generation's heightened religious stringency not as an attempt to create a more authentic Judaism through a critique of the past, but as a new set of disciplines required today in order to reach the spiritual level of their great grandmothers in Eastern Europe and their foremothers in the Bible.

When Hasidic women describe differences between Jews, Gentiles, and secular North Americans, they reproduce and invert English terms that are intrinsic to the Western narrative of secular modernity. These include primitive versus civilized, animals versus humans, and backward versus contemporary. In their story of Western modernity, religious practice, not secular knowledge, is the civilizing force. The very re-signification by Hasidic women of the term "modern," with its historical roots in the European social and political movements that led so many Jews away from traditional Judaism, is significant. To be modern, in the Hasidic sense, is to be more like a Gentile, to live, talk, eat, and dress like a Gentile, someone who is less "refined" because he or she lacks the religious discipline to fulfill God's commandments.

Hasidic women and girls' description of other Jewish women offers insight into the anxieties stemming from being stringently observant

Jews living in New York City. For Hasidic women and girls I worked with—Bobovers, the unaffiliated, and fellow travelers—there are Jewish feminine others who also represent what not to be. Girls who are not sufficiently fluent in the secular world are called in English "primitive or backward," and they are an embarrassment in front of other Jews and Gentiles. However, girls who are "too modern" are equally problematic, as they are too close to living like Gentiles. Ambivalence defines this Jewish othering, which seems, according to those I asked, to be exclusive to women and girls.

Accounting for nonliberal religious women's lives requires moving beyond a notion of agency premised on progressive liberal conceptions of autonomy and freedom. Hasidic mothers and teachers I worked with teach their daughters to engage with what are often assumed to be modern institutions, activities, and forms of knowledge. They smoothly navigate the national vernacular, consumption, developmental psychology, education, and self-help, as well as the leisure pursuit of reading fiction and the language of romantic love. The task for girls is to develop the self-discipline to participate in, yet change, the very meaning of these forms, so that secular modernity can facilitate the one and only Jewish *emes* 'truth'. This is done not through the "childish and selfish" freedoms of secular modernity, they claim, but through disciplined submission to a social and divine hierarchy. If we are to account for nonliberal women's agency, our portraits must include analyses of both gendered structures of power and nonliberal women's own goals for piety through discipline.

The everyday experiences of Hasidic women and girls also require us to rethink how to conceptualize and describe those who participate in religious enclaves and are simultaneously cosmopolitan urbanites. The lives of Hasidic women and girls today are marked by increasing religious stringency and an increasing participation in bourgeois consumption practices. For example, over the ten years that I have been visiting Boro Park, I have seen striking changes to the neighborhood: on a recent visit, I sat sipping an iced-cappuccino, something I had been unable to do in the mid-nineties, in a trendy new lunch spot that served panini, salmon teriyaki, and lattes. Construction can be seen on every side street, with shtotty townhouses going up. Stores are packed with elegant, high-priced shoes, clothes, lingerie, linens, baby clothes, and even some high-end chain stores such as Jacardi and Benneton. There is an ever growing market for shiny games and books for Jewish children, revealing the manufacturers' keen eyes for successful North American children's toys. And yet, from my observations, the Hasidic residents of Boro Park have not become less observant. The owner of a hat store told me that women's headscarves, the most religiously stringent head coverings, are becoming more popular. As the sales clerk in a new women's clothing store explained to me, "This store has very Hasidic clothing, very tsnies, *and* it looks like a store in Manhattan." Indeed, the all-white, spare store would not look out of place in Soho, but all the clothing is modest. For these women the ideal Hasidic femininity is with it, but not modern, increasingly stringent *and* increasingly fluent in the secular world and all it has to offer.

I have argued that attending to talk between adults and children, and between children themselves, offers a grounded methodology for ethnographically studying how an authoritative, alternative religious modernity is taught to the next generation of Hasidic women. These are women who will one day be responsible for physically and ideologically reproducing the next generation.[4] My approach pushes the anthropology of religion to go beyond assumptions about what should constitute its object of study. A focus on language socialization and childhood more broadly requires that the categories of the religious and the secular themselves become areas for investigation. Prayer and ritual, for example, are important sites for Hasidic girls' socialization into particular ways of speaking and being, but so, too, are monopoly games and playing jump rope. The focus on everyday interaction with children and adults, however, must strive to account, more than it has, for the ways that micro-level interactions are always about historical and cultural versions of morality, knowledge, and power.

An implication of my approach with nonliberal women and children is to break down the existing boundaries between the study of language and the study of religion and culture. Although I began my research with an interest in Hasidic girls' shift to English, I could not ignore how girls' language was embedded in broader concerns with modesty, in language, clothing, comportment, and access to knowledge. This has pushed me to go beyond an exclusive focus on language in order to account for what Hasidic women and girls themselves care about. I emphasize the importance of attending to sites where language and other semiotic media interact. This opens up an avenue for exploring relationships between language, the body, and material culture. An approach that includes space for how talk interacts with other semiotic media has the potential for gnerating new ways of understanding how a nonliberal religious community creates its own gendered narrative of truth across the life cycle.

AN ETHICAL ANTHROPOLOGY

Anthropology is premised on the relationship between the observer and the observed.[5] My claims to being the observer in Boro Park, however, were tenuous and contested by the Hasidic women I worked with. The blog I introduced at the beginning of this coda makes the "real" issue for my presence not my research but my own Jewishness, something that many of my Hasidic friends and acquaintances did as well, albeit more gently. How Jewish am I, where did I get my information, and where do my allegiances lie? As one of the posted comments wondered, am I really a "frum girl" who pretended to be an outsider? Ayala Fader is a *heimishe* name, or is it? Ayala could also be a name that secular Israelis might choose for their daughter, which, in fact, is what my own secular Israeli mother did. These kinds of interactions locate my personal history, including my academic interest in Hasidic Jews and my "secular" analysis, as part of broader debates about authenticity and modernity among contemporary North American Jews.

My work with Hasidic women has the same problem of translation and accountability as other "insider" or "native" ethnographies do, but it also has unique power dynamics inherent to research in nonliberal communities.[6] This is because nonliberal communities challenge and reject liberal beliefs about the person, autonomy, and difference that are the bedrock, not only for more liberal religions, but also for anthropology and the social sciences in general. Anthropologist Susan Harding (2000), for example, notes the struggle over power and knowledge in her study of Jerry Falwell and the Moral Majority, where conversion of the anthropologist was a real goal for those being studied. Harding suggests that when the anthropologist is a potential convert or returnee, the ethnographic encounter can be an active struggle between community members and the ethnographer to claim the "true" or "real" interpretive framework for why the ethnographer has come to the community, as well as what the anthropologist ultimately writes.

This description of competing frameworks, however, reproduces the very categories—religious and secular, observer and observed—that nonliberal religious women challenge in their everyday lives. In my research in Boro Park, the "true" or "real" interpretive framework was not always clear to me or to the women and girls I met. Even around the issue of friendship, competing interpretive frameworks came into play. For example, I invited Suri, an unusual Hasidic woman who left and then returned to her community, to my upcoming wedding, but she said she probably would be unable to come because a woman rabbi was conducting the ceremony. I was hurt, having assumed that she felt as I did, that our friendship would transcend our religious differences. I had traveled to Brooklyn because I wanted to understand another kind of Judaism. Wouldn't she want to come to Manhattan to see mine? I have come to realize, though, just how "located and partial," to use

Donna Haraway's words (1991), my own assumptions were, mired as they are in secularist understandings of religions as equally valid, private, and individualized (Asad 1993).

The Hasidic women I write about in this book have political and religious convictions that are troubling to me personally and professionally. Because they share with me the social space of New York City, there is the issue of contested citizenship; we have different notions of community and civic responsibility. But my position as an anthropologist requires a different stance from my position as a Jewish New Yorker. These issues are competing, but not mutually exclusive, interpretive frameworks that all have a powerful voice in North American politics today.

Now with children of my own, rather than studying Hasidic children's questions, I find myself confronting those of my children. Visiting Boro Park recently, I brought along my six-year-old daughter, Talia. I knew I could not bring my long-haired son, Simon, a nine-year old with no payes or yarmulke. My daughter, whom I had dressed in a skirt and blouse, would be less obvious, I thought. She had come with me when she was younger, as had Simon. But upon our arrival, Talia, a tiny girl with a booming voice, began to ask questions. "Why are these girls all wearing skirts?" I tried to explain, as we walked behind a young matron pushing a stroller listening intently to our conversation. "They're religious, so they have to dress modestly," I said. "What's religious? What's modesty?" Talia asked. As I stammered a weak answer, the matron smiled at me and said, "That's a smart little girl you have there." Talia's questions continued throughout the afternoon, not only exposing me, I felt, but also making me wonder about my obligations for "bringing up the next generation of Jews." At one point she asked me, as we strolled with a friend, Adina, "Do we follow what's in the Bible?" I decided to be frank, "No, not really." "Do you?" she asked Adina. "I try to," Adina responded. As I begin to teach my own daughter about her rights and obligations as a Jewish girl, what other kinds of questions will she ask and what will I answer?

In what has been called an "engaged anthropology," research and advocacy are complementary. An ethical anthropology is different, although both raise similar questions about the politics of scholarship. Working with nonliberal Jews complicates exactly what constitutes advocacy and where anthropologists' responsibilities lie. The challenge for an ethical anthropology is to make competing interpretive frameworks explicit and to highlight dilemmas over representations. Multiple loyalties and audiences remain salient issues. As a Jewish woman anthropologist, where should my loyalties lie? With the Hasidic women I worked with? With liberal Jews? With anthropologists? With the fight against racism and injustice regardless of race, religion, or ethnicity? Similar to Jacobs-Huey's (2002:797) discussion about loyalty among "insider" anthropologists, I, too, am ambivalent to "air dirty laundry" or to write about topics which Hasidic women themselves find problematic, although I have clearly done so in some cases. For example, when I asked Rifky, Esty, and Raizy to read some chapters I wrote for their comments, their responses surprised me. I had thought that they would not like to see their beliefs about Gentiles aired or comparisons drawn between them and other nonliberal religious communities. These matters proved relatively unproblematic. Instead, they were concerned about how they looked to outsiders, especially other Jews. They did not want me to include "superstitious" beliefs, which I did remove. More important, they did not want me to discuss the divisions between Orthodox Jewish women. They wanted to present a united Jewish community. After much thought, I decided that discussion of these divisions is critical to the narrative I want to tell.

Might we use anthropology not as a cultural critique of ourselves but of those whom we study, or is this ethically problematic? Harding (1991) has argued that ethnography of fundamentalist Christians that challenges the opposition between observer and observed potentially contributes to political critiques that academics might make of fundamentalists. Can accounts of Hasidic women include a critique of nonliberal Judaism made by a Jewish liberal woman anthropologist? If an ethical tenet of anthropology is not to harm the people we work with, what constitutes harm? Who decides? There are no easy answers. However, ethnography with nonliberal religious groups here at home continues to raise new, important questions for anthropology when the people we write about turn around and critique, not only our representations of them, but the very value of anthropology itself.

In this book I have tried to understand the projects that Hasidic women work toward as they raise their children to continue on as the faithful. There can be unexpected consequences in contemporary nonliberal religious movements, outcomes, and arrangements that challenge liberal assumptions about the religious, the secular, gender, agency, and modernity. Analyses in nonliberal religious communities push social scientists to rethink the very categories our studies are based on, as well as the ways we are personally implicated in the politics of representation, and in politics more generally. In *Mitzvah Girls* I tell a story about the struggle of nonliberal Hasidic women and girls to redefine the narrative of civilization. An ethical anthropology looks for new ways to account for the stories of both anthropologists and nonliberal religious groups as they are told to the next generation and beyond.

Notes

1. Bobover, who originated in what is now Poland, are one of many Hasidic sects.

2. Saba Mahmood (2005) uses the term "nonliberal" in her study of Muslim women in Egypt. I find it the most accurate historically and the least problematic politically. Since 9/11, the term "fundamentalism" has acquired violent and often racist undertones, especially in the popular press. See also Nagata (2001) for a discussion of the problems with the current use of the term "fundamentalism," which include the conflation of religious nationalism with fundamentalism. Using the term "nonliberal" to describe the religious movement is also helpful, because it requires explicit elaboration of, and comparison with, liberalism that emerged out of a specific Western European history.

3. This is not to suggest that the desire for freedom or autonomy is an invention of liberalism or the European Enlightenment. Rather, as Saba Mahmood points out, liberalism's particular contribution is the explicit connection between self-realization and individual autonomy so that self-realization is founded on realizing what one's true will desires (2005:13).

4. Lila Abu-Lughod (1998) and Lara Deeb (2006) each show that women's pious modernity is entangled with, and not simply a rejection of, liberal feminist discourses.

5. Spitulnik (2002) has noted the importance of using linguistic data in analyses of local modernities, as well as the potential pitfalls of translating terms into English from other languages. For Hasidic Jews, the terms "modern" and "secular" are used in English, but they still have different meanings from scholarly and more popular mainstream uses, adding yet another layer to the challenges of translation.

6. I use the term "alternative religious modernity" to account for the ways that a number of scholars implicate nonliberal religious movements into the very processes of modernity which they critique. These nonliberal religious movements are not simply throwbacks to some imagined premodern religious way of life. See, for example, Ammerman 1987 and Harding 2000.

7. For discussions of the difficulties of defining the analytical category of the modern and modernity, see, for example, Chakrabarty 2002; Deeb 2006; Keane 2007, and Knauft 2002. Keane (2007:48) suggests, and I agree, that despite the difficulties of settling on a definition, the "idea" of the modern has become critical to the stories that people in a wide range of contexts tell about themselves, their pasts, and their futures. This merits, I believe, ethnographic investigation of the ways that different communities use these categories in their own moral narratives.

8. The secularization theory prominent in the social sciences of the 1950s predicted that, as the world became increasingly modern, religious life would become less relevant or, at least, increasingly privatized. The unexpected reinvigoration of religious movements since the 1970s in North America and elsewhere has proven otherwise. The secularization theory may actually be read as a legacy of the particular relationship between modernity, the social sciences, and an understandings of religion as privatized and apolitical (see Asad 1993).

9. For studies of charismatic and evangelical Christian women in North America and Latin America, see, for example, Brusco 1995; Neitz 1987; Stacey and Gerard 1990.

10. The liberalism that Mahmood describes posits that a person is free if she is able to act according to her own will. A woman who freely chooses to submit herself to a patriarchal religion, then, is still free (2005:13).

11. See, for example, Deeb 2006; El-Or 2002; Jacobson 2006; Levine 2003; Mahmood 2001, 2005; and Mariz and Machado 1997.

12. Joel Robbins (2004a) notes in his review article on Pentecostal and Charismatic Christianity that we know little about how gender is constructed in these communities.

13. See, for example, Allison, Jenks, and Prout 1998; Burr 2006; Goodwin 2006; Lewis 2003; Pollack 2005; and Stephens 1995.

14. For ethnographic research on the everyday lives of Christian fundamentalists in North America that examines schooling, child rearing, and marriage see Ammerman 1987; Peshkin 1986; and Rose 1988.

15. See, for example, Mead 1954 [1928]. For a review of earlier socialization literature, see Kulick and Schieffelin 2004.

16. In contrast to Ashkenazic Jews from Europe, Sephardic (Hebrew, "Spanish") Jews were expelled during the Spanish Inquisition in the fifteenth century and were dispersed across the Mediterranean and parts of North Africa. Both their histories and cultural and religious practices differ from those of Ashkenazic Jews.

17. For a discussion of the historical context and its implications for Jewish life in Europe, see Katz 1973.

18. A substantial and growing body of literature has emerged on the history of Hasidic Judaism; I merely sketch out the most basic history. For further reading, see, especially, Hundert 1991 and Rosman 1996.

19. While always messianic, historically there have been different levels of messianic "tension" (Mintz 1992:248). For a fuller discussion of messianism, see Scholem 1988.

20. I draw on a number of sources, including Belcove-Shalin 1989; Ettinger 1991; Heilman 1992; and Kirshenblatt-Gimblett 1995.

21. Before the war smaller communities of Hasidic Jews came to the United States and Israel, among other places. These communities survived, but it was not until the great influx of Hasidic Jews after the war that the communities began to flourish as they have today. For a discussion of Satmar who came to New York before the war, see, for example, Rubin 1997.

22. One of the exceptions is Mintz's *Hasidic People: A Place in the New World* (1992), which discusses the differences and conflicts between a number of Hasidic courts in New York.

23. Mintz (1992) notes this for Bobover Hasidim, and Rubin (1997) notes it for Satmar. I also recorded several family histories that focused on the complex ties and backgrounds of Hasidim who came from Europe after World War II to the United States. One Hasidic woman, for example, reported that, before the war, her father, who had been born in Hungary, had been Orthodox but not Hasidic. Upon arriving in New York after the war, he became a follower of the Satmar rebbe, whose charisma and warm community appealed to him. Today, however, many of his children, though still Hasidic, no longer consider themselves Satmar, partly because of the political in-fighting over lines of rabbinic succession.

24. Ethnographies of Satmar Hasidic Jews in Williamsburg, Brooklyn, include Belcove-Shalin 1995; Kranzler 1995; Poll 1962; and Rubin 1972, 1997.

25. Ethnographies of Lubavitchers, who are the most open to outsiders, are most common in the literature. Good resources include Fishkoff 2003; Goldschmidt 2006; Harris 1988; Koskoff 2001; Levine 2003; and Morris 1998.

26. Men are forbidden to hear a woman sing, as it might incite unwanted desire. For this reason, concerts are segregated by gender, although women are allowed to hear men singing, which I discuss further in chapter 6.

27. Bobover Hasidim are discussed in Belcove-Shalin 1988, 1995; Epstein 1987; Heilman 2006; Kamen 1985; and Mintz 1992.

28. For a discussion of a community of Litvish Jews, see Helmreich 1986.

29. For an ethnographic study of a Reform congregation in North America, see Furman 1992. On Jewish Conservative congregations, see Jack Wertheimer 2000.

30. Many scholars now use the Hebrew term *haredim* 'those who tremble before God' (a reference to shared characteristics among the Ultra-Orthodox) as an analytical category. I avoid this term, however, because, although it is helpful in characterizing specific historical forces, as a Hebrew term it inhibits cross-cultural comparison with other nonliberal religious groups, further marginalizing Jewish studies. In addition, it is a category much more commonly used in Israel by both scholars and community members. This is not the case in North America, which has its own categories as I discuss.

31. Soloveitchik's work focuses on Litvish Jews in North America. I believe that his work holds true for Hasidic Jews as well. For a related argument, see also Heilman 2006 and Friedman 1993.

32. Barbara Kirshenblatt-Gimblett uses this term (personal communication).

33. Simultaneously the Bobover rebbe ruled that only some Yiddish names should be given to children. He told his followers that Yiddish names such as Kloynemos should not be given, as they might lead to teasing by other Hasidic children. Kloynemos is a Yiddish name but its origins are Greek. Hyperbolization includes cleansing unwelcome "foreign" influences, although, as I discuss in chapters 4 and 5, there is little linguistic purism in everyday language use.

34. The blacks in Crown Heights with whom Goldschmidt worked understood conflicts with their Hasidic neighbors more generally in terms of race, not religion, conflating whiteness and Jewishness.

35. In the Talmud, according to one community member, Gentiles who abide by the Noachide laws, which prohibit, for example, stealing, murdering, and adultery, will also be rewarded in the afterlife.

36. An exception is any Muslims, all called "Arabs" by Hasidic women. Some of the women's comments implied that Arabs share many racialized traits with African Americans. I assume that these attitudes toward Arabs are based on Israel's history. Most Hasidic women I met supported Israel, not the secular state so much as the large communities of observant Jews who live there.

37. See, for example, Boyarin 1993; Kugelmas 1988; and Myerhoff 1982.

38. See, for example, Belcove-Shalin 1988; Davidman 1991; El Or 1994; Kaufman 1991; Levine 2003; and Morris 1998.

39. For more on boys' education, see Heilman 2000; Kamen 1985; and Rubin 1997.

40. Satmar are an exception to girls' schooling histories both in Europe and in North America, as I discuss in Chapters 4 and 5. See Rubin (1997:174–181) for an interesting discussion of Satmar girls' schooling.

41. This contrasts to El-Or's (1994) study of new educational opportunities for Ger Hasidic women in the Ger community in Israel, known for being homogenous and especially stringent.

42. As noted earlier, Lubavitchers interact most often with other kinds of Jews because they do the most outreach. This has made them the most fluent in North American popular culture.

43. Hasidic Jews respond differently to the contemporary state of Israel, founded by secular Zionists. The Satmar Hasidic Jews, for example, burn the Israeli flag on the streets of Williamsburg every year, whereas the Lubavitchers actively support the state while simultaneously hoping to influence it religiously.

44. At other times Hasidic Jews have stormed the local police station making charges of police brutality in a borough with a long history of local conflicts with the police.

45. Hikind's remarks (personal communication) actually echo those made by anthropologist Susan Harding (1991) in her work with Fundamentalist Christians in the United States. She notes that although academics and others support the right of minorities in the U.S. to be heard, often they do not extend the same invitation to "repugnant others" or religious minorities.

CHAPTER TWO
FITTING IN

1. I recognize that the term "North American" and "secular" as used here and elsewhere glosses over the complex differences that constitute these categories. However, I have tried to use the terms used by the Hasidic women

I worked with, which include their erasure of important distinctions of race, class, ethnicity, and so on. I understand their use of the term as an idealized type, either referring to Gentiles in contrast to Jews or as a way to distinguish between their experiences and those of their great-grandparents in Eastern Europe.

2. Drawing on fieldwork from the early 1980s, Mark Kamen noted that male Bobover Hasidic educational practices in contexts of early education—classroom activities, games, toys, and psychological models of development—were often influenced by non–Hasidic North American childrearing practices (Kamen 1985: appendix). I suggest that these are also gendered contexts, as the teachers are almost always women.

3. This cultural give and take between Jews and Gentiles has a long and varied history. Cultural borrowing can take many forms and have different outcomes. Bratslaver Hasidic Jews, for example, as Jerome Mintz (1968) notes, often used Polish storytelling genres in their own Hasidic tales, and also emulated the royal court aesthetic in their own Hasidic court life. In much of the Jewish Studies literature, as historian Elisheva Baumgarten (2004: 11) notes, Jewish and Gentile communities are too often treated as discrete units. She offers a less reified approach to the study of Jews living in non-Jewish contexts by framing medieval Jewish family life as one inflection of broader European culture. I aim to do this as well with my discussion of Hasidic Jews as a nonliberal religious community.

4. Some members of Rifky's family had been influenced by Lubavitcher philosophy, and perhaps this explains her explicit reference to the Messiah. She told me, however, and interviews with Bobover or unaffiliated Hasidic women bear this out, that although reference to the Messiah is more muted in Hasidic circles other than Lubavitch, the ongoing hope for redemption remains relevant to all Hasidic Jews.

5. Language socialization studies that have focused on morality include, for example, Clancy 1986; Fung 1999; Rydstrom 2004; and Smith-Hefner 1999.

6. See, for example, Gonzalez (2001) for a similar critique of the language socialization literature. Kulick (1992) is an exception to this discussion.

7. Foucault's work on ethics specifically focuses on early Christianity and its transition from Greek philosophy, but, as a theoretical framework it has implications for other contexts.

8. For example, a strong ascetic tradition runs through Hasidic philosophy that frequently denigrates the body and is concerned with the potentially polluting effects of the body and bodily desires, but I did not hear these kinds of accounts. Perhaps women did not discuss these issues with me because I was an outsider who might misinterpret the information, or perhaps because I was exposed predominantly to interactions between women and children, sexuality or acestism would have been considered inappropriate issues to discuss.

9. Most likely Gitty is implicitly referring to a passage from the Babylonian Talmud, Kiddushin 40b: "One who eats in the *shuk* 'market' resembles a dog; and some say he is disqualified from giving testimony."

10. Language socialization studies have shown that the qualities valued in children reflect central cultural concerns for adults. This has led to important

distinctions of race and class in North American childrearing practices. In North American white working-class families, for example, adults routinely tease children in order to toughen them up to survive a world that their parents perceive as dangerous and challenging (Heath 1983; Kusserow 2004; and Miller et al. 1992).

11. Michael Wex (2005) notes that in rabbinic commentary the *yaytser-hure* is also a force for creativity, as it is the source of passion. In Hasidic women's interactions with young children I did not hear the evil inclination framed this way.

12. On Fundamentalist Christians, see, especially, Susan Harding 2000; and on haredi (ultra-Orthodox) Jews in Israel, see Menachem Friedman 1987, 1990, 1993.

13. Language socialization studies of morality have similarly noted the centrality of emotion. However, these studies have generally limited their conception of morality to local practices and beliefs. This approach does not address morality as historically produced and emerging from particular relationships of power.

14. Language socialization, with its focus on everyday talk between adults and children, offers a grounded, practice-based approach to the study of morality, which is currently lacking in the anthropology of religion (Lambek 2000).

CHAPTER THREE
DEFIANCE

1. Barbara Benedict, in a cultural history of the concept of curiosity in eighteenth-century England shows how it is bound up with emerging European modernity. She writes, "Curiosity was the anxious subject of conflicting emerging views of humanity, culture, nature and consequently was always informed by competing cultural representations as individuals and groups struggled to possess, reject, define and reformulate it (2001:22).

2. A number of scholars in different disciplines have discussed how the formation of subjectivities includes the elaboration of undesirable subjects. For example, Judith Butler (1990) suggests that the production of subjectivities rests on the repudiation of other subjects. The work of discursive psychologist Michael Billig similarly suggests that every time a parent tells a child to do something, the inverse is implied. Thus, when parents teach children to say "thank you," they are simultaneously socialized to understand the inverse, rudeness in this case. Billig suggests that this may, in fact, create a desire for the repudiated subject (cited in Kulick and Schieffelin 2004).

3. See also Mahmood's (2005) discussion of how religious ritual is a technology of the self.

4. Nancy Ammerman's 1987 study has similarly noted that members felt it was important to consistently display happiness and satisfaction as part of witnessing to those not yet born again. Among other believers, cheerfulness in the face of trial provided evidence of the extent of their trust in God.

5. An intriguing avenue for investigation, for a male researcher with access, would be to see how Hasidic boys in school learn the skills of Torah study, which are based on argumentation and questioning, while simultaneously learning not to question the authority of the texts themselves.

6. Recently I observed that, in a number of New York City public schools, the language of "choice" shapes discipline in the classroom. Children are praised, for example, when they "make a good choice" about their behavior but are given a warning for a "bad choice." This discourse implies that the individual child has the agency to choose whether to obey classroom rules. In contrast, in Bnos Yisruel, teachers often reprimand a child by saying, *me darf folgn a teacher* (you have to obey a teacher).

7. For example, see Ammerman 1987; Heilman 2000, 1995; Kamen 1985; Peshkin 1986; Rose 1993; Rosenak 1993; and Sivan 1995.

8. Yiddish baby talk, a simplified mix of Yiddish and English, is used to talk to Hasidic babies (described further in chapter 4).

9. Samuel Heilman (2000:192–194) describes how the same biblical commentary was told to a group of haredi boys in an Israeli kindergarten. The teacher in the school used the contemporary categories of Gentiles relevant to Israeli children: Americans and Arabs.

10. Additional stories of Hasidic "misfits"— Hasidic Jews who cannot fit in—are profiled in Winston 2005.

CHAPTER FOUR
MAKING ENGLISH JEWISH

1. For example, see Mintz 1968:13–14 for Gentile sources for Hasidic tales.

2. Here I merely discuss the bare bones, selective version of Yiddish, which has a long and complicated history. For rich resources on Yiddish, see Fishman 1981; Weinreich 1980; Harshav 1990; and Shandler 2005.

3. Harshav (1990:xiii) notes that, historically, not all Ashkenazic European Jews spoke Yiddish, although the vast majority did.

4. Poll (1962) points out that Satmar Hasidic women were most fluent in Hungarian. Based on my conversations with Hasidic women, I believe that most Hungarian Hasidic women no longer speak Hungarian.

5. Vilna was a major Jewish cultural center whose prominence was reinforced by the great Lithuanian yeshivas, famous Jewish Enlightenment (*haskalah*) authors, religious and secular publishing houses, the emergent socialist organization (the Bund), modern Yiddish and Hebrew schools, and YIVO (Harshav 1990:80).

6. Kathryn Woolard's elaboration of simultaneity draws on the work of Mikhail Bakhtin (1981, 1984), who has influenced recent scholarship in linguistic anthropology.

7. Woolard (1998) does not discuss borrowing, but, in the Hasidic case, distinctions between code switching and borrowing are not clear and follow the same processes.

8. Woolard (1998), drawing on Blom and Gumperz (1972), notes the distinction between metaphorical and situational forms of code switching. In situational code switching, the shift in languages redefines the context of interaction. Myers-Scotton (1993, 2002) notes that these kinds of switches are often intersentential, that is, speaking one language in one sentence and another in the next. The shift in languages either creates or marks a shift in the context or highlights another set of relationships. The form of code switching of concern in this chapter is often referred to as "metaphorical code switching." This kind of code switching, Myers-Scotton (1993, 2002) points out, is often intrasentential, that is, using two languages within the same sentence. See Woolard 1998:16–18 for a full discussion of different approaches to code switching among sociolinguists and linguistic anthropologists.

9. For a discussion of language ideologies, see, for example, Schieffelin, Woolard, and Kroskrity 1998; Kroskrity 2000; and Woolard and Schieffelin 1994.

10. Rifky most likely meant to say "quibble" here.

11. The Hebrew script signals Yiddish phonology, but there are no diacritics in this text, which leaves the pronunciation of the vowels rather ambiguous because Yiddish vowel pronunciation depends on the dialect of spoken Yiddish.

12. Although this man suggests that making German Jewish was a positive move to preserve Jewish life, Sander Gilman (1991) has noted that the ineluctably Jewish ways of speaking German, called Mauscheln, often became fodder for anti-Jewish humor in early twentieth-century Germany.

13. Notably the editor argues that the Yiddish language is one way that Jews keep themselves apart from Gentiles. This contrasts to Max Weinreich's (1980) position that Yiddish was a critical factor in the development of a diaspora Jewish culture.

14. The author writes "bother" in Hebrew script, which has no character that corresponds to the English /th/, or in the international phonetic alphabet [ð]; [ð] is transliterated as ד (daled or Hebrew /d/), which is pronounced [d]. "Bother" becomes "boder" in Hebrew script and is inflected like a Yiddish verb in its infinitive form, "_bodern_."

15. Angermeyer (2005), in his examination of Russian-American classified advertisements, has noted the salience of script choice in bilingual communities with two different scripts.

16. In texts for children, diacritical markings are included. Perhaps because the book was published in Israel and there is a greater orientation toward a more Hebraized Yiddish, the transliteration of English follows Hebrew diacritic rather than a phonetic transliteration of Yiddish.

17. This is noted by Woolard 1998 and Alvarez-Caccamo 1998.

18. This is especially true since /r/ is often dropped in Hasidic Yiddish, making _der_ often sound like _de_. I have noticed, at least in the context of speaking, that there has been a simplification of article usage or a convergence with the English usage of articles which are invariable. In Yiddish, articles are declined according to the gender of the noun. In standard Yiddish, for example, "the child" is translated as _dos kind,_ where _kind_ is a neutral noun that takes the neutral form of 'the', _dos,_ rather than the masculine form _der_ or the feminine

form *di*. Although Bnos Yisruel's Yiddish primers have some basic instruction in the gender of nouns and the appropriate article form, I never heard any correction of girls' usage which mostly seemed to be the ambiguous, bivalent *de*.

19. See, for example, Myers-Scotton 1993; Thomason 1997; and Poplack 1980, 1981.

20. Those studying conversational code switching (not usually called syncretic) have noted the frequency with which discourse markers are used in another language, see for example, Auer 1998.

21. At the *upshern*, boys' hair, previously left untouched, is shaved although the sidelocks are left long. Boys receive the ritual garments that mark them as Jewish males, a *kapl* "yarmulke" and *tsitses* (ritual fringed undergarment). The rebbe cuts the hair and then the child is wrapped in a *tales* 'prayer shawl', brought to *khayder* (boys' school), and taught a few Hebrew letters. The child is given candies during the instruction to show how sweet it is to learn. Boys then return to kindergarten and have an "*upshern* party."

22. There is no precedent for the -y suffix in either the baby talk of native European Yiddish speakers or for speakers of European languages. The use of the suffix -y as a diminutive marker is influenced by English; Mordkhe Schaechter, personal communication).

23. Yiddish names, as noted, are often inflected with the English diminutive as well. These include Shiffy (Shifre), Rukhy (Rukhl), Avromy (Avrom), and Malky (Malke).

24. Sarah Benor (personal communication) suggests that da-da might come from the Hungarian *dac* which means defiant or bad. This especially makes sense since baby-talk registers often create specialized words that include repetition, for example, boo-boo, *kuts-kuts* 'cough-cough', poo-poo, and, perhaps, da-da. Hasidic women I asked did not know the word's origin.

25. For discussions of the politics of Jewish memory, see also J. Boyarin, 1991, 1992, 1994a.

26. See, for example, the case of the Arizona Tewa, (Kroskrity 1998). For discussions of language loss/death, see, for example, Dorian 1981; and Kulick 1992.

27. Previously, the store clerk noted, reading material for children and young adults was translated from Hebrew and was mainly nonfiction. Today Jewish English fiction is written either by an individual woman or a group of women, often based in Israel or Brooklyn, and supervised by rabbis who ensure that books are kosher.

28. The Web site of the English-language Judaica Press is www.JudaicaPress.com.

29. For a more in-depth discussion of literacy among Hasidic women and girls, see Fader 2008.

CHAPTER FIVE
WITH IT, NOT MODERN

1. Agha (2004) calls this a metapragmatic stereotype.

2. For example, see Gal 1979.

3. Hasidic explanations for the Holocaust itself are complicated and troubling. Some women and a few men told me that the Holocaust was God's punishment for the European Jews who had allowed their Jewish brethren to become secular or, to use the Yiddish word, *modern*. A few others told me that the Holocaust was God's way of bringing Jews together at a time when they were so divided by competing beliefs about citizenship, modernity, and Jewish religious practice. These attempts at explanation can be seen as part of a broader effort to figure out God's plans (see chapter 3). See Mintz 1968, among others, for a further discussion of Hasidic explanations of the Holocaust.

4. This practice can be traced to the Talmud, but it is an especially important aspect of nineteenth-century Jewish educational practices in Eastern Europe.

5. These, in my experience, were often abridged stories of sages in a variety of Yiddish that had a great deal of interference, in Woolard's (1998) sense, from loshn-koydesh or even modern Hebrew, as the books were generally published in Israel. These books were often considered too difficult for girls to read alone, because they had less familiarity with Hebrew than boys do.

6. This is most likely because a speech therapist has considerable flexibility in terms of a work schedule that suits the life of an Orthodox woman whose calendar is determined by ritual obligation. I also believe that careers for Orthodox women remain the extension of caregiving in a professionalized context. Speech therapists most often work in schools or homes with children. In contrast, a common profession for Hasidic men is that of an accountant or a businessman, both of whom also make their own hours. The aim of a profession for Hasidic men is to earn enough money to provide for a family or even, if successful, to return to full-time Torah study.

7. Another term and actual ongoing party for Hasidic youth, primarily Lubavitchers, I believe, who are experimenting with leaving their communities is "Cholent Party."

8. El-Or's (1993, 1994) work with Hasidic women in Israel similarly emphasizes the threat of "luxury" that is particular to the postwar generation of Hasidic Jews who have prospered. For further discussion of her argument, see chapter 6.

Chapter Six
Ticket to Eden

1. Lila Abu-Lughod (2002) and Saba Mahmood (2001, 2005) have both criticized Western feminism for generalizing cultural and historical progressive notions of the self as universally applicable to all women.

2. Theoretically the discussion of modesty engages debates in social theory as to how to understand the body and its signifiers (clothing, hair, and comportment). Mahmood (2005:29) contrasts Bourdieu's notion that the body is a medium of signification to Foucault's emphasis that the body is the tool through which the self is formed. As discussed in this chapter, Hasidic womens and girls' modesty is both an embodied language of signification and the medium through which modest selves are formed.

3. See Levine 2003 for a similar discussion.

4. Keane (2007) develops the concept of semiotic ideology which is an extension of linguistic ideology (see Schieffelin, Woolard, and Kroskrity 1998). By ideology, Keane emphasizes the ways that reflexive awareness is part of the production and change of social phenomena (17). He suggests that the notion of a semiotic ideology offers a way to situate "words, things, and persons (along with other agentive beings such as spirits) dynamically within the same world with one another" (18).

5. For a discussion of how modesty mediates inter- and intra-communal differences in Israel, see El-Or 1993, 1994. For discussions of these topics in Williamsburg, Brooklyn, in the 1960s, see Mintz 1968 and Poll 1962.

6. El-Or, in her study of Ger Hasidic women in Israel, suggests that modesty offers women "the ability to participate within limits in the experience of modern life while simultaneously negating modernity" (1993:587; see, too, 1994). This is experienced as a form of power (dignity and meaning) for the women she worked with. She suggests, however, that modesty is actually an ideology (in Marx's sense of false consciousness) that upholds "a new form of patriarchy which reproduces women's subordination" through the rejection of luxury (1993:595). Although this interpretation raises important relationships between gender and power, and religion and economics, it does not address how and why Hasidic girls come to participate in modesty, aside from fear for their reputations or a "false" understanding of their own subordination.

7. I refer to the *Code of Jewish Law*, because several women recommended it to me when I asked for sources about modesty that they themselves used. In fact, the book is used in the Bobover high school and in the Teachers' Seminary of Boro Park to prepare young women who will teach in the school system.

8. For an excellent discussion of Russian and Lithuanian Jewish women's dress prior to the nineteenth century, see Wengeroff 2000:248–252.

9. This contrasts to Goldschmidt's suggestion that for Jews in Crown Heights, Brooklyn, the immorality of the city streets is in opposition to the morality of the privacy of the Jewish home (2006:123). However, perhaps because Orthodox Jews dominate the streets in Boro Park far more than they do in Crown Heights, women in Boro Park described two public spheres: Gentile and Jewish. The Jewish public sphere includes the street as well as the synagogue, and both belong to men. The Gentile public sphere and the Jewish home are the responsibility of Hasidic women.

10. Shaving one's head at marriage is an example of heightened stringency around Jewish ritual practice. Because the religious law dictates that a married woman must submerge herself in a *mikve* 'ritual bath' every month at the end of her menstrual cycle, with the water touching every part of her body, some Hasidic women shave their heads to ensure that a strand of hair does not escape submersion.

11. The category of *loshn-hure* 'evil talk' (gossip or slander) is an explicit aspect of girls' learning self-control. In summer camp and on school walls there are signs warning girls to monitor how they speak. Peers and teachers remind one another not to speak badly about others simply by saying "loshn- hure!" Inspirational lectures on loshn-hure are also available for women. It is under-

stood that loshn-hure is potentially dangerous and can do harm to oneself and others.

12. For a more extensive discussion of Queen Esther, see Fader 2007a.

13. Anthropologist Jerome Mintz (1968:65) notes this as well when he cites a Hasid in Brooklyn who says, "When children are older they have to have an explanation (i.e., for Jews who act like Gentiles). We tell them secular Jews were not brought up to be observant, it's not their fault. We hope one day they will learn more, they will become religious."

14. Rifky theorized that *yunchy* is derived from the Hungarian word for "Johnny," which implies looking like everyone else, like every "Tom, Dick, or Harry."

15. Hasidic Jews make frequent and relatively unproblematic use of fertility treatments. For a discussion of Orthodox Jews and fertility treatments in Israel, see Kahn 2000.

16. Hirshkind (2001), Mahmood (2005), and Faubion (2001) have made similar arguments.

CHAPTER SEVEN
BECOMING HASIDIC WIVES

1. Jewish ethnographers who have written about what is variously termed "social status" or "class" in Hasidic communities in Williamsburg, Brooklyn, tend to emphasize the importance of male piety (e.g., Kranzler 1995; and Poll 1962). This literature describes levels of stringency, involvement in the leadership of the rebbe's court, and community activities or services that create a ranking system for Hasidic men. Rubin (1997) has pointed out that wealth also plays a role in determining status, but he suggests that wealth is diminishing in importance as Hasidic communities grow and are less dependent on non-Hasidic sources of status. This does not seem accurate today, given that Hasidic Jews in North America are becoming increasingly bourgeois. Further, Rubin discusses wealth from worldly success as a bleeding in of "secular" American values rather than an intrinsic part of Hasidic social organization. This position assumes that the secular and the religious, the material and the spiritual, are discrete categories. By focusing on women's interpretations and experiences of social class, I show that it is this very distinction between the secular and the religious, the material and the spiritual, that Hasidic women challenge.

2. See Rubin 1997, for a discussion of matchmaking among Satmar; and see Heilman 2000, for a discussion of two case studies among haredim in Israel.

3. Personal communication, Paul Glasser.

4. As a woman, I could not observe or participate in groom classes. Several women told me, however, that grooms most often sit down one-on-one with a teacher (often an expert on this topic). The teacher explains to the boy his new ritual and physical responsibilities as a Jewish husband. From my conversations with a few women, it seemed as if boys receive less elaboration about the rewards they will receive for the discipline required in a Jewish marriage.

See Heilman 2000, for a discussion of how one young Israeli Hasid learned about the facts of life from a teacher.

5. The speech quoted from these classes is based on handwritten notes and not a tape-recorder.

6. For example, see Giddens 1992; and Lindholm 1998.

7. Laura Ahearn's (2001) study of love letters in Nepal, for example, shows that in some contexts romantic love is associated with development and modernity.

8. For girls who are somewhat more modern, the dangers must be even greater. For example, I saw an Orthodox but not Hasidic young woman openly reading a racy romance novel one Shabbes afternoon.

9. In fact, as already noted, most Hasidim do not watch movies. Morah Margolis, however, was not raised Hasidic as I noted. She married into a Hasidic family. She told me privately that she and her husband occasionally rented a video and watched a movie when the children were asleep.

Coda

1. Note the use of nonstandard English, which includes the mixing of Yiddish and English and a disregard for Standard English rules of punctuation and spelling, particularly of Hasidic Yiddish words in English.

2. See, for example, the work of Appadurai 1996; Chakrabarty 2002; Gaonkar 2001; Knauft 2002; Larkin 1997; among others. This literature, as Knauft (2002:24) notes, attempts to engage the global with the local. This includes attending to the impact of political economy in conjunction with cultural orientations and subjective dispositions.

3. For example, see Deeb 2006.

4. Ginsburg and Rapp (1995) make a similar argument for attending to the politics of reproduction.

5. Feminist critiques of anthropology have made important contributions to our understandings of the politics of fieldwork. See, for example, Fader 2007b, a special issue of *Signs* 2005 (S. Harding and K. Norberg, eds.); and Wolf 1996.

6. A seminal article is Narayan 1993. Other references include Kondo 1990; Pissaro 1997; and Williams 1996.

Glossary

baal tshuva (fem. baales tshuva; pl. baaley tshuvas), also called bt (pl. bts). — Returnees to the faith.

balebatish. — Bourgeois

Bobover. — The Polish/Galician Hasidic sect

capl/yarmulke. — Male head covering

derekh-eyretz. — Polite behavior

emune. — Belief or faith

ffb(s). — Abbreviation for "*frim/frum from birth,*" in contrast to a bt.

fray. — Free, meaning nonobservant Jews

frim/frum. — Observant Jews

goy (pl., *goyim*). — Gentiles

haymish. — Homey, meaning Jews who share a commitment to strict Orthodoxy

kale. — Bride

khilel-hashem. — Shaming God

khinekh. — Moral education

khitspe. — Defiance

khsidish/Hasidish. — Hasidic

khusn. — Groom

kosher (*kashres*). — Jewish dietary laws. The term is also used metaphorically to denote secular culture which has been checked for inappropriate content.

Litvish. — Lithuanian Jews, Orthodox but not Hasidic. Also called *misnagdim* 'opposed', meaning opposed to Hasidic Judaism.

loshn-koydesh. — Holy language, Hebrew and Aramaic

Lubavitch. — Originally a Russian Hasidic sect, now known for its outreach to less observant Jews

mides. — Personal traits or characteristics

mikve. — Jewish ritual bath

mitsves. — Commandments, also good deeds

morah. — Teacher

moshiakh. — Messiah

nebby. — Nerdy, a loser, unpopular

neshume. — Soul

rebbe. — The charismatic leader of a Hasidic sect

Satmar/Hungarian. — A Hasidic sect originally from Hungary

shabes. — Sabbath

shaytel. — Wig

shtotty. — Sophisticated, fashionable, trendy

tahares-hamishpukhe. — The laws of family purity

tsitsis. — The ritual fringed garment worn under a shirt by men and boys older than three years

tsnies. — Modesty

yayster-hatoyv. — Inclination for good

yayster-hure. — Inclination for bad

yikhes. — Illustrious lineage

References

Abu-Lughod, Lila. 1986. *Veiled Sentiments: Honor and Poetry in Bedouin Society.* Berkeley: University of California Press.

———. 1998. Introduction: Feminist longings and postcolonial conditions. In *Remaking Women: Feminism and Modernity in the Middle East,* ed. L. Abu-Lughod, 3–31. Princeton, N.J.: Princeton University Press.

———. 2002. Do Muslim women really need saving? Anthropological reflections on cultural relativism and its others. *American Anthropologist* 104 (3): 783–790.

Agha, Asif. 1998. Stereotypes and registers of honorific language. *Language in Society* 27 (2): 151–194.

———. 2004. Registers of language. In *A Companion to Linguistic Anthropology,* ed. A. Duranti, 23–45. Malden, Mass.: Blackwell.

Ahearn, Laura. 2001. *Invitations to Love: Literacy, Love Letters, and Social Change in Nepal.* Ann Arbor: University of Michigan Press.

Alvarez-Caccamo, Celso. 1998. Switching code to code-switching: Towards a reconceptualization of communicative codes. In *Code-Switching in Conversation: Language, Interaction, and Identity,* ed. P. Auer, 29–50. London: Routledge.

Ammerman, Nancy. 1987. *Bible Believers: Fundamentalists in the Modern World.* New Brunswick, N.J.: Rutgers University Press.

Angermeyer, Philipp. 2005. Spelling bilingualism: Script choice in Russian American classified ads and signage. *Language in Society* 34 (4): 493–531.

Appadurai, Arjun. 1996. *Modernity at Large: Cultural Dimensions of Globalization.* Minneapolis: University of Minnesota Press.

Asad, Talal. 1993. *Genealogies of Religion.* Baltimore, Md.: Johns Hopkins University Press.

———. 2003. *Formations of the Secular: Christianity, Islam, Modernity.* Stanford: Stanford University Press.

Auer, Peter, ed. 1998. *Code-switching in Conversation: Language, Interaction, and Identity.* London: Routledge.

Bakhtin, Mikhail M. 1981. *The Dialogic Imagination: Four Essays.* Edited by M. Holquist. Translated by C. Emerson and M. Holquist. Austin: University of Texas Press.

Baquedano-Lopez, Patricia. 1997. Creating social identities through doctrina narratives. *Issues in Applied Linguistics* 8 (1): 27–45.

Baumgarten, Elisheva. 2004. *Mothers and Children: Jewish Family Life in Medieval Europe.* Princeton, N.J.: Princeton University Press.

Belcove-Shalin, Janet. 1988. Becoming more of an Eskimo. In *Between Two Worlds: Ethnographic Essays on American Jewry,* ed. J. Kugelmass, 77–102. Ithaca, N.Y.: Cornell University Press.

Belcove-Shalin, Janet. 1989. A quest for wholeness: The Hasidim of Brooklyn. Ph.D. dissertation, Cornell University.

———, ed. 1995. *New World Hasidim: Ethnographic Studies of Hasidic Jews in America.* Albany: State University of New York Press.

Benedict, Barbara. 2001. *Curiosity: A Cultural History into Early Modern Inquiry.* Chicago: University of Chicago Press.

Benor, Sarah Bunin. 2004a. Second style acquisition: The linguistic socialization of newly Orthodox Jews. Ph.D. dissertation, Stanford University.

———. 2004b. Talmid chachams and tsedeykeses: Language, learnedness, and masculinity among Orthodox Jews. *Jewish Social Studies* 11 (1): 147–170.

———. n.d. Yeshivish, Yinglish, or Orthodox Jewish English in America. Unpublished paper.

Blom, Jan-Peter, and John J. Gumperz. 1972. Social meaning in linguistic structures: Codeswitching in Norway. In *Directions in Sociolinguistics*, ed. J. Gumperz and D. Hymes, 407–434. New York: Holt, Rinehart and Winston.

Bogoch, Bryna. 1999. Gender, literacy, and religiosity: Dimensions of Yiddish education in Israeli government supported schools. *International Journal of the Sociology of Language* 138:123–160.

Boyarin, Daniel. 1993. Placing reading: Ancient Israel and Medieval Europe. In *The Ethnography of Reading*, ed. J. Boyarin, 10–37. Berkeley: University of California Press.

Boyarin, Jonathan. 1988. Waiting for a Jew: Marginal redemption at the Eighth Street shul. In *Between Two Worlds: Ethnographic Essays on American Jewry*, ed. J. Kugelmass, 52–76. Ithaca, N.Y.: Cornell University Press.

———. 1991. *Polish Jews in Paris: The Ethnography of Memory.* Bloomington: Indiana University Press.

———. 1992. *Storm from Paradise: The Politics of Jewish Memory.* Minneapolis: University of Minnesota Press.

———. 1994a. *Remapping Memory: The Politics of Timespace.* Minneapolis: University of Minnesota Press.

———. 1994b. Death and the minyan. *Cultural Anthropology* 9 (1): 3–22.

———. 2002. Circumscribing constitutional identities. In *Powers of Diaspora*, ed. J. Boyarin and D. Boyarin, 105–157. Minneapolis: University of Minnesota Press.

Brink, Judy, and Joan P. Mencher, eds. 1997. *Mixed Blessings: Gender and Religious Fundamentalism Cross-culturally.* New York: Routledge.

Brodkin, Karen. 1998. *How Jews Became White Folks and What That Says about Race in America.* New Brunswick, N.J.: Rutgers University Press.

Brusco, Elizabeth. 1995. *The Reformation of Machismo: Evangelical Conversion and Gender in Colombia.* Austin: University of Texas Press.

Burr, Rachel. 2006. *Vietnam's Children in a Changing World.* New Brunswick, N.J.: Rutgers University Press.

Butler, Judith. 1990. *Gender Trouble: Feminism and the Subversion of Identity.* New York: Routledge.

Cavanaugh, Jillian. 2005. Accent matters: Material consequences of sounding local in Northern Italy. *Language & Communication* 25 (2): 127–148.

————. 2006. Little women and vital champions: Gender and language shift in Bergamo, Italy. *Journal of Linguistic Anthropology* 16 (4): 194–210.

Chakrabarty, Dipesh. 2002. *Habitations of Modernity: Essays in the Wake of Subaltern Studies*. Chicago: University of Chicago Press.

Clancy, Pat. 1986. The acquisition of communicative style in Japanese. In *Language Socialization across Cultures*, ed. B. B. Schieffelin and E. Ochs, 213–250. Cambridge: Cambridge University Press.

Davidman, Lynn. 1991. *Tradition in a Rootless World: Women Turn to Orthodox Judaism*. Berkeley: University of California Press.

————. 2002. Truth, subjectivity, and ethnographic research. In *Personal Knowledge and Beyond: Reshaping the Ethnography of Religion*, ed. J. Spickard, J. Landres, and M. McGuire, 17–26. New York: New York University Press.

Davidman, Lynn, and Janet Stocks. 1995. Comparative fundamentalism. In *New World Hasidim: Ethnographic Studies of Hasidic Jews in American*, ed. J. Belcove-Shalin, 142–164. Albany: State University of New York Press.

Deeb, Lara. 2006. *An Enchanted Modern: Gender and Public Piety in Shi'i Lebanon*. Princeton, N.J.: Princeton University Press.

Dinur, Benzion. 1991. The origins of Hasidism and its social and messianic foundations. In *Essential Papers on Hasidism: Origins to the Present*, ed. G. Hundert, 86–208. New York: New York University Press.

Dorian, Nancy. 1981. *Language Death*. Philadelphia: University of Pennsylvania Press.

Dubnow, Simon. 1991. The beginnings: The Baal Shem Tov (Besht) and the center in Podolia. In *Essential Papers on Hasidism: Origins to the Present*, ed. G. Hundert, 58–87. New York: New York University Press.

El-Or, Tamar. 1993. The length of slits and the spread of luxury: Reconstructing the subordination of Ultra-Orthodox Jewish women through the patriarchy of men scholars. *Sex Roles* 29 (9/10): 585–599.

————. 1994. *Educated and Ignorant: Ultra-Orthodox Women and Their World*. Boulder, Colo.: Lynne Riemer.

————. 2002. *Next Year I Will Know More: Literacy and Identity among Orthodox Jewish Women in Israel*. Detroit: Wayne State University Press.

Elster, Charles. 2003. Authority, performance, and interpretation in religious reading: Critical issues of intercultural communication and multiple literacies. *Journal of Literacy Research* 35 (1): 663–692.

Epstein, Shifra. 1987. Drama on the table: The Bobover Hasidic pirimspiel. In *Judaism Viewed from Within and from Without*, ed. H. Goldberg, 195–219. Albany: State University of New York Press.

Ettinger, Shmuel. 1991. The Hasidic movement—reality and ideals. In *Essential Papers on Hasidism: Origins to the Present*, ed. G. Hundert, 226–243. New York: New York University Press.

Fabian, Johannes. 1983. *Time and the Other: How Anthropology Makes Its Object*. New York: Columbia University Press.

Fader, Ayala. 2001. Literacy, bilingualism, and gender in a Hasidic community. *Linguistics and Education* 12 (3): 261–283.

————. 2006. Learning faith: Language socialization in a Hasidic community. *Language in Society* 35 (2): 205–228.

Fader, Ayala. 2007a. Reclaiming sacred sparks: Linguistic syncretism and gendered language shift among Hasidic Jews. *Journal of Linguistic Anthropology* 17(1): 1–22.

———. 2007b. Reflections on Queen Esther: The politics of Jewish ethnography. *Contemporary Jewry* 5 (27): 112–136.

———. 2008. Reading Jewish signs: The socialization of multilingual literacies among Hasidic women and girls in Brooklyn, New York. *Text and Talk* 28 (5): 621–641.

Faubion, James D. 2001. *The Shadows and Lights of Waco: Millenialism Today.* Princeton, N.J.: Princeton University Press.

Ferguson, Charles A. 1996. Babytalk in six languages. In *Sociolinguistic Perspectives: Papers on Language in Society, 1959–1994,* ed. Thom Heubner, 103–114. New York: Oxford University Press.

Fishkoff, Sue. 2005. *The Rebbe's Army.* New York: Schocken Books.

Fishman, Joshua, ed. 1981. *Never Say Die: A Thousand Years of Yiddish in Jewish Life and Letters.* The Hague: Mouton.

———. 1985. The sociology of Jewish languages from a general sociolinguistic point of view. In *Readings in the Sociology of Jewish Languages,* ed. J. Fishman, 1–21. Leiden: E. J. Brill.

———, ed. 1989. *Language and Ethnicity in Minority Sociolinguistic Perspective.* Clevedon, England: Multilingual Matters.

Foucault, Michel. 1980. *Power/Knowledge. Selected Interviews and Other Writings, 1972–1977.* Edited by C. Gordin. New York: Pantheon Books.

———. 1984. *The Foucault Reader.* Edited by P. Rabinow. New York: Pantheon Books.

———. 1997. On the genealogy of ethics: An overview of work in progress. In *Essential Works of Foucault,* Vol. 1. *Ethics: Subjectivity and Truth,* ed. P. Rabinow, trans. R. Hurley et al., 281–301. New York: New Press.

Fox, Richard G., ed. 1991. *Recapturing Anthropology: Working in the Present.* Santa Fe, N.M.: School of American Research Press.

Friedman, Menachem. 1986. Haredim confront the modern city. In *Studies in Contemporary Jewry,* ed. P. Medding, 2:74–96. Bloomington: Indiana University Press.

———. 1987. Life tradition and book tradition in the development of Ultra-Orthodox Judaism. In *Judaism Viewed from Within and from Without,* ed. H. Goldberg, 235–256. Albany: State University of New York Press.

———. 1990. Jewish zealots: Conservative versus innovative. In *Religious Radicalism and Politics in the Middle East,* ed. E. Sivan and M. Friedman, 127–142. Albany: State University of New York Press.

———. 1993. The lost kiddush cup: Changes in Ashkenazic haredi culture—A tradition in crisis. In *The Uses of Tradition: Jewish Continuity in the Modern Era,* ed. J. Wertheimer, 175–187. New York: Jewish Theological Seminary of America; distributed by Harvard University Press, Cambridge, Mass.

Fuchs, Menucha. 2002. *The Shabbos Queen and Other Shabbos Stories.* New York: Judaica Press.

Fung, Heidi. 1999. Becoming a moral child: The socialization of shame among young Chinese children. *Ethnos* 27 (2): 180–209.

Furman, Frida. 1987. *Beyond Yiddishkeit: The Struggle for Jewish Identity in a Reform Synagogue*. Albany: State University of New York Press.

Gal, Susan. 1979. *Language Shift: Social Determinants of Linguistic Change in Bilingual Austria*. New York: Academic Press.

Ganzfried, Solomon. 1996. *Code of Jewish Law, Kitzur Shulhan Arukh: A Compilation of Jewish Laws and Customs*. Translated by Hyman E. Goldin. New York: Hebrew Publishing.

Gaonkar, Dilip Parameshwar, ed. 2001. *Alternative Modernities*. Durham, N.C.: Duke University Press.

Garrett, Paul B., and Patricia Baquedano-Lopez. 2002. Language socialization: Reproduction and continuity, transformation and change. *Annual Review of Anthropology* 31 (1): 339–361.

Giddens, Anthony. 1992. *The Transformation of Intimacy: Sexuality, Love, and Eroticism in Modern Societies*. Stanford: Stanford University Press.

Gilman, Sander. 1991. *The Jew's Body*. New York: Routledge.

Ginsburg, Faye. 1987. When the subject is women: Encounters with Syrian Jewish women. *Journal of American Folklore* 100 (398): 528–539.

Ginsburg, Faye, and Rayna Rapp, eds. 1995. *Conceiving the New World Order*. Berkeley: University of California Press.

Gilroy, Paul. 1993. *The Black Atlantic: Modernity and Double Consciousness*. Cambridge, Mass.: Harvard University Press.

Glinert, Lewis, and Miriam Isaacs, eds. 1999. Pious voices: The language of Ultra-Orthodox Jews. *International Journal of the Sociology of Language*. Special Volume, no. 138.

Glinert, Lewis, and Yaacov Shilhav. 1991. Holy land, holy language: A study of an Ultra-Orthodox Jewish ideology. *Language in Society* 20(1):59–86.

Goffman, Erving. [1955] 1972. On face-work: An analysis of ritual elements of social interaction. In *Strategic Interaction*, ed. J. Laver and S. Hutcheson, 319–326. Philadelphia: University of Pennsylvania Press.

Gold, David D. 1985. Jewish English. In *Readings in the Sociology of Jewish Languages*, ed. J. Fishman, 280–298. Leiden: E. J. Brill.

Goldberg, Harvey, E. 1987. Introduction: Judaism in Israel. In *Judaism Viewed from Within and from Without*, ed. H. Goldberg, 220–234. Albany: State University of New York Press.

Goldman Carrel, Barbara. 1993. Hasidic women's fashion: Undressing a paradox. Master's thesis, New York University.

———. 1999. Hasidic women's head-coverings: A feminized system of Hasidic distinction. In *Religion, Dress, and the Body*, ed. L. Arthur, 63–180. New York: Berg.

Goldschmidt, Henry. 2006. *Race and Religion among the Chosen Peoples of Crown Heights*. New Brunswick, N.J.: Rutgers University Press

Goldsmith, Emanuel S. 1976. *Architects of Yiddishism at the Beginning of the Twentieth Century: A Study in Jewish Cultural History*. Rutherford, N.J.: Fairleigh Dickinson University.

Gonzalez, Norma. 2001. *I Am My Language: Discourses of Women and Children in the Borderlands*. Tucson: University of Arizona Press.

Goodwin, Marjorie Harness. 2006. *The Hidden Lives of Girls*. Malden, Mass.: Blackwell.

Greenzweig, David. 1990. *We Can Read and Understand*. Brooklyn: Bnos Zion of Bobov.

Griffith, R. Marie. 1997. *God's Daughters: Evangelical Women and the Power of Submission*. Berkeley: University of California Press.

Gumperz, John J. 1982. *Discourse Strategies*. Cambridge: Cambridge University Press.

Haraway, Donna. 1991. *Simians, Cyborgs, and Women: The Reinvention of Nature*. New York: Routledge.

Harding, Susan Friend. 1991. Representing fundamentalism: The problem of the repugnant cultural other. *Social Research*, 58 (2): 373–393.

———. 2000. *The Book of Jerry Falwell*. Princeton, N.J.: Princeton University Press.

Harding, S., and K. Norberg, eds. 2005. New Feminist Approaches to Social Science Methodologies. Vol. 30, No. 4. Special issue of *Signs: Journal of Women in Culture and Society*.

Haeri, Niloofar. 2003. *Sacred Language, Ordinary People*. New York: Palgrave.

Harshav, Benjamin. 1990. *The Meaning of Yiddish*. Stanford: Stanford University Press.

Heath, Shirley Brice. 1983. *Ways with Words: Language, Life, and Words in Communities and Classrooms*. Cambridge: Cambridge University Press.

Heilman, S. and M. Friedman. 1991. Religious fundamentalism and religious Jews: The case of haredim. In *Fundamentalisms Observed*, ed. M. Marty and R. Scott Appleby, 197–264. Chicago: University of Chicago Press.

Heilman, Samuel C. 1981. Sounds of modern Orthodoxy: The language of Talmud studies. In *Never Say Die!* ed. J. Fishman, 227–258. The Hague: Mouton.

———. 1995. The vision from the madrasa and bes medrash: Some parallels between Islam and Judaism. In *Fundamentalisms Comprehended*, ed. M. Marty and R. Scott Appleby, 71–95. Chicago: University of Chicago Press.

———. 1998a. *People of the Book*. Edison, N.J.: Transaction.

———. 1998b. *Synagogue Life: A Study in Symbolic Interaction*. Edison, N.J.: Transaction.

———. 2000. *Defenders of the Faith: Inside Orthodox Jewry*. Berkeley: University of California Press.

———. 2006. *Sliding to the Right*. Berkeley: University of California Press.

Heilman, Samuel C., and Steven M. Cohen. 1989. *Cosmopolitans and Parochials: Modern Orthodox Jews in America*. Chicago: University of Chicago Press.

Heller, Monica. 1999. *Linguistic Minorities and Modernity: A Sociolinguistic Ethnography*. New York: Longman.

Helmreich, William B. 1986. *The World of the Yeshiva: An Intimate Portrait of Orthodox Jewry*. New Haven, Conn.: Yale University Press.

Hendershot, Heather. 2004. *Shaking the World for Jesus: Media and Conservative Evangelical Culture*. Chicago: University of Chicago Press.

Hill, Jane H. 1998. "Today there is no respect": Nostalgia, "respect," and oppositional discourse in Mexicano (Nahuatl) language ideology. In *Language Ide-*

ologies: Practice and Theory, ed. B. B. Schieffelin, K. Woolard, and P. Kroskrity, 68–86. New York: Oxford University Press.

Hill, Jane H., and Kenneth C. Hill. 1986. *Speaking Mexicano*. Tucson: University of Arizona Press.

Hirshkind, Charles. 2001. The ethics of listening: Cassette-sermon audition in contemporary Cairo. *American Ethnologist* 28 (3): 623–649.

Hundert, Gershon, ed. 1991. *Essential Papers on Hasidism: Origins to Present*. New York: New York University Press.

Irvine, Judith, and Susan Gal. 2000. Language ideology and linguistic differentiation. In *Regimes of Language: Ideologies, Polities, and Identities*, ed. P. Kroskrity, 35–84. Santa Fe, N.M.: School of American Research.

Isaacs, Miriam. 1998. Yiddish in Orthodox communities in Jerusalem. In *Politics of Yiddish*, ed. D. Kerler, 85–96. Oxford: Avon.

———. 1999. Haredi, haymish, and frim: Yiddish vitality and language choice in a transnational, multilingual community. *International Journal of the Sociology of Language* 138:9–30.

Jacobs-Huey Lanita. 2002. The natives are gazing and talking back: Reviewing the problematics of positionality, voice, and accountability among "native" anthropologists. *American Anthropologist* 104 (3): 791–804.

Jacobson, Shari. 2006. Modernity, conservative religious movements, and the female subject: Newly Orthodox Sephardi women in Buenos Aires. *American Anthropologist* 108 (2): 112–119.

Jakobson, Janet, and Anne Pelligrini. 2000. World secularisms. *Social Text* 18 (3): 1–23.

James, Allison, Chris Jenks, and Alan Prout. 1998. *Theorizing Childhood*. New York: Teachers College Press.

Jochnowitz, George. 1981. Bilingualism and dialect mixture among Lubavitcher children. In *Never Say Die!: A Thousand Years of Yiddish*, ed. J. Fishman, 721–737. The Hague: Mouton.

Kahn, Susan. 2000. *Reproducing Jews: A Cultural Account of Assisted Conception in Israel*. Durham, N.C.: Duke University Press.

Kamen, Mark. 1985. *Growing Up Hasidic: Education and Socialization in the Bobover Hasidic Community*. New York: AMS.

Katz, Dovid. 2004. *Words on Fire: The Unfinished Story of Yiddish*. New York: Basic Books.

Katz, Jacob. 1973. *Out of the Ghetto*. New York: Schocken Books.

Kaufman, Debra Renee. 1991. *Rachel's Daughters: Newly Orthodox Jewish Women*. New Brunswick, N.J.: Rutgers University Press.

Keane, Webb. 2007. *Christian Moderns: Freedom and Fetish in the Mission Encounter*. Berkeley: University of California Press.

Kirshenblatt-Gimblett, Barbara. 1990. Performance of precepts and precepts of performance: Hasidic celebrations of Purim in Brooklyn. In *By Means of Performance: Intercultural Studies of Theatre and Ritual*, ed. R. Schechner and W. Appel, 109–117. Cambridge: Cambridge University Press.

———. 1995. Introduction. In *Life Is with People: The Culture of the Shtetl*, ed. M. Zborowski and E. Herzog, ix–xlviii. New York: Schocken books.

Klein, Leah. 1993. *Secrets!* B. Y. Times series, no. 15. Southfield, Mich.: Targum/ Feldheim.

Knauft, Bruce M., ed. 2002. *Critically Modern: Alternatives, Alterities, Anthropologies*. Bloomington: Indiana University Press.

Kondo, Dorrine. 1990. *Crafting Selves: Power, Gender, and Discourses of Identity in a Japanese Workplace*. Chicago: University of Chicago Press.

Koskoff, Ellen. 2001. *Music in Lubavitcher Life*. Urbana: University of Illinois Press.

Kranzler, George. 1961. *Williamsburg: A Jewish Community in Transition*. New York: Phillip Feldheim.

———. 1995. The economic revitalization of the Hasidic community of Williamsburg. In *New World Hasidim: Ethnographic Studies of Jews in America*, ed. J. Belcove-Shalin, 181–204. Albany: State University of New York Press.

Kroskrity, Paul. 1998. Arizona Tewa kiva speech as manifestation of a dominant language ideology. In *Language Ideologies: Practice and Theory*, ed. B.B. Schieffelin, K. Woolard, and P. Kroskrity, 103–121. Oxford: Oxford University Press.

———, ed. 2000. *Regimes of Language: Ideologies, Polities, and Identities*. Santa Fe, N.M.: School of American Research.

Kugelmass, Jack, ed. 1988. *Between Two Worlds: Ethnographic Essays on American Jewry*. Ithaca, N.Y.: Cornell University Press.

Kulick, Don. 1992. *Language Shift and Cultural Reproduction: Socialization, Self, and Syncretism in a Papua New Guinean Village*. Cambridge: Cambridge University Press.

———. 1998. Anger, gender, language shift, and the politics of revelation in a Papua New Guinean village. In *Language Ideologies: Theory and Practice*, ed. B. B. Schieffelin, K.Woolard, and P. Kroskrity, 87–102. New York: Oxford University Press.

Kulick, Don, and Bambi B. Schieffelin. 2004. Language socialization. In *A Companion to Linguistic Anthropology*, ed. A. Duranti, 349–368. Malden, Mass.: Blackwell.

Kusserow, Adrie. 2004. *American Individualisms: Child Rearing and Social Class in Three Neighborhoods*. New York: Palgrave.

Lal, Jayati. 1996. Situating locations: The politics of self, identity, and "other" in living and writing the text. In *Feminist Dilemmas in Fieldwork*, ed. D. Wolf, 32–71. Boulder, Colo.: Westview.

Lambek, Michael. 2000. The anthropology of religion and the quarrel between poetry and philosophy. *Current Anthropology* 41 (3): 309–320.

Lanclos, Donna Michelle. 2003. *At Play in Belfast*. New Brunswick, N.J.: Rutgers University Press.

Larkin, Brian. 1997. Indian film and Nigerian lovers: Media and the creation of parallel modernities. *Africa* 67:406–440.

Lewis, Amanda. 2003. *Race in the Schoolyard: Reproducing the Color Line*. New Brunswick, N.J.: Rutgers University Press.

Levine, Stephanie Wellen. 2003. *Mystics, Mavericks, and Merrymakers: An Intimate Journey among Hasidic Girls*. New York: New York University Press.

Lindholm, Charles. 1995. Love and structure. *Theory, Culture, and Society* 15 (3): 243–263.

Mahmood, Saba. 2001. Feminist theory, embodiment, and the docile agent: Some reflections on the Egyptian Islamic revival. *Cultural Anthropology* 16 (2): 202–237.

———. 2005. *Politics of Piety: The Islamic Revival and the Feminist Subject*. Princeton, N.J.: Princeton University Press.

Makihara, Miki. 2004. Linguistic syncretism and language ideologies: Transforming sociolinguistic hierarchy on Rapa Nui (Easter Island). *American Anthropologist* 106 (3): 529–540.

Males 'Virtues'. 1998. *A Magazine for the Jewish Home*, no. 3:3–4. Monsey, N.Y.

Marcus, George, and Michael Fischer. 1986. *Anthropology as Cultural Critique: An Experimental Moment in the Human Sciences*. Chicago: University of Chicago Press.

Mariz, Cecilia Lareto, and Maria das Dores Campo Machado. 1997. Pentecostalism and women in Brazil. In *Power, Politics, and Pentecostals in Latin America*, ed. E. Cleary and H. Stewart-Gambino, 41–54. Boulder, Colo.: Westview.

Marmon, Naomi, 1999. Reflections on contemporary miqveh practice. In *Women and Water: Menstruation in Jewish Life and Law*, ed. R. Wasserfall, 232–254. Hanover, Mass.: Brandeis University Press.

Martin, Ann. 1988. *Kristy and the Snobs*. The Babysitter's Club series, no. 11. New York: Scholastic.

Marty, Martin, and R. Scott Appleby, eds. 1991. *Fundamentalisms Observed*. Chicago: University of Chicago Press.

———, eds. 1993a. *Fundamentalisms and Society*. Chicago: University of Chicago Press.

———, eds. 1993b. *Fundamentalisms and the State*. Chicago: University of Chicago Press.

Mayer, Egon. 1978. *From Suburb to Shtetl: The Jews of Boro Park*. Philadelphia: Temple University Press.

Mazel Tov: Wedding! Seven Blessings. n.d. Workbook, part 1. Jerusalem: Matzlichim.

Mead, Margaret. 1954 [1928]. *Coming of Age in Samoa*. New York: Morrow Quill.

Miller, Peggy J., Julie Mintz, Lisa Hoogstra, Heidi Fung, and R. Potts. 1992. The narrated self: Young children's construction of self in relation to others in conversational stories of personal experience. *Merrill-Palmer Quarterly* 38:45–67.

Mintz, Jerome 1968. *Legends of the Hasidim*. Chicago: University of Chicago Press.

———. 1992. *Hasidic People: A Place in the New World*. Cambridge, Mass.: Harvard University Press.

Mitchell, Bruce. 2006. *Language Politics and Language Survival: Yiddish among the Haredim in Postwar Britain*. Paris/Louveen: Peters.

Morris, Bonnie. 1998. *Lubavitcher Women in America: Identity and Activism in the Post-War Era*. Albany: State University of New York Press.

Myerhoff, Barbara. 1978. *Number Our Days*. New York: Touchstone.

Myers-Scotton, Carol. 1993. *Social Motivations for Codeswitching*. Oxford: Oxford University Press.

———. 2002. *Contact Linguistics: Bilingual Encounters and Grammatical Outcomes*. Oxford: Oxford University Press.

Myhill, John. 2004. *Language in Jewish Society: Towards a New Understanding*. Clevedon, England: Multilingual Matters.

Nagata, Judith. 2001. Beyond theology: Toward an anthropology of fundamentalism. *American Anthropologist* 103 (2): 481–498.

Narayan, Kirin. 1993. How native is the native anthropologist? *American Anthropologist* 95:671–685.

Neitz, Mary Jo. 1987. *Charisma and Community: A Study of Religious Commitment within the Charismatic Renewal*. New Brunswick, N.J.: Transaction.

Ochs, Elinor. 1988. *Culture and Language Development: Language Acquisition and Socialization in a Samoan Village*. New York: Cambridge University Press.

———. 1992. Indexing gender. In *Rethinking Context: Language as Interactive Phenomenon*, ed. A. Duranti and C. Goodwin, 335–358. Cambridge: Cambridge University Press.

Ochs, Elinor, and Bambi B. Schieffelin. 1984. Language acquisition and socialization: Three developmental stories. In *Culture Theory: Essays in Mind, Self, and Culture*, ed. R. Shweder and R. LeVine, 276–320. Cambridge: Cambridge University Press.

Ong, Aiwa. 1995. Postcolonial nationalism: Women and retraditionalization in the Islamic imaginary, Malaysia. In *Feminism, Nationalism, and Militarism*, ed. C. Sutton, 43–50. Arlington, Va.: Association for Feminist Anthropology/American Anthropological Association Press.

Orsi, Robert. 2005. *Between Heaven and Earth*. Princeton, N.J.: Princeton University Press.

Palmer, Susan, and Charlotte Hardman. 1999. *Children in New Religions*. New Brunswick, N.J.: Rutgers University Press.

Peshkin, Alan. 1986. *God's Choice: The Total World of a Fundamentalist Christian School*. Chicago: University of Chicago Press.

Peskowitz, Miriam, and Laura Levitt. 1997. *Judaism since Gender*. New York: Routledge.

Pissaro, Joanne. 1997. "You can't take the subway to the field": "Village" epistemologies in the global village. In *Anthropological Locations: Boundaries and Grounds of a Field Science*, ed. A. Gupta and J. Ferguson, 147–162. Los Angeles: University of California Press.

Poll, Solomon. 1962. *The Hasidic Community of Williamsburg: A Study in the Sociology of Religion*. New York: Schocken Books.

———. 1965. The role of Yiddish in American Ultra-Orthodox and Hassidic communities. *YIVO Annual of Jewish Social Sciences* 13:125–152.

———. 1995. The charismatic leader of the Hasidic community: The zaddiq, the rebbe. In *New World Hasidim: Ethnographic Studies of Jews*, ed. J. Belcove-Shalin, 257–276. Albany: State University of New York Press.

Pollack, Sheldon. 1998. India in the vernacular millennium: Literary culture and polity, 1000–1500. *Daedalus* 127 (3): 41–74.

Poplack, Shana. 1980. Sometimes I'll start a sentence in Spanish y termino en Español: Toward a typology of code-switching. *Linguistics* 18 (7/8): 581–618.
———. 1981. Syntactic structure and social function of code-switching. In *Latino Language and Communicative Behavior,* ed. R. Duran, 169–184. New York: Ablex.

Pratt, Mary Louise. 1992. *Imperial Eyes: Travel Writing and Transculturation.* New York: Routledge.

Prell, Riv-Ellen. 1988. *Prayer and Community: The Havurah in American Judaism.* Detroit: Wayne State University Press.

Pufall, Peter, and Richard Unsworth. 2004. *Rethinking Childhood.* New Brunswick, N.J.: Rutgers University Press.

Rampton, Ben. 1995. *Crossing: Language and Ethnicity among Adolescents.* New York: Longman.

Riesbrodt, Martin, and Kelly Chong. 1999. Fundamentalisms and patriarchal gender politics. *Journal of Women's History* 10 (4): 55–78.

Robbins, Joel. 2004a. The globalization of Pentecostal and Charismatic Christianity. *Annual Review of Anthropology* 33:117–143.
———. 2004b. *Becoming Sinners: Christianity and Moral Torment in a Papua New Guinea Society.* Berkeley: University of California Press.

Rose, Susan. 1988. *Keeping Them Out of the Hands of Satan: Evangelical Schooling in America.* New York: Routledge.

Rosen, David. 2005. *Armies of the Young: Child Soldiers in War and Terrorism.* New Brunswick, N.J.: Rutgers University Press.

Rosenak, Michael. 1993. Jewish fundamentalism in Israeli education. In *Fundamentalism and Society,* ed. M. Marty and R. Scott Appleby, 374–414. Chicago: University of Chicago Press.

Rosman, Moshe. 1996. *Founder of Hasidism: A Quest for the Historical Ba'al Shem Tov.* Berkeley: University of California Press.

Rotman, Risa. 2008. *Fit for a Princess.* Brooklyn, N.Y.: Hachai.

Rubin, Israel. 1972. *Satmar: Island in the City.* Chicago: Quadrangle Books.
———. 1997. *Satmar: Two Generations of an Urban Island.* New York: Peter Lang.

Rydstrom, Helle. 2004. *Embodied Morality: Growing Up in Rural Vietnam.* Honolulu: University of Hawaii Press.

Schaechter, Mordkhe. 2004. *Yiddish II: An Intermediate and Advanced Textbook.* 4th ed. New York: League for Yiddish.

Schick, Marvin. 1979. Borough Park: A Jewish settlement. *Jewish Life* (winter): 186.

Schieffelin, Bambi B. 1990. *The Give and Take of Everyday Life.* New York: Cambridge University Press.
———. 1994. Code-switching and language socialization: Some probable relationships. In *Pragmatics: From Theory to Practice,* ed. L. E. Hewett, R. M. Sonnenmeier, and J. F. Duchan, 20–42. Englewood Cliffs, N.J.: Prentice Hall.
———. 2000. Introducing Kaluli literacy: A chronology of influences. In *Regimes of Language: Ideologies, Polities, and Identities,* ed. P. Kroskrity, 293–327. Santa Fe, N.M.: School of American Research Press.

Schieffelin, Bambi B., and Elinor Ochs. 1986. Language socialization. *Annual Review of Anthropology* 15:163–191.

Schieffelin, Bambi B., Kathryn Woolard, and Paul Kroskrity, eds. 1998. *Language Ideologies: Theory and Practice*. New York: Oxford University Press.

Scholem, Gershom. 1988. *Major Trends in Jewish Mysticism*. New York: Schocken Books.

Seidman, Naomi. 1996. *A Marriage Made in Heaven: The Sexual Politics of Hebrew and Yiddish*. Berkeley: University of California Press.

Sered, Susan. 1996. She perceives her work to be rewarding: Jewish women in a cross-cultural perspective. In *Feminist Perspectives on Jewish Studies*, ed. L. Davidman and S. Tenenbaum, 169–190. New Haven: Yale University Press.

Shaffir, William. 1974. *Life in a Religious Community: The Lubavitcher Chassidim in Montreal*. Toronto: Holt, Rinehart, and Winston of Canada.

———. 1995. Boundaries and self-presentation among the Hasidim: A study in identity maintenance. In *New World Hasidim: Ethnographic Studies of Jews*, ed. J. Belcove-Shalin, 31–68. Albany: State University of New York Press.

Shandler, Jeffrey. 2005. *Adventures in Yiddishland: Postvernacular Yiddish Culture*. Berkeley: University of California Press.

Sharot, Stephen. 1982. *Messianism, Mysticism, and Magic: A Sociological Analysis of Jewish Religious Movements*. Chapel Hill: University of North Carolina Press.

Sivan, Emmanuel. 1995. The enclave culture. In *Fundamentalism Comprehended*, ed. M. Marty and R. Scott Appleby, 11–86. Chicago: University of Chicago Press.

Smith-Hefner, Nancy. 1999. *Khmer-American: Identity and Moral Education in a Diaspora Community*. Berkeley: University of California Press.

Soleveitchik, Hayim. 1994. Rupture and reconstruction: The transformation of contemporary orthodoxy. *Tradition* 28 (4): 64–130.

Sontag, Deborah. 1998. Orthodox neighborhood reshapes itself. *New York Times*, January 7.

Spitulnik, Debra. 2000. The social circulation of media discourse and the mediation of communities. In *Linguistic Anthropology: A Reader*, ed. A. Duranti, 95–118. Malden, Mass.: Blackwell.

———. 2002. Accessing "local" modernities: Reflections on the place of linguistic evidence in ethnography. In *Critically Modern*, ed. Bruce Knauft, 194–219. Bloomington: Indiana University Press.

Stacey, Judith, and Stacey Gerard. 1990. We are not doormats: The influence of feminism on contemporary Evangelicals in the United States. In *Uncertain Terms: Negotiating Gender in American Culture*, ed. F. Ginsburg and A. Tsing, 98–117. Boston: Beacon.

Steinmetz, Sol. 1987. *Yiddish and English: A Century of Yiddish in America*. Tuscaloosa: University of Alabama Press.

Stephens, Sharon. 1995. *Children and the Politics of Culture*. Princeton, N.J.: Princeton University Press.

Stroud, Christopher. 1992. The problem of intention and meaning in code-switching. *Text* 12 (1): 127–155.

Thomason, Sarah. 1997. *Contact Languages: A Wider Perspective*. Amsterdam: John Benjamins.

Thorne, Barrie. 1993. *Gender Play: Girls and Boys in School.* New Brunswick, N.J.: Rutgers University Press.

Trudgill, Peter. 1974. *Sociolinguistics: An Introduction.* New York: Penguin Books.

Urciuoli, Bonnie. 1996. *Exposing Prejudice.* Boulder, Colo.: Westview.

Von Hirsh, Eva. 1995. The Jews of Gateshead, England. Ph.D. dissertation, University of Linkoping, Sweden.

Weinreich, Max. 1980. *The History of the Yiddish Language.* Translated by J. Fishmann and S. Noble. Chicago: University of Chicago Press.

———. 2008. *The History of the Yiddish Language.* Vols. 1 and 2. New Haven, Ct.: Yale University Press.

Weinreich, Uriel. 1956. Notes on the Yiddish rise-fall intonation contour. In *For Roman Jakobson,* ed. M. Halle, 633–643. The Hague: Mouton.

———. 1990. *College Yiddish.* New York: YIVO Institute for Jewish Research.

Weiser, Chaim. 1995. *Frumspeak: The First Dictionary of Yeshivish.* Northvale, N.J.: Jason Aronson.

Wengeroff, Pauline. 2000. *The World of a Russian Jewish Woman in the Nineteenth Century.* New York: Capital Decision.

Wertheimer, Jack, ed. 2000. *Jews in the Center.* New Brunswick, N.J.: Rutgers University Press.

Wex, Michael. 2005. *Born to Kvetch.* New York: St. Martin's.

Wexler, Paul. 1981. Jewish interlinguistics: Facts and conceptual framework. *Language* 57 (1): 99–149.

Williams, Brackette. 1996. Skinfolk, not kinfolk: Comparative reflections of the identity of participant-observation in two field situations. In *Feminist Dilemmas in Fieldwork,* ed. D. Wolf, 72–95. Boulder, Colo.: Westview.

Winston, Helle. 2005. *Unchosen: The Secret Lives of Hasidic Rebels.* Boston: Beacon.

Wolf, Diane. 1996. *Feminist Dilemmas in Fieldwork.* Boulder, Colo.: Westview.

Woolard, Kathryn. 1998. Simultaneity and bivalency as strategies in bilingualism. *Journal of Linguistic Anthropology* 23:55–82.

Woolard, Kathryn, and E. Nicholas Genovese. 2007. Strategic bivalency in Latin and Early Modern Spain. *Language in Society* 36 (4): 487–509.

Woolard, Kathryn, and Bambi B. Schieffelin. 1994. Language ideology. *Annual Review of Anthropology* 23:55–82.

Zentella, Ana Celia. 1997. *Growing Up Bilingual: Puerto Rican Children in New York.* Malden, Mass.: Blackwell.

Index

Note: Page numbers in italic type indicate photographs.

higher education, 25, 84, 137, 139, 169, 175
Hikind, Dov, 30
Holocaust, xiii, 8, 110, 122, 230n3
Hungarian Hasidim, 8, 9, 151, 176
Hungarian Yiddish, xiv, 131
Hungary, xiv
hyperbolization of difference, 14

imagination, 56–58
inclinations, for good or evil, 43–48, 111, 145, 161, 226n11
individuality, 38–41, 58–59
inspirational lectures (*shiers*) , 25, 36, 64–65, 83, 87, 172, 198
intention, 89
interference, in language, 92, 94–98, 101–5
intermarriage of Hasidim, 181
intonation, 101–2, 106
Isaacs, Miriam, 93
Israel, 224n36

Jacobs-Huey, Lanita, 219
Jewish difference: comportment and, 159–62; emphasis of, 13–14; Gentiles and, 14–15, 38, 47, 69–71, 93, 136–37, 147, 159–66; Hasidic communities and, 31; Hasidic Yiddish and, 93–101; innate traits of, 38–39; language and, 96, 118; modesty and, 158–64; researcher role and, 16–21; semiotics and, 19, 121, 136–37; socialization of girls into, 32; speech and, 162–64
Jewish English, 101–5
Jochnowitz, George, 93
Judaica Press, 112
Judaism: Conservative, 13; continuum of, 138–39, 170–73; and language, 89–91; modernity and European, 7; Modern Orthodox, 13; in North America, 12–13; Reconstructionist, 13; Reform, 13. *See also* Jewish difference; Orthodox Judaism

Kahn, Susan, 17
kale 'bride,' 180, 192, 197–208
Kamen, Mark, 225n2
kapl 'yarmulke,' 54, 229n21
Karlin-Stolin Hasidim, 28
Kaufman, Debra Renee, 25
Keane, Webb, 2, 61, 147, 178, 221n7, 231n4

khevrise 'study partner,' 193
khilel-hashem 'blaspheming God's name,' 41
khinekh 'moral education,' 34–86; defiant behavior and, 74–82; "fitting in" and, 56–59; gender and, 41–43, 54–56, 71–74; goals of, 39–40, 60–61; inclinations and, 43–48; individuality and, 56–59; personality traits and, 38–43; physical/material world and, 37–38; praise and rewards in, 48–56; questioning and, 62–74, 82–86; and self-making, 34–35, 60–61; and unquestioning faith, 65–68. *See also* childrearing
khitspe 'willful defiance,' 69, 74–82
khukhem 'wise child,' 69
khumre. See religious stringency
khusn 'bridegroom,' 192, 197–98, 232n4
kidesh-hashem 'sanctifying God's name,' 41
Kinder Shpiel Inc. 'Child's Play' Inc., 110
kin names, 106
kinship, 180–82. *See also* family
kiruv 'Jewish outreach,' 10–11, 17–18, 20
Kiryas Joel, New York, 10
kosher: metaphorical uses of, 129, 136, 168–69; religious observance of, 26, 44
Koskoff, Ellen, 89
Krasna Hasidim, 28
Kulick, D., 86, 120

Lakewood, New Jersey, 13
language: appropriate speech, 162–64, 202, 231n11; associative networks of, 120, 126; borrowing in, 92, 99–104; function of, among Hasidim, 32; gender and, 21, 88, 90, 93, 120, 124–30, 143; in the home, 124–28; modernity and, 114, 116–17; and multilingualism, 91; purism in, 89, 94, 108, 110; sacred, 114, 116; in schools, 22–23; sexuality and, 201–2; simultaneities in, 91–93; syncretic, 88–89, 92, 105, 108–10, 116–17; vernacular, 87–88, 114, 116. *See also specific languages*; language socialization
language ideologies, 92
language socialization : baby talk and, 105–7, 124, 126; and childrearing practices, 225n10; games and books for, 110–12, *113*, 114; in the home, 124–26; and morality, 35, 226n14; in school, 108–10, 126–30, 132–34; theoretical approach based on, 6, 35
Latinos, 9

258 • Index